# MILLAIS AND THE RUSKINS

To  A. Viruly
whose letters from across the North Sea
have so encouraged me

# CONTENTS

# Contents

# ILLUSTRATIONS

❈

# Illustrations

# FOREWORD

This book, like *Effie in Venice*,* depends for its chief source on the collection of letters, known as the Bowerswell Papers, acquired by the Pierpont Morgan Library of New York from Effie's grandson, Sir Ralph Millais, Bt, in 1950. Therefore my first expression of gratitude must be to the Trustees of the Pierpont Morgan Library and to its Director, Mr F. B. Adams, Jr, for permission to use the letters and to work in their library. Dr Helen Gill Viljoen has again allowed me to use this material although she has spent so much time in studying and annotating it for her own forthcoming biography of Ruskin and I am deeply grateful to her for this and for providing me with the portrait on page 163.

There is, however, a great deal of other unpublished material throwing light on the events narrated in this story which I have been given the privilege of using. First must come the collection of letters from Millais to Holman Hunt which are in the possession of Mrs Elizabeth Burt, Holman Hunt's grand-daughter; then the Ruskin letters in Yale University Library, the account books and diaries of John James Ruskin at the Ruskin Galleries, Bembridge School, Isle of Wight, and letters to F. J. Furnivall at the Huntington Library, San Martino, California. To the owners of all these I tender thanks and, so far as Bembridge is concerned, a very special word of gratitude to Mr James Dearden, the Curator, for his invaluable assistance and to Mr R. G. Lloyd, C.B.E., Q.C., the Chairman of the Educational Trust Ltd, who so wonderfully carry on the Ruskin tradition initiated by the late J. H. Whitehouse.

The letters themselves, though, would be a barren field without the co-operation of the Millais family. I wish, therefore, to express my appreciation of their unfailing help, particularly in the case of

*Effie in Venice* (to which reference is made in this volume) was published in the United States by The Vanguard Press under the title *Young Mrs. Ruskin in Venice*.

Sir Ralph Millais, Bt, his sister, Mrs Esmé Prowse, her daughter Miss Thea Prowse and their cousin Admiral Sir William James, G.C.B. I am much in debt, moreover, to another member of the family, the Hon. Clare Stuart Wortley, who died in 1945 but who spent much time before her death in transcribing most of the Bowerswell Papers and adding notes to them on family matters. Sir Ralph Millais has very kindly lent me these transcriptions and allowed me to quote from them freely.

A host of kind people have patiently suffered my questioning on matters in which they are expert and even shown me paths which would lead to a shaft of light I would otherwise have missed: Miss Rosalie Glynn Grylls, Mrs Virginia Surtees, Mr Ian Lowe of the Ashmolean Museum, Miss Jane Boulenger, Miss Elizabeth Davison of the Arts Council, Dr H. C. Harley, Mrs Janet Camp Troxell, Mr Tim Hilton, Mrs Margaret Munro, Mrs Patrick Gibson, Miss Mary Bennett of the Walker Art Gallery, Liverpool, Lady Trevelyan, Mr John Musgrove, M.S., Mr T. E. Chester Barratt, C.B.E., Mr Alister Wedderburn, Sir John Murray, K.C.V.O., D.S.O., Viscountess Mersey, Mr Richard Ormond of the National Portrait Gallery, Mrs Léonie Ormond, the Countess of Birkenhead, Lady Jean Fforde, the Countess of Longford and Mr E. Ll. St J. Couch. I wish also to thank the Matron of the Eventide Homes, Bowerswell, the Editor of *Debrett*, the Archivist of British Transport Historical Records, the librarians of the Public Library of Dundee, Caithness County Library and the Central Public Library, Edinburgh, Messrs William Blackwood & Sons, Ltd, Stibbard, Gibson & Co, and also my excellent typist, Mrs Job.

Permission to quote from published and unpublished Ruskin material has been kindly granted by Messrs George Allen and Unwin Ltd, John Ruskin's Literary Trustees.

It has been my object to let the characters speak for themselves through their letters in which the emotional stress which underlies them so often shows through the day-to-day trivia of suburban life and a momentous holiday in the Highlands. I have provided the minimum of linking passages, and all source authorities (except to the footnotes) together with the history of the letters are to be found at the end of the book.

It has been necessary to punctuate Effie Ruskin's and Millais's letters for the sake of clarity; their spelling, emphases, capitals and exclamation marks have, however, been retained. John Ruskin's punctuation and that of his father is given exactly as written because it is so much a part of their style. Deletions of irrelevant passages are indicated by dots, and the obtrusive ampersand which they all used throughout has been changed to the complete word.

All letters are hitherto unpublished except where otherwise indicated in the source notes. Abbreviations for sources are given on pages 274-5.

# RETURN FROM VENICE

❋

It was in July, 1852, that John and Effie Ruskin went to live in their new south London home, 30 Herne Hill, Camberwell. They had been married for over four years and had just returned from their second trip to Venice—a ten-month sojourn during which Ruskin had been gathering material for the second and third volumes of *The Stones of Venice*.

Effie, a very pretty and attractive young woman of twenty-four, had been a great success in Venice, admired by Field-Marshal Radetzky, the pet of Marshal Marmont, the belle at all the balls: her letters home had been full of Counts and Countesses, Princes, Archdukes, Grand Dukes and Pretenders. She possessed a special gift for getting on with foreigners, being neither stiff nor shy, and as she was always very attentive to the women the admiration she received never aroused their jealousy. Moreover, she had been able to go out on her own. John's unsociability had been tolerantly accepted; he had merely been thought eccentric.

A greater contrast than between Venice and suburban Camberwell would be hard to imagine, and it was not only Effie who had misgivings about going to live there. John had them for her (though not for himself; *he* could be happy anywhere so long as he was not disturbed in his work or dragged into society), but it was John's father, John James Ruskin, who had the gloomiest forebodings.

The old Ruskins lived at Denmark Hill, half a mile away towards Camberwell Green, in a comfortable Georgian house in seven acres of garden and orchard with a small farm attached. John, nearly ten years older than Effie, was their only child and the object of their adoration and over-care. Effie as a daughter-in-law had fallen heavily between two stools; she was neither the high-born heiress they had aspired to for their brilliant son, nor the malleable girl to whom they had reconciled themselves when at last they gave in to John's determination to marry her, and as they were unaware that the marriage had never been consummated they must have been bitterly disappointed that she had failed to give them a grandchild, especially Mrs Ruskin, who adored babies.

Effie was the eldest daughter of a very old friend of John James Ruskin, George Gray, a Writer to the Signet* in Perth, whom Mr Ruskin had been in a position to patronise at the time of the marriage because he had nearly ruined himself by speculating in railway shares. As John's books were not yet producing an income, the young couple were entirely dependent on Mr Ruskin's bounty, a fact he never let them forget and which he seemed to think gave him the right to criticise Effie in a way he would have hesitated to do had she been possessed of a dowry. At the time of the marriage Mr Ruskin had given John £10,000 which John had settled on Effie. The interest on this capital was the young people's basic income, but as well as this Mr Ruskin gave them an allowance and paid all their travelling expenses.

During the past four years many letters had been exchanged between Mr Ruskin and Mr Gray in which Effie's conduct had been censured and defended, and much of Mr Ruskin's criticism had been passed on to Effie by her mother. This, more than anything, had stirred in Effie a deep resentment against her in-laws. When she was with them she got on with them well enough, for they rarely criticised her to her face; they attacked her behind her back, and that she could not forgive. If the Grays had had the good sense to keep Mr Ruskin's abuse to themselves and pass on only the praise, which was sometimes forthcoming, the marriage might not have come to grief so soon, for John and Effie were not as yet unhappy together. They had learnt to go their own ways and never to interfere with each other. John was completely absorbed in his great work, and Effie's social talents had been fully employed in Venice. She had gone out of her way in her letters home to praise John's kindness in little things—her complaints while they were in Venice were all against his parents—while he for his part was extremely proud of her looks and of her success in Austrian and Italian society; and as she had behaved, in spite of her freedom, with the most scrupulous propriety, he was perfectly satisfied with her conduct. He had written to her during their engagement when he was most in love with her, 'I find

* Principal class of Solicitor in Scotland, so called because at one time it was their business to prepare charters, warrants, etc., for the King's signet.

work good for me and when I am busy upon architecture or mathematics I sometimes very nearly forget all about you!—and retain merely a kind of pleasant sense of all's being right.'[1] That was John at his happiest.

The following letters from Mr Ruskin to Effie's father, written while the young people were still in Venice, best give the situation they found themselves in on their return, and are the perfect introduction to Mr Ruskin himself, a man of sixty-seven, suffering from a chronic stomach complaint, still travelling regularly to the north of England for the wholesale wine business, Ruskin, Domecq and Telford, which had made him rich after years of early poverty and struggle.

Preston. 30th March 1852

My dear Sir

You may have heard from Phemy\* that we have taken a House for her and John adjoining our former Residence on Herne Hill, the counterpart of that House†—we have been induced to do this for the reason of my Son requiring in pursuit of his Literary Occupations to be near London for a few years to come and also that his Mother and I, getting old, my son inclined to give us a share of his Company but from Phemy not being happy or comfortable at our House, he could best do so by living—*near* us not *with* us. Now this Scheme as you well know will involve Great Expense—I am getting the House *well* but plainly furnished with a stile of Furniture that will suit any residence they may move to at home or abroad—I confess

---

\* As Effie had been called as a child. Her full name was Euphemia Chalmers—Chalmers being the maiden name of her maternal grandmother.

† No. 28. The Ruskins had lived there from 1823 till 1842 when they moved to Denmark Hill and the house was let. After the death of his parents, when Ruskin moved to Brantwood, he gave the house to his ward, Joan Severn, and occupied his old room there whenever he came to London. Nos 28 and 30 were joined together on one side and detached on the other. They were demolished in about 1906 and in 1923 two small houses were built on the site of each. Those on the site of No. 28 are now numbered 26 and 28 and in the garden of 26 is a commemorative plaque to Ruskin. The site of No. 30, where Effie lived with Ruskin, is now occupied by Nos 30 and 32. The Denmark Hill house was demolished in 1947. Its place has been taken by a block of flats almost opposite Ruskin Park.

to you however that I have great misgivings as to the propriety
of trying the Scheme at all—John merely dropped a few words
in a late Letter that Phemy did seem a little melancholy at the
prospect of a quiet suburban villa near London—You know
the Life they have been leading and the Society they have enjoyed, especially Phemy who has daily taken advantage of the
good Company in her power—I confess I have great fears of
Phemy being able contentedly to live at Herne Hill without
even the opportunity of seeing Visitors which Park Street* gave
—I have indeed myself written to John expressing sympathy in
the loss of the Society they were about to leave—Mrs Ruskin
and I differ on this subject as much as we ever do differ. She
thinks Phemy ought to be, and will be, happy enough—If she
could live alone as we do, with John and a little Company, this
might be, but Phemy is young and Society likes her and she
loves Society. I have no hope of her yet leading a very domestic
Life though I would not conclude that her present Life was a
very happy one. My object in writing to you is to ask the
favour of your candid opinion of our plan. You and Mrs Gray
know much more of Phemy's sentiments than we do—John's
Mother thinks that an only son should do something for his
aging parents.† On the other hand there seems to exist some
idea that the young people in order to be quite happy should be
quite let alone—that any interference on our part does harm—
I admit that the young people seem to go on pretty well on their
present plan of letting each other do as they chuse—and I
doubt if it were tried whether Phemy could find enough in
John's Society and the small addition the Herne Hill House
would give them—to make Life agreeable—They never appeared to me to have more than a decent affection for each
other, John being divided betwixt his wife and his pictures and
Phemy betwixt her Husband and her Dress—So that to hope to
make them happy and comfortable in a Life which suits Mrs

* Mr Ruskin had taken for them 31 Park Street, Mayfair, for three years
so that they might have a chance of going into Society in London. They
had lived there for sixteen months between their trips to Venice.

† Mrs Ruskin was four years older than her husband. He was her first
cousin. When she was about twenty-three she had gone to live with his
parents in Scotland and had married him in 1818 when she was thirty-six
after a nine-year engagement.

Ruskin and me, seems quite chemerical and I am really at a loss what to do *with* them or for them—My desire is to promote their happiness but this must be done in their way—not ours. Mrs Ruskin is very sanguine about the Herne Hill plan—I am both fearing and doubting—If from the Knowledge you possess of your Daughter's sentiments you can suggest any thing more certain than another to conduce to her happiness, if not destructive of her Mother in Law's hopes and happiness, you would serve me greatly by communicating your ideas to me—I beg the favour of a reply to this Letter if possible by Friday addressed Adelphi Hotel, Liverpool. With kindest regards to Mrs Gray I am My dear Sir

Yours very truly
John James Ruskin[2]

Liverpool. 2nd April 1852

I am extremely obliged by your Letter of 31 March which so far satisfies me in your not appearing to have any doubts of the Scheme of Life proposed for the next few years for our Son and Daughter suiting their tastes, though from your light way of treating the subject and from the tone of your Letter I have no great hope of your lending your aid in bringing about the change which may be wanting to render this quite probable or certain—However dark my views may be of many things—it does not alter facts—The young people spend nearly double their Income—in a ceaseless round of dressing and gaiety—I have not yet seen two days spent quietly without weariness and I have seen this perpetual restlessness and want of Excitement cause much suffering to Mrs Ruskin who gets much more Love and enjoys more of the Society and kind attentions of all other young women than of Phemy—What have my views to do with this? I perhaps view things more brightly than I should do for I give them all they ask for—I see Phemy as yet very young and being beautiful and admired and an ornament to Society, naturally fond of being much in it—She does not lead the Life I could have wished my Daughter in Law to lead but she may come to do so—She will get tired of her present Life and in the meantime my Son is not unhappy. He is proud of his wife and pleased to see her shine in Society . . .

It is easy to tell me it is all nonsense minding the change and that a man should control and dictate to his Wife—I do not believe that either you or John could make Phemy lead any Life but what she was herself disposed to lead—but I do think some effect may be gradually produced by the kindly given advice or remonstrance of her Mother and yourself—I have heard Mrs Ruskin say that any advice from her was pointedly rejected which is *very* likely for I daresay Phemy thinks she knows as much of the world as her Mother in Law, neither do I want to force my opinions on you.[3]

London 3 May 1852

I ought sooner to have thanked you for your kind and particular Letter of 5 April. It will be useless to enter further on the chief subject of it—I plead guilty to being myself pleased with John and Phemy going into good Society—Mrs Ruskin was not so satisfied—but their going into the highest Society could all have happened in a more prudent manner. Talented and professional men of very limited means manage to go and take their family too into the most select company—In fact as I once before said, had they kept a little back—had Phemy dressed much more quietly, they would have been at parties higher than they ever reached, but the old and high families repel any new people attempting to be on an exact equality or trying to dress up to them or I would say beyond them for they are distinguished for quietness of Demeanour; but all this is a matter of Opinion just as I also have the Opinion which I trust may prove a wrong one that Phemy will not take at all to Herne Hill, nice and pretty as the house will be—I saw them go into high Company and was flattered—I now think with Mrs Ruskin that I have committed a mistake and for the Consequences I shall blame myself more than Phemy—You seem to ask if I wish them to give up the Style and live quietly—not exactly—but I would have them resolutely in the face of the world fix what would be a right Expenditure and keep to it and if the world would not receive them on these terms—be satisfied to be less in it—I am quite sure they would be courted as much and loved even more.

Mr Ruskin had taken 30 Herne Hill on a thirty-four-year lease at £95 a year and had given Mr Snell, an upholsterer and house agent of 27 Albemarle Street, more than £2,000 and *carte blanche* to decorate and furnish it, so that when John and Effie arrived from Venice with their two servants (John's valet, George, and Effie's maid, Mary) the house was ready for them. Nevertheless, they stayed a few nights at Denmark Hill before moving in, and continued to dine there until Effie found a cook. Effie's letters tell us just what the house was like.

> Denmark Hill
> [Postmarked London July 14 1852]
>
> My dearest Mama
>
> I received your kind and very comforting letter* on the road as I was going to see my new house which you know Mrs Ruskin would call a good omen although nothing could induce her to go with us, so like her, isn't it? She said we must not think it any want of feeling but that she was so unlucky a person that nothing would prevail on her to go. We therefor accompanied Mr Ruskin and went all over the place and found every thing in its place, all being new and clean. You must remember their old house next door for it is exactly the same. What especially delighted me was a little bit of garden at the back and a very diminutive Conservatory about four feet square but which has a vine and some flowers which pleases me very much. I will give you a description of the house and furniture when I have more time and am less tired for I had a fatiguing day yesterday and the evening before a horrid passage from Boulogne, cold, miserable and rough, everybody sick, and that takes a day or two to recover from.

On Sunday, July 18, she wrote from Herne Hill to her brother, George, eighteen months younger than herself, who worked in his father's legal firm in Perth:

> Now to our House—when we returned I found what I expected, viz, that Mr R had given Mr Snell a large sum of

---

* Comforting because Effie's little brothers and sisters, who had had scarlet fever, were now recovering. Three of Effie's younger sisters had died of this illness in 1847 within a few weeks of each other so naturally the Grays had been extremely worried.

money to do up the House—which Mr Snell had naturally done up as cheaply and vulgarly as he could and put the half of the money in his pocket. I, of course, said nothing but praised what I could and found fault with nothing but John was enraged and said that he had never before felt ashamed to ask his friends to come and see him, that it was only fit for a Clerk to live in. I told him he had better not get angry before his Father but make Mr Snell change some of the Carpets and all the Crockery which he is to do, and we have chosen some we like better, but it would be difficult for you to imagine how we feel the extreme cleanliness and vulgar trimness of every thing we see. In Italy we drove in nails and pasted things on our walls* without minding where or how, here it seems horrible the mere idea of touching any place, everything is so dreadfully in order. I am very much amused at the Ruskins (entre nous). I think they have been looking over John's account books since we returned and I imagine see what he spent and what I spent the year we have been away—at any rate they made me a proposal if I liked to take the charge of our income and give John out of it £200 a year for all his expenses—my having all the rest to manage with as I could. I said I would try for six months, and as I have neither a carriage nor rent to pay for, I must try and save, for John is far too Liberal and I suppose they see that.

And on the 22nd she wrote to Rawdon Brown, their great friend in Venice, who had lived there for the last nineteen years:

Dear Mr Brown
I have had so much to do since returning home that I have not been able till now to acknowledge your kind note. If you can imagine me in a small ugly brick house partly furnished in the worst possible taste and with the most glaring vulgarity, with ten workmen pulling down walls and making such improvements as we can, with only George and Mary for servants, you can partly imagine the state I am in . . . I have said nothing at all not to vex anybody, and to say the truth John was so furious at the evident dishonesty of the upholsterer, who I

* They had lived in an apartment of the Casa Wetzlar, on the Grand Canal, now the Gritti Palace Hotel.

should say has put the best half of the money in his pocket, and the smallness of the house, that he said at first he would not go into it, and was going to such extremes that I have done my best to calm him and he is now partly reconciled and hopes by means of his casts* and drawings to make himself happy and the house more bearable. I have no carriage but Mrs Ruskin permits me to go into town once a week in hers, and I shall take that opportunity of seeing a few people whose friendship I should be sorry to lose.[4]

And to her mother on July 26:

The weather is very fine and the sun hot. My little garden is in much need of watering by the time we get home in the evening.† We have lots of workmen still about us and I don't think we shall be comfortable for long for we are to change the Dining room and Drawing room carpets, and a partition wall in John's study is being moved to throw two rooms into one. My bedroom is very small. Altogether the place is inconceivably cockney after Venice as you may imagine but my flowers amuse me and after Venice I think all London looks equally hideous and smoky.

And again to her mother on August 2:

Today I am getting put down in the dining room two very pretty Turkey carpets and rods on the walls for Pictures. We chose the carpets to get rid of the frightful Kidderminster Mr Snell put, and in two days the same will be done in the drawing room. I have chosen a very gay French looking one with bouquets of flowers on white ground and a broad velvet sort of border attached to match all round. It looks like Tapestry and yet there is no difference in the price to the hideous one down.‡ Fancy putting for a very small drawing room which ought to

* Ruskin had had plaster casts made in Venice of the capitals on the columns of the Doge's Palace, and had shipped them home in advance.
† From dining at Denmark Hill. Dinner there was at six.
‡ An entry in Mr Ruskin's account book shows that he had to pay Mr Snell £31 extra for these carpets, and £26 for extra work done to the house. He also paid another £20 for a piano. (Bembridge.)

look as airy and light as possible a carpet dark purple with small green and white spots at regular distances of half a yard all over, the effect being quite *funereal*. On the centre table I have got them to make, for a beautiful lace border that I bought at Venice, a table cover of purple Utrecht velvet, and with one or two things of taste we will materially alter the present vulgar newness of the house.

This is the background of the story which follows.

# TROUBLES AT HERNE HILL

Apart from the house itself and the general change in their living conditions, Effie had other troubles when they got home. One of them was to do with the unpleasant circumstances of their departure from Venice: Effie's jewels had been stolen on the day they were to leave and a friend of their own, whom they had seen constantly, an Englishman called Foster, serving in an Austrian regiment stationed at Verona, was suspected of the theft. Although it was the police who accused him, the officers of his regiment became bitterly hostile towards the Ruskins, and Foster's best friend, Count Franz Thun, aide-de-camp to Radetzky, with whom they had been particularly friendly, went so far as to challenge John to a duel. The scandal got into the London papers a fortnight after they arrived home and John was obliged to write a letter to *The Times* explaining the circumstances.

Another worry was that Mrs Gray's younger brother, Melville Jameson, a widower with three children who lived in Perth, committed the enormity of marrying his housekeeper and was so ashamed of his own conduct that he thought of giving up his legal practice in Perth and emigrating to Australia. But perhaps the greatest cause for anxiety was the danger that John might become a Roman Catholic. In Venice he had met Lord Feilding, the eldest son of the Earl of Denbigh, a recent 'pervert', as it was then called, who had travelled home with them and done his best to convert them.[1]

About the robbery, Effie wrote to Rawdon Brown on July 22:

My father in law is dreadfully angry about the challenge at Verona [Mr Ruskin had not heard about it until after they got home]. I never saw him in such a state and he was so nervous yesterday and said such things that I was quite frightened at the vehemence of his indignation and grief for the insult his son had received. In this state he naturally used much stronger language than was necessary which provoked John and his

mother very much as they are quite indifferent about refusing
to fight any number of times, and I was very sorry indeed for
Mr Ruskin and thought they did not at all sympathise with
his wounded feelings and his great pride in his son and told
them so for which Mr Ruskin thanked me and said he knew
he had very worldly notions but even John having to justify
himself for anything in conduct hurt him dreadfully. I thought
his feelings very natural.

On July 27 Mr Ruskin himself was writing to Mr Gray:

In the Mg. Chronicle of 21 July and in the Church and State
Gazette of 23 July are paragraphs with false statements of the
affair at Venice, making my Son the Accuser—and not the
police, and in a small newspaper attached to the Gardeners
Chronicle of Saturday last 24 July is a paragraph to same effect
giving my Sons name in full—which *alone* he will have to notice
... I hope you have got all particulars from Effie as you will
hear many remarks and it is very important to put the facts
clearly before people (of course nothing is known by any one
of the Verona affair [the challenge]) but for your Daughters
sake it should be known that *several* [ *jewel*] *Cases* were emptied
in the room for we have not good peoples remarks to meet but
all that Scandal and malice can suggest, and from the way it
appears in the papers—some will say—the Lady has been visiting the Barracks and merely dropped her Jewels and that her
Husband, angry and jealous, has accused an Officer—or they
may make another story and say she gave the man Jewels.
John only considers the whole a great Bore—He does not take
proper charge of his wife and the utmost Innocence without
discretion and Circumspection will not save young people from
such scrapes. Mrs Ruskin has been very unwell since their return
and fears a serious effect on their Character—I feel it less because I have been always prepared for something though I got
displeased about a Dog being brought, given by Count Thun*

---

* This dog had been given to Effie; she called it Zoe. When she left
John she abandoned the dog too. John changed its name to Wisie and it
lived with him for many years. He wrote about it in *Praeterita*, Vol. III,
Chap. II.

—but we are all very well as to agreeing to make the best of it—
The young people are very pleasant at present dining with us
every day.

Mr Ruskin wrote again on Monday, August 2:

You will see by today's Times—John has answered the various remarks in papers—It was talked of at all Clubs and parties and it became necessary and it is cautiously and modestly
done*—There was a vulgar bad paragraph again in the Globe
of last Tuesday . . . Please say nothing of the affair beyond what
paper [*The Times*] gives.

There was a great party, 1200 at the Rooms of Royal
Academy last Wednesday.—John and Effie should have been
there. Sir Charles Eastlake† said no Tickets were left—This
may be true—He and Lady Eastlake dine with me on Thursday and I shall judge of this—I observe that Samuel Rogers‡
where their Card was left 14 days ago and who is at home—
does not notice them. This may be an accident but I am rather
sensitive since this Jewel and officer story—They luckily are not,
and though I have my opinion and draw conclusions, as both
may be wrong I say not a word to them—Effie has dined most
days with us—twice without John and we go on very well. I
don't like that young Ford, a sort of man about Town, coming
calling but I should only make mischief by interfering. I think
it proper however to give you and Mrs Gray my thoughts.

Young Ford was Clare Ford, the only son of Richard Ford,
author of a *Hand-book for Travellers in Spain*. When the Ruskins were
living at 31 Park Street the Fords had been neighbours at No. 123,
and Effie had made great friends with Richard Ford's two eldest
daughters and had chaperoned them to parties. Their brother,

* It is a short letter stating that it was not he, Ruskin, who had accused
the officer but the police.

† President of the Royal Academy, 1850–65. His wife was soon to become
a close friend of Effie's.

‡ Ruskin had known Samuel Rogers (1763–1855) for nearly twenty
years, but since his marriage to Effie he had been asked more frequently
to the old poet's famous breakfasts, Effie being a great favourite of his.

Clare, then a spoilt dissipated young man, had fallen in love with Effie, and through her influence had given up his commission in the army and gone abroad to study for the Foreign Office. Effie's brother, George, who had come to London in 1851 to see the Great Exhibition, gossiped about Effie and Clare when he got home which brought forth an indignant protest from Effie. She declared that George was merely jealous of Clare whom he had not even met.[2] And now Clare was back again in London.

On July 19 Effie had written to her mother: 'My much abused friend Clare has been living for a year in the Pyrenees studying and drawing, improving himself immensely. He has just been nominated attaché to the Embassy at Naples by Lord Malmesbury and I suppose will return to London shortly preparatory to going out. I am very glad and think he will do well.' He did so well that in due course he became Ambassador to Madrid, Constantinople and Rome, and was knighted in 1886.

Mr Ruskin's 'giving his thoughts' to the Grays about the young man's visits evidently resulted in some kind of warning from them to Effie which was answered by John himself. This letter is of particular interest in view of the fact that John was later accused of trying to get rid of Effie by deliberately compromising her with other men. Effie certainly had no such belief at this time, though George Gray maintained for the rest of his life that Clare Ford was one of the men with whom John had tried to get her into trouble.

John's letter, addressed to Mr Gray, was written from Herne Hill on August 8. It is difficult not to believe in its complete sincerity:

You are very good not to be angry with me for never writing to you or Mrs Gray—but indeed I have given up writing to any one for a long time . . . but I wished to write to you at present in order as far as may be to set your mind at rest respecting the acquaintance of Effie with Mr [Ford] which she says, appears to cause you considerable uneasiness—I quite agree in all you say of the necessity of great caution in a young married lady of Effie's beauty and natural liveliness, but I am happy to be able to assure you that I have never seen the slightest want of caution on her part in the course of her various relations with young men of every character, but on the contrary, the greatest shrewdness and quickness in detecting the slightest want of proper feeling on their part followed by fearless decision in forbidding or otherwise preventing their farther intrusion upon her in cases which required such severity—so that she runs much more chance of being found fault with for prudery than coquetry. In Mr [Ford]'s case I think she has acted and is acting with perfect prudence as well as kindness and I believe she may have more cause to look back with pleasure to the intercourse she has permitted in this instance than to any other of her London acquaintanceships—for she has done the young man already infinite service—has prevailed upon him to give up his town life—to work in a quiet country place in the Pyrenees for nearly a year—and to prepare himself for a place in the [Foreign] Office . . . I should also think it great selfishness in any young woman to forego the *chance* of doing so great a good, merely because it was possible that some ill natured people might laugh at her—On the other hand it is equally necessary that she should distinguish efforts to please her made with an occult motive, from efforts to please her made —as they are daily and innocently made—under the natural influence of womanly tact and gentleness—And I believe that Mr [Ford] while indeed he is much readier to hear and act upon a lecture from Effie than anybody else is as honorable and upright in all his purposes and feelings respecting her as her admirers of the ages of 70 and 86—I see nothing whatever likely to cause the slightest harmful talking—in her permitting his occasional visits more especially as I am going to give him some hints about his drawing and shall be at home much more than I was in Park Street, but it would cause talk to some extent if she were abruptly to check an intercourse of so long standing.[3]

Mr Ruskin's fears that John and Effie had been passed over by Samuel Rogers and Sir Charles Eastlake because of the 'Jewel and Officer story' were groundless. They were soon breakfasting with the old poet, and Lady Eastlake was soon writing to John Murray, the publisher, 'We dined at Denmark Hill last Thursday [August 5] and enjoyed ourselves much. The old people are much kinder to their pretty daughter-in-law than they were and look to her to keep their son from going through some Ruskin labyrinth to Rome.'[4]

On the subject of John's possible conversion Effie had written to her mother on July 26:

Mrs R goes to such extremes of anti-popery that I am really afraid of her tormenting John into being more with them than he otherwise would, for his vanity is terribly hurt at her speaking to him exactly like a child and she does talk such nonsense that I cannot help laughing. She says we have been living for a year amongst idolators and infidels and that for that time we have not heard a word of truth. She abuses the Austrians and holds up the Hungarians and Italians by the Hour and if we say anything she says we know nothing but lies. John says he never heard anything like her and that you are nothing to her, now she abuses the Jesuits far more than ever you did. She said to me the other day, 'My dearest Effie, I wish you would use your influence with mine to prevent your Husband keeping company with these Idolators for they are most insidious.' I said I thought she was quite right but that the less she said to John about it the better for it only made him angry. She promised not to speak any more and she does not directly to him, but every day after dinner she commences a tirade against Religion in general that would amuse you to hear. She won't let any body else speak.

On August 2 Effie told her mother that John was lunching that day with 'Archdeacon Manning'* which Mrs Ruskin thought highly dangerous; every Roman Catholic acquaintance he made was 'entirely destroying' her. Mrs Gray was also very perturbed, apparently, about this meeting with Manning and on August 3 Effie replied to a letter of hers:

Your valuable letter of yesterday I read to John. He said he thought it astonishingly clever and is going to answer it himself.

* Henry Edward Manning (1808–92) had been Archdeacon of Chichester before his secession to Rome in 1850. He had first appeared as a Roman Catholic priest on June 10, 1852, in a little chapel in Horseferry Road, Westminster. Rather surprisingly, he was asked to Denmark Hill; there is an entry in Mr Ruskin's diary-notebook for August 9: 'Archdeacon Manning at luncheon.' (Bembridge.) Soon after this he went to Rome where he lived for the next three years.

Mrs Ruskin told me yesterday that no one knew what she had suffered since he had had to do with these people. Now mind, I clearly see the danger as well as you do—but I thought it would never do to speak as his parents did or to act like them, as if I had done so and he had hinted it to them, the Papists, they might have made him begin a system of deception which would be fatal. For instance he goes into London nearly every morning and stays till five or six. *How* do we know that if he likes he may not visit Mr Manning whenever he chuses? Now I know he neither receives letters nor goes near them. The Feildings are in Wales and never write. Manning is out of town and goes shortly to Rome. I do not believe that John will have further personal intercourse with them—but what *I* dislike about him is his wish to understand the Bible throughout— which nobody in this world will ever do—and unless they receive it as a little child it will not be made profitable to them. He wishes to satisfy his intellect and his vanity in reading the Scriptures and does not pray that his mind and heart may be softened and improved by them. He chuses to study Hebrew and read the *Fathers* instead of asking God to give him Light. His whole desire for knowledge appears to me to originate in Pride and as long as this remains and his great feeling of *Security* and doing every thing to please himself he is ready for any temptation and will be permitted to fall into it. I do what I can but I require to be very careful what I say; for he has no respect for what his Mother says and yet it worries him intensely feeling that she thinks so differently. He says that he thinks it most painful to see how narrow-minded some excellent people [are]. Now if I were not very careful he would shut himself up and I would not know either what he was thinking or doing. Believe me I shall watch him most closely. Some of these stories of miracles he is not persuaded are false and he wishes very much to be assured that the Stone of St Januarius at Naples is really an imposture. You know the Papists say that the stone on which the saint was beheaded at Pozzuoli turns red when the blood in the bottle at Naples liquefies.*

* St Januarius, or Gennaro, was martyred under Diocletian. Two jars containing his blood are preserved in the church called after him in Naples. Three times a year the liquefaction of this blood is said to take

Now he says Protestants are very unjust and won't examine these facts and he has a number of ideas of this kind which I think most dangerous as his mind is naturally so imaginative and he is fond of mystery—short stories and every thing that savours of the marvellous, but now I must conclude.

Next day came the news of Melville Jameson's marriage to his housekeeper. Effie wrote back by return:

Dearest Mother

How truly I sympathize with you in this sad trial. I am perfectly overpowered with it and I can easily imagine what *your* feeling must be, which this dreadful affair must touch so nearly. How Melville ever could have acted in this way I cannot divine. The idea of his considering his duty to such a woman in comparison to those to his own children and last wife, and then the madness of giving up every prospect of earthly prosperity and at the same time encreasing his responsibilities makes me really think your idea of putting him in the Asylum if you could have managed it in time not a bad one for his intellect must be impaired—What on Earth is to become of him and these dear children of *Jessie's** I cannot think. When one only glances back at all the scenes in Croft House to think what a wife he had and how in every thing she was perfect for him to imagine that He—Her own Husband—should be the only one that would ever disrespect her memory is most astonishing and makes me have a worse opinion of men than ever I had before —I have often seen bad men, brutal *and* foolish men, unfeeling and selfish, but a man like Melville, so good and so kind always and so connected with all my young days, to think of *Him* so disgracing himself is wonderful and very instructive to see what even a good man may do. But you see there is great natural weakness of character for since he has given up yours and my

---

place, and whether the process is rapid or slow is considered a good or bad omen for the following year.

* His first wife, *née* Duncan, who had died in September, 1848. She had been much beloved by Effie. She left a daughter and two sons. At her death, Melville had broken his partnership with Mr Gray and joined his father-in-law's legal firm.

Water-colours of Millais by Holman Hunt,
painted on April 12, 1853.
painted in December, 1853.
In the eight months between these two portraits Millais had fallen in love with Effie.

*The Order of Release* by Millais.

Father's advice he has made greater and greater errors, trusting in his own strength when he had none . . .

The woman seems to me stupid as well as bad, for were she ambitious or had any spirit she never would have approved of his throwing away his means and becoming a beggar. For you it would be better did he never return—but for himself it appears to me the only thing to save him from ruin—for it is all very well to be hopeful but what is he to do? And although his professional character may be unspotted, marrying such a woman is sufficient to give every stranger distrust . . . It seems so hopeless to think of him at all now—for that creature will lead him a miserable Life and he must feel continual remorse and she can in no way compensate for what he has sacrifised, and probably she will manage him completely which he never allowed *Jessie*, who was an Angel, to do. I remember hearing her say myself once that men were far oftener managed by their servants than their wives . . . John thinks his letter shows him to be much in Love with the woman. I don't and think him miserable already. What is she like?*

A fortnight later John wrote to Mrs Gray a beautifully sane letter about these two topics—Melville's marriage and Roman Catholicism:

Herne Hill 28th August 1852
Saturday

My dear Mrs Gray

I have been hoping—ever since Effie read to me your wise letter about Romanism to be able to write a few words to you to relieve you as far as I could from anxiety on that head—and finding myself at last more peacefully and quietly at home than I have been for these many months (I might almost say years) I must try whether I cannot do so—though I have first to acknowledge that your letter was perfectly right and wise, and that there *is* some little danger in the spirit of contradiction which very little opposition will arouse, sometimes, in obstinate people like me. Still—there is no fear of such a feeling as this

---

* The new Mrs Melville Jameson had a son in June, 1853, followed by three daughters. These children never got on with Jessie's children.

influencing me to the extent that you dread, in so important
a matter. I simply set it down as something to the discredit of
Protestantism that my mother is afraid after having bred me up
in its purest principles for thirty four years, to let me talk for
half an hour with a clever Catholic: but I shall certainly not
permit this fact to tell for more than its simple worth—and that
worth is really not much—for my mothers anxiety about my
religion is much like that which she shows with respect to my
health or safety—rather a nervous sensation than a definite and
deliberately entertained suspicion of danger in this or the other
circumstance. Only I see that I must not blame Catholics for
illiberality in refusing to argue with, or listen to Protestants.

The beginning of these perilous speculations of mine was only
this—that one evening in St Mark's place [Venice]—getting
into an argument with Lady Feilding—I was completely
silenced by her—had not a word to say for myself—and out of
pure shame, I determined at once to know all that could be
said upon the subject—and fit myself better for battle another
day: as well as to look into some statements made by Protestant
writers, which I had hitherto accepted undoubtingly, but which
I found the Catholics denied just as indignantly as the Protestants affirmed them positively. And this I must do before I can
write any more against the Catholics—for as I have received
all my impressions of them from Protestant writers, I have no
right to act upon these impressions until I have at least *heard*
the other side. But I do not see why this should make either
you—or any of my Protestant friends anxious. I can most
strongly and faithfully assure you that I have no hidden leaning or bias towards Popery: that on the contrary I hate it for
abusing and destroying my favourite works of art: my name
and what little reputation I have, are entirely engaged on the
Evangelical side, my best friends are all Puritans—including
my wife—and all my life has been regulated by Protestant
principles and habits of independent thought—I am as cool
headed as most men in religion—rather too much so: by no
means inclined either to fasting or flagellation:—past the age
of Romance—and tolerably well read in my Bible: And if under
these circumstances—you are afraid when you hear that I am
going to enquire further into points of the Romanist doctrines

of which I am ignorant—it seems to me that this is equivalent
to a confession that Protestantism is neither rational nor defen-
sible—if fairly put to the proof—but a pasteboard religion
which the first sword cut will demolish like Mambrine's helmet.*
I do not ask you to think better of me or to put confidence in me
—I hold myself certainly no stronger nor better than many
who have gone over. But I ask you to have confidence in Protestantism—that it can bear the enquiry of an unprejudiced
mind—for I believe those who have gone over *were* prejudiced
in every instance—bred in a false and semi-Protestantism
—with an inward leaning to Rome, from their childhood. I
don't look upon myself as venturing into 'temptation' as my
mother calls it—in the pride of strength—but as merely inquir-
ing which, of two statements—is most accordant with commonsense—and I should think myself no Protestant at all if I were
not always ready to do this—but merely a Catholic under a
wrong name. I don't suppose—if all I have been taught of
Protestantism be true—that there can be the slightest chance
of my being made a Catholic by hearing the other side—and
if it be untrue—the sooner I find this out the better.

However—enough of this—for I have hardly left myself time
to say a word about poor Melville—I have been much less
shocked than anybody else by the whole affair—a good deal
surprised, certainly: but I have long held it for a fixed law of
human nature that the best and wisest of men may lose their
*heads* as well their hearts—and what is worse their consciences:
—to a woman. I suppose people were a good deal surprised
when David and Solomon did so—but I don't think we have
any right to be surprised—since their time, and so I have got
rid even of my astonishment. They say St Benedict conquered
the fiend in him, by rolling himself into a bed of nettles—poor
Melvilles nettles are just growing—He is much to be pitied—
but I think ought on no account to leave Perth—and I am
sorry to hear of his being so ashamed of himself—going by back

* Mambrine or Mambrino was a Moorish king, celebrated in the French
and Spanish medieval romances of chivalry. His enchanted helmet of pure
gold rendered him invulnerable until the hero Renault struck it off. Don
Quixote believed he saw Mambrine in his helmet but it turned out to
be a travelling barber with a brass pot on his head to keep off the rain.

streets and so on—as if that would do any good: Myriads of
people marry their servants—and if they choose to do so—no one
has any right to quarrel with them on that account any more
than for any other kind of bad taste. If Melville were here—
I should ask him and his wife to dinner forthwith and make
much of them both. The woman may be a bad kind of person—
but if every bad kind of woman was to be kept out of society—
it would be very awkwardly thinned. However I think—when
Melville begins to recover his wits—you should point out to him
the curious sophistry of self will. He excuses himself for marrying this woman because he has given her a promise—and cannot "be a scoundrel". Now he gave *you* a promise to send the
woman entirely away: and his keeping this promise to you was
I believe quite as essential to *your* happiness as his faith to the
servant was to hers. But he appears never to have thought there
was anything binding or sacred in a promise made to his sister.
It must be kept only when made to his maid. However if he
will only now mind his business—give up his own philanthropy
—hold up his head—and assume a general "what business is it
of yours" look, he will get on capitally, and is well quit of
Duncans and Blaikies.*

I am very sorry to hear of poor George's being still confined—
but there is much to be thankful for in the comparatively gentle
dealing of the fever with him. I hope by the time this letter
reaches you his penance will be over—and he will [be] able to
receive my congratulations, give him my love—and love with
a kiss to Sophy and Alice—though, tell them they are very
naughty to carry off my wife from me . . .

Ever affectionately yours

J. Ruskin[5]

As this letter shows, Effie was already planning to go home on a
visit to Bowerswell, the house in Perth which her father had bought
on his marriage in 1827 and which had been rebuilt in the last few
years while the family were still living in it. Indeed Effie would have
gone home sooner if Mr Ruskin had not forbidden it on account of
the infection in the house. Effie's younger sisters, Sophie and Alice,

---

* One of his Duncan sisters-in-law had married a Blaikie.

aged nine and seven, and her three small brothers, John, Melville and Albert, of six, five and two, had all had the fever very badly. Now her eldest brother, George, was down with it, so her visit would have to be postponed until he was fully recovered.

# EFFIE'S DISCONTENT

❋

Effie must have felt very much of a prisoner at Herne Hill, 'let in' to London only one day a week—Wednesday—and all her friends away for August even when she did go in. John was able to escape from the horrid little house whenever he wanted to. Every morning he walked over to Denmark Hill to work in his old study, surrounded by his beloved Turners, and most afternoons he went up to London by omnibus in his capacity as one of Turner's executors. Turner had died on December 19, 1851, and at first John was thrilled to be let loose in his studio in Queen Anne Street, but he was soon sickened by disputes over the will and on August 24, after breakfasting with Samuel Rogers at 22 St James's Place, Effie reported to her mother that John had gone to sign his name at Doctors' Commons* renouncing the executorship. 'I saw Rogers do the same this morning,' she went on, 'remarking that he and John were the only two out of the eight worth anything and that the rest might perhaps put *butter* on the drawings and eat them for what they knew. Certain it is that already Turner's lawyer has *stolen* a bag of drawings.'

Although Rogers was at that time ninety, and two years before had been run over by a brougham and broken his hip, Effie described him as being 'as brisk as possible, paying me all manner of compliments and saying clever things. I think he would like us to go every day but it is a trouble going so far so early in the morning. . . . He abused John for carrying Mrs Browning's poem—"Casa Guido Windows"—in the carriage with him and going to Kentish Town to see her . . . but old Rogers is so jealous of every other man or

* College of Doctors of Law at Bennet's Hill, Upper Thames Street, finally demolished in 1867. The Prerogative Court where wills and testaments were proved was one of the five courts at Doctors' Commons before the institution in 1857 of the Court of Probate, Divorce and Admiralty as a division of the High Court.

woman who writes verse that he sometimes is very amusing in his criticism.'*

In her next letter Effie told her mother that she was practising economy 'which my worthy John don't do in the least as he has bought £160 of Liber Studiorum† in these six weeks he has been home so that I am glad I have the charge of the money and he has to go to his Father who approves—But I do not—I think it foolish for a man of his fortune to wish to have a finer set of Turner plates than any body in England. If he will spend money and have a Turner Mania I would rather it were pictures.'

By the end of September all danger of infection at Bowerswell was over and, as their servant George was leaving them and the new one, Frederick Crawley, a young man whom Effie had been all the way over to Hampstead to interview, could not come until the end of October, this seemed the perfect moment for her visit home. She could not possibly stay in the house with only two women to do all the work, she told her mother. Moreover another uncle, Andrew Jameson, was returning home to Edinburgh after a visit to Holland and she would be able to travel under his escort: her father-in-law would never allow her to travel alone.

Effie left London on September 24 and was away for about seven weeks during which time John presumably stayed at Denmark Hill. They must have written to each other but their letters have not survived, and there are no letters from Effie to her mother after she got back to Herne Hill until November 17. When she returned she brought with her for a long visit her two little sisters, Sophie and Alice, and their French nursery governess, Delphine. The first news

---

* Ruskin was to have been introduced to the Brownings by Coventry Patmore at The Grove, Highgate, but on this occasion only Robert Browning turned up. In September John went to call at Welbeck Street where the Brownings were staying in lodgings, bringing (according to Elizabeth Browning) 'his pretty natural sprightly wife with him . . . Pretty she is and exquisitely dressed—*that* struck me—but extraordinary beauty she has none at all, neither of feature or expression.' (*Robert Browning* by Betty Miller, p. 172. Murray, 1952.)

† Turner's great series of engravings in etching and mezzotint, made under his own control from drawings prepared specially for this purpose. The seventy-one prints were issued between 1807 and 1819 at prices from 15/- to 2 gns each. When Turner's work was partly dispersed after his death, Ruskin was willing to pay up to 50 gns for proofs touched by the Master himself.

of their arrival is in a letter of November 10 from John to his father-in-law:

I have been too long in expressing to you my sense of the trust you have given me in your two sweet little daughters—and in assuring you that as far as in me lies, I will take care of them—and try to give you them back in good health—and with no injury to their gentle and affectionate dispositions: I believe they will be very glad to come back to you—for London seems rather to confuse than delight them—and our house here is dull—and small—and the air close and relaxing. Still—Sophy has more colour than when she came—and I believe the change of air after their late illness will be good for both. They speak French admirably—and Delphine seems every way a good governess, and a good girl—you are exceedingly fortunate in getting such an one . . .

I am partly happy—partly sorry that Effie has persuaded you to come up to the Duke's funeral*—Glad I always am and shall be, to see you—but I am sorry that it is at this time—for I am neither master at present of my time nor my wits—I am just winding off the tangled skein of all my Venice work—and am much puzzled and good for nothing; and I cannot help feeling that there is some truth in what my father says, that so valuable a life as yours ought not for so slight a cause as this ridiculous and tiresome pageant, to be imperilled among flights of excursion trains such as will be rushing up from all parts of the country at the period in question. However, I doubt not that after the hard work you have lately gone through, you are much in need of relaxation—and I hope you will not doubt that I shall be most happy to see you—though I could have enjoyed your visit more at another time. You must miss your little Girls sadly—and it was very good of you to let Effie steal them. I think she looks the better of her journey—though I wish she could find health in English air.[1]

This wish of John's that Effie could find health in 'English air' covered a long history of irritation with Effie's perpetual indisposi-

* The Duke of Wellington had died on September 14 and it had taken two months to arrange his funeral.

tion. Effie had fallen ill during Christmas, 1848, while they were
staying at Denmark Hill, eight months after their marriage, and she
had never really recovered. It was difficult for anyone to make out
what was wrong with her; she was tired and hoarse, with blisters on
her throat and inflammation of the stomach; she caught frequent
colds and was more influenced by the weather than most people. In
May, 1849, while John was with his parents on a three-month tour
of Switzerland, she had consulted Dr James Simpson (the originator
of chloroform) who was then Professor of Midwifery at the University
of Edinburgh. He diagnosed some nervous complaint of long standing and said she would be better if she had children. Although she
was afterwards to blame all her physical ills on the unnatural
married life she led with John, she was frequently indisposed even
before they were engaged, suffering from headaches and sleepless-
ness. She was always worse at Denmark Hill and invariably better
when she was enjoying herself. John in the same way fell ill whenever he stayed at Bowerswell, or indeed when he did anything he did
not like, but even if their ailments were largely psychosomatic they
were no less real. Effie moreover felt that no one understood her
debility, least of all the Ruskins, whereas John received abundant
and, to Effie's way of thinking, most irritating sympathy from his
parents for the slightest indisposition.

John and Effie had been asked to the Duke of Wellington's
funeral at St Paul's on November 18 by the Dean's wife, Mrs
Milman, whom Effie had known since 1848. John refused to go so
Effie was able to take her father who came to London in spite of
John's regrets that he should choose such a moment for his visit.
Effie wrote to her mother on Wednesday, November 17:

Although Papa says that he does not intend writing to you
till he returns, I think I may as well inform you that he arrived
quite safely and looking very well after passing all the night in
playing whist with the town council of Edinburgh, but all his
Luggage has got lost somewhere and he arrived without an
article of any sort, so today we have been at Nichol's* to get
a frock coat and mourning tie and he will look quite the
thing at the Deanery where I understand a very large and

* H. J. & D. Nichol of 114–20 Regent Street and 22 Cornhill were
men's tailors with a large ladies' department.

distinguished party are to assemble at breakfast and after the ceremony to dinner which I am glad of to show Papa the way they entertain which is very good, but only fancy what a day we shall have. We leave this 5 A.M., get to the Deanery between eight and nine, to the Cathedral at ten and not out till 5 P.M. But we shall not be sitting all the time as having two Galleries we can Parade outside and in—and every one is envying our good fortune in getting such places. All London today is one Mass of Black and White Calico hung in festoons which looks very funereal, and I never saw such a mob of mustachoed men, women in black, every one is in mourning today and every one seems driving or lounging about. Never on any other day did I see such mobs of people and carriages. Mary was at the Deanery yesterday for our tickets and said the Whole Hall was full of gentlemen entreating for tickets and the servants turning them out and saying they had none. Poor Mrs Milman is half dead with fatigue having had such quantities of writing to do, and I have no doubt everybody will be thankful when it is all over—Papa is very much pleased with my house and thinks the position charming and that I should be very happy here—so I would be if he and the children would remain . . . We are all to dine at Denmark Hill at six and Papa left me at one after buying a stereoscope to go to the City on business, and to Chelsea, to see the last of the lying in State, I suppose to prepare his mind for tomorrow.* I am sorry he can't stay longer with us. He makes John laugh very much with his way of speaking *out*.

Effie gave her mother no account of the funeral, probably because Mr Gray carried back all the news. On January 21 of the following year, 1853, she met the second Duke of Wellington at a dinner-party at Richard Ford's and wrote at length to her mother about it on the following day.[2] After this there is a long gap in her letters home. Mrs Gray, who kept all her letters from Venice, seems to have preserved very few from this period. It is not until February 22 that there is another letter from her and then it is to Rawdon Brown

* The great hall of Chelsea Hospital where the Duke was lying in state had been open to the public since November 13. On the first day the crowd was so great and so uncontrolled that several people were killed.

acknowledging a manuscript she had received from him—the despatches of Sebastian Giustinian written from England while Venetian Ambassador at the Court of Henry VIII between 1515 and 1519, which Brown had translated and edited. Effie sent the manuscript for him to Smith, Elder—Ruskin's publishers—with a strong recommendation from Ruskin, and thereafter frequently reported on its slow progress into print.

She ended her letter: 'John is spending all his money in Missals [illuminated manuscripts]—he has a perfect mania in that line just now. Goodbye dear Mr Brown. I wonder if you are looking out at your beautiful view* of water and Bridges with golden setting sun, just golden everything. I have it all before me, although outside the thick snow flakes are rapidly falling and the poor little Robins are coming nearer and nearer the house to be fed.'

Perhaps it was the snow which accounted for the melancholy of her next letter to her mother—a letter in which for the first time she showed her deep unhappiness:

> Herne Hill
> [Postmarked 'Perth Feb 25th 1853']
> I have not been able to write to you for some days past, because I have been unwell with a bad cough and cold which has kept me in bed several mornings . . . One thing you will be sorry at, I have not been again to Claudet's† but every Wednesday has been so dark and I thought it would be better to wait till summer and get another of myself done if Papa wished it very much by someone else, but you know Kilburn‡ did the Blue one of me and you do not like it much I am afraid. They will all have a sad expression—The Ruskins are bothering me now because I won't visit at all without John or go to Balls alone. How is one to please them? I have never asked John to

---

* Brown lived at the Ca' Grimani della Vida on the Grand Canal, opposite the Ca' Pesaro.

† Antoine Claudet (1797–1867), a Frenchman settled in London, had received instruction under Daguerre himself and had bought from him in 1839 the first licence to practise the daguerreotype in England. He had a great success and in 1853 was given the Royal Warrant.

‡ William Edward Kilburn had in 1846 opened his daguerreotype studios at 234 Regent Street. His 'photographic miniatures' were much advertised.

go to a single place nor told them of many of the kind invitations
I have had, yet they know from John I get them. What should
I do? If I do go—I must be fatigued, spend money in carriage
hires and go alone. If I don't they say that it is my own fault
if I have not society and that I may go wherever I like or do
what I choose provided I don't *degrade* John by taking him into
society. In fact they don't care any of them what becomes of
me or what I do so that they are left to enjoy themselves sel-
fishly alone. John and his Father go on buying Missals at a
most extravagant rate, and there is another one at £170 that
they seem bent on acquiring and which will soon be added to
the collection which he's carefully locked up for fear of mortal
fingers touching them so that I have no good of them at all. I
never saw such a trio. If I had bookmaking powers I should
certainly write about them. This going out is the last thing
they are grumbling at me for—and I think of sending all my
invitations to D.H. [Denmark Hill] to be decided upon, for
which ever way I do is sure to be wrong and that seems to me
the only way to make them say exactly what they think. They
will naturally—as they generally have done—say to do what I
like best and then abuse me afterwards—so I intend to say no,
I leave you to decide with the distinct understanding that I
have no will on the subject at all—and having been so unfortunate as not to please you in what I thought would in this
matter, you will now tell me exactly what you desire me to do.
Be so good as to tell me if you think this would be wise? For
my own part I would much rather not go out at all; it subjects
me to many inconveniences and great fatigue of Body, but I
think I must do as I have said, for they use all their influence
against me and wish to make me Mary Richardson* over
again. They will be kind to me but then I must be their Slave
in return. I must praise them as three perfect people and
be treated as a fool or a child, whichever suits me best, but
then I must never complain or else get a torrent of insults in
return.

* Mr Ruskin's orphaned niece whom he had adopted in 1821 when she
was thirteen and who had been Mrs Ruskin's slavish companion until her
marriage to Parker Bolding in 1847. She had died two years later leaving
a son.

About my Cook,* her wages at £14–14 wages, £2–2 for tea—
but Beer besides. Alice [her younger sister] is in great feather
speaking the funniest French. They will leave Wednesday and
I hope will have a quiet passage.³

The children returned home on March 2 and Effie went to Downes
Wharf to see them off. Mr Gray was a director of the Dundee, Perth
and London Shipping Company which ran a weekly service, leaving
Dundee and London every Wednesday, and the Grays suffered a
martyrdom of sea-sickness for passages at reduced rates on these
paddle-steamers which took forty hours to do the journey.

After seeing them off Effie lunched with Sir Charles and Lady
Eastlake at their house, 7 Fitzroy Square. 'Lady Eastlake quite
thinks with you,' she reported next day to her mother, 'and advises
me to try and see some of my particular friends when I can, but not
to go out without John, to keep to my point about that.'

Lady Eastlake was to play a leading part in the drama of Effie's
flight from John, and it appears from the passage above that Effie
was already consulting her about her marital problems. Born
Elizabeth Rigby in 1809 she was the daughter and sister of distinguished obstetric physicians, both called Edward Rigby. Before her
marriage to Charles Eastlake in April, 1849, she had lived in Edinburgh, travelled widely in Germany and stayed for two years in
Russia with a married sister. Her letters to her mother written from
Russia were published in 1841 as a book, *A Residence on the Shores of
the Baltic*, which had considerable success. Through John Murray,
her publisher, she met John Gibson Lockhart, Scott's son-in-law and
editor of the *Quarterly Review*, and from 1842 she became for many
years the only female contributor to the *Quarterly*, writing for it
regularly on such diverse subjects as Dress and Cologne Cathedral.†
She was also a distinguished amateur artist.

Effie had first met her at the Richard Fords' in June, 1850, and
had described her as 'a striking looking woman with penetrating
black eyes and a fine intelligent face', and after another meeting,
when she had befriended Effie at a large party at Devonshire House,

---

* Mrs Gray was trying to find a Scotch cook for her.

† Her most famous contribution was an article in the issue of December,
1848—*Vanity Fair and Jane Eyre—Governesses*—in which she reviled Currer
Bell and Jane and praised Becky Sharp.

Effie told Rawdon Brown, 'She is one of my beauties and so charming in every way, so good and so womanlike, so clever and not in the least of a blue.' Effie did not mention that she was also almost six feet tall. (Lockhart christened her 'Lofty Lucy'.) She was twenty years older than Effie; she had not married until she was forty and her husband fifty-six, and she had no children, so probably Effie appealed to her frustrated maternal feeling. One of Effie's daughters, Alice Stuart Wortley, always maintained that it was Lady Eastlake who 'found out' the truth about Effie's marriage, told her how wrong it was and urged her to escape from such an unnatural situation.[4] 'Found out' seems to imply that Effie was at first reluctant to talk about her physical relationship with John and that Lady Eastlake overcame her scruples. Having been brought up in medical circles, Lady Eastlake was no doubt better informed and more outspoken on such delicate matters than most women of her time.

Perhaps it was on this very day, March 2, when lunching at Fitzroy Square, while Effie was feeling sad and lonely after the departure of the children, that Lady Eastlake drew out the truth from her.

But the melancholy mood did not last. Soon a brightening new interest came into her life. She began to sit as a model for Millais.

# ENTER MILLAIS

John Everett Millais was not yet twenty-four when Effie sat to him for *The Order of Release* in March, 1853. They had first met seven years before at a dance at Ewell Castle, near Epsom, belonging to Mr Gadesden, an old friend of the Grays. Effie had been staying there and Millais had been close by staying with some friends from Jersey, the Lemprières. He had asked to be introduced to the lovely girl with the auburn hair, but as he was only sixteen, Effie at seventeen had been haughty and bored.[1] When she next met him in 1851 he must still have appeared to her a mere boy, especially as he was very young looking for his age.

As a child he had been extremely small and delicate, and even now, though grown to six feet, he still weighed only nine stone according to his brother William, and referred to himself as 'a specimen of a living paper knife'.[2] He suffered from headaches, biliousness, insomnia and rheumatism brought on from sitting so much out of doors to paint realistically. But in spite of his extreme thinness he was from all accounts wonderfully good looking, with the profile of an angel, a full cupid's bow mouth and such a mass of thick curly fair hair that he had difficulty in parting it and called it his 'cockatoo crop'.[3] (In the many sketches he made of himself in 1853–4, he shows his hair parted down the *back* of his head.) He was always conventionally and neatly dressed as he disliked looking like an artist. Where most other artists of the day appeared in velveteen jackets, open-neck shirts and flowing ties, he always wore a long frock-coat and high-standing collar. His voice, however, according to William Rossetti, 'hardly corresponded to his countenance; it was harsh rather than otherwise. In talk he was something of what one calls a rattle; saying sprightly things in an offhand way, but not entering into anything claiming the name of conversation.'[4] He must have had great charm, though, and a power of quickly endearing himself. His luck was proverbial and he was the kind of man, his best friend, Holman Hunt, tells us in his reminiscences, who always got other people to carry his parcels for him.

Born on June 8, 1829, the son of John William Millais, whose family had been settled in Jersey for many generations, his first years were spent at St Helier and then at Dinan in Brittany, but by 1839 his precocious talent for drawing had shown itself so remarkably that his parents were advised to move to London so that he might be properly taught. This they did with a letter of introduction to Sir Martin Archer Shee, P.R.A., whose immediate pronouncement was: 'Better make him a chimney sweep than an artist.' As soon as he had seen some of the boy's work, however, he declared that it was the parents' duty to fit him for the vocation for which nature had evidently intended him.[5] For a couple of terms, therefore, he went to Mr Sass's art school in Bloomsbury as well as to the British Museum for several hours' copying every day. At the age of eleven this prodigy entered the Royal Academy Schools,* the youngest student ever to be admitted. He remained there for the next six years, carrying off every prize and honour. In Holman Hunt's opinion he was an utterly dedicated and superbly trained artist.

In 1848, when only nineteen, he founded with two of his fellow Academy students, Holman Hunt and Dante Gabriel Rossetti, the Pre-Raphaelite Brotherhood, a movement which aimed at an ideal form of naturalistic painting, abandoning all the old tricks of the Academicians such as painting on a dark brown ground to obtain an antique effect. Millais himself summed up their purpose as having 'but one idea—to present on canvas what they saw in Nature'.[6] Four other friends were granted the right to put the secret initials PRB on their work,† and although there were others on the fringe of the movement who subscribed to the same ideals, these seven were the only recognised members of the Brotherhood. It was, however, Millais and Hunt, two years older than Millais, who were the closest friends—so close indeed that when they were both working on pictures for exhibition at the Academy, Hunt would bring his canvas to Millais's studio and they would work together all through

---

* Then, as now, entrance to the schools was by competitive examination, no fees ever having been charged.

† Thomas Woolner (1825–92), James Collinson (1825–81), Frederick George Stephens (1828–1907), and William Michael Rossetti (1829–1919). The last, in fact, never painted and Woolner was a sculptor.

Effie with foxgloves in her hair painted by Millais at Glenfinlas.
(*See p. 64*)

*A Wet Day's Pastime.* Drawing by Millais of the party at Glenfinlas. Playing at the table are William Millais (left) and Ruskin. In the doorway are Mr Monteath, the Minister, and Effie. Millais in back view; his bandaged left thumb dates this sketch after July 25. *(See pp. 72–3.)*

the night, talking, doing bits of each others' pictures and drinking coffee.

Such an intense friendship between two young men might be questioned today but at that time people were far less ready to jump to the conclusion that any very close friendship between members of the same sex must be suspect, and Hunt and Millais, therefore, had no self-consciousness about openly showing their devotion to each other. Hunt was later to call theirs a 'sacred friendship' and Millais was not ashamed to cry for a whole morning in front of the Ruskins when he heard that Hunt was going off to the Holy Land. Moreover neither of them had been to a public school where even in those days young gentlemen were taught that any open demonstration of feeling was unmanly.

By 1853 Millais had already painted three of his most famous pictures—*Lorenzo and Isabella*, *The Huguenot* and *Ophelia*. He was living with his parents at 83 Gower Street where he also had his studio.* Although his family were not at all well off, he was rich compared with Hunt or Rossetti. Hunt, for instance, was in danger at one time of having to give up professional painting altogether and return to working as a clerk in the City as he had done as a youth, but then Hunt's father was opposed to his taking up art as a profession whereas Millais was encouraged in every way by his family who, recognising him as a future breadwinner, made many sacrifices for him as well as being intensely proud of his genius. The life of the household revolved round his 'painting room' as he called it; his mother read aloud to him or sat beside him sewing while he worked, and every member of the family sat to him over and over again as a model in various poses and costumes.

Millais's father, a gentle and extremely handsome man who had been for many years an officer in the Jersey Militia, was a gifted musician.† He played the guitar particularly well and was always ready to play to his children's friends when they came to the house. Millais's mother, born Emily Mary Evamy, was a more dominating

---

* The house is now No 7, near the Bedford Square end of the street on the west side. Millais's studio was on the ground floor built out into the garden at the back.

† He was described in some early letters as 'incurably musical' and as 'undoubtedly a musician who might have made a name for himself had he cared to enter the competition and criticism of public life, but he lacked energy'. (Millais, Vol. II, p. 417.)

character than her husband. She had been married before to a Mr
Enoch Hodgkinson by whom she had had two sons. It was she who
had the greatest influence on Millais; he had been too delicate as a
child to go to school and she had educated him herself. The rest of
the family consisted of a girl, Emily, who married an American and
went to live in America, and a boy, William, a year older than
Millais, who possessed a fine tenor voice and was a good water-
colour painter, though without Millais's application and industry.*
The brothers were devoted to each other and William always
looked after the more delicate and sensitive Johnny or Jack as
Millais was called in the family.

It was in 1851 that Ruskin threw the weight of his influence into
the Pre-Raphaelite cause. Millais had exhibited three pictures at the
Royal Academy that year—*Mariana, The Woodman's Daughter* and
*The Return of the Dove to the Ark*—and Hunt had exhibited one—*Two
Gentlemen of Verona*. All four pictures were furiously attacked in the
press, the critics, who seemed to be personally affronted by them,
objecting principally to the bad drawing, bad perspective, morbidity
of subject, and stiffness and awkwardness of composition. Ruskin, at
the instigation of Coventry Patmore (a mutual friend with a special
interest since the subject of *The Woodman's Daughter* had been taken
from a poem of his), wrote two letters to *The Times* in their defence
which were published on the 13th and 30th of May.† He even asked
his father to buy *The Return of the Dove* but it had already been
sold.

Holman Hunt tells us in his reminiscences that 'after letting a
sufficient interval to follow Ruskin's last letter in *The Times* to make
sure we should not be influencing in any degree or manner the
judgement of the writer, Millais and I posted a joint letter to thank
him for his championship. The address in Gower Street was given in

---

* He never sang professionally although he had many offers to do so.
He was able to make a modest living from his painting. Later on, when his
brother became famous and showed his work in his studio on the first
floor of Palace Gate, William would have an exhibition of his own work
in the hall and catch prospective buyers as they went in and out.

† Ruskin's first letter occupies three-quarters of a column on the back
page of *The Times* and is signed and dated 'Author of *Modern Painters*.
Denmark Hill, May 9.' He begins it by disclaiming all personal acquaintance with the artists. His second letter is shorter and merely a continuation
of the first.

the letter, and the next day John Ruskin and his wife drove to the house, they saw my friend, and after a mutually appreciated interview carried him off to their house at Camberwell and induced him to stay with them for a week.'[7]

This story has been repeated in many accounts of Millais's meeting with the Ruskins, and although the first part of it is no doubt accurate, Millais almost certainly did not go and stay with them. They were then living in Park Street, and although Denmark Hill was in Camberwell, the Ruskins did not stay there themselves at all during the spring and summer of 1851, and to have asked Millais to stay in Park Street would have been pointless. Moreover, none of the three concerned mentions any such visit. Undoubtedly, however, they became very friendly* and Millais was writing to a friend on July 2, 1851, 'I have dined and taken breakfast with Ruskin, and we are such good friends that he wishes me to accompany him to Switzerland this summer.'[8] The Ruskins went to Switzerland at the beginning of August on their way to Venice but Millais was too busy to go with them.

Unfortunately there is no account from Effie herself of this meeting in 1851, though family tradition has it that after calling at Gower Street they took Millais back with them to Park Street to dinner and that Effie was delighted with his youth and gaiety.[9] She does not mention him at all in her letters until September 1, 1852, and then it is merely to remark that his *Ophelia* had been painted in one of the fields belonging to Mr Gadesden of Ewell whom Effie still visited occasionally. When next she writes of him it is from Herne Hill on Sunday, March 20, 1853, to tell her mother that he is painting her for one of his pictures to be sent in to that year's Royal Academy Exhibition:

These last days I have been sitting to Millais from immediately after breakfast to dinner, thru all the afternoon till dark which gave me not a moment, and now I am rather tired and a stiff neck but I was anxious to be as much help to him as possible as the whole importance of this picture is in the success

* According to Mr Ruskin's diary for 1851, Millais was asked to dinner at Denmark Hill on June 20, and dined there on June 22. He did not go there again until October 31 when Effiie was in Scotland. (Large, leather-bound exercise book containing notes as well as diary entries. Bembridge.)

of this head, and as he has only two in the year it is like half his year's work and as he must have them both sent in in ten days he has little enough time. He found my head like every one who has tried it immensely difficult and he was greatly delighted last night when he said he had quite got it. The features are at once so curious and the Expression so difficult to catch that he wanted—half a smile. He says he is to do me for another picture next year for another kind of expression. He paints so slowly and finely that no man working as he does can paint faster. The picture he will not show us until it is quite finished. He says nobody has painted me at all yet, that the others have cheated themselves into making me look pensive in order to escape the difficulties of colour and expression.*

And on the following Sunday, March 27, she wrote again:

I went into Millais's studio yesterday to give him a last sitting as he was not quite satisfied with the head when he got it into his own room.† He finished it quite to his own satisfaction and mine. I saw both his pictures—"The Proscribed Royalist", the one he first intended me for and "The Ransom", the one I am in.‡ I really do not know which I like best, they are both so wonderful, the first as a grand study of nature, trees, moss,

* G. F. Watts had made two drawings of Effie in 1851, and Thomas Richmond (George Richmond's brother) had painted her in the same year. This portrait, and Watts' larger picture in crayons (now at Wightwick Manor, Wolverhampton), had both been exhibited in the 1851 Academy. Thomas Richmond had also painted her in December, 1848, and Ruskin himself had made a drawing of her in Venice in March, (now at the Ashmolean Museum, Oxford).

† This seems to show that the previous sittings had taken place at Herne Hill.

‡ The name of this picture, which had been commissioned for Joseph Arden through Thackeray, was soon changed to *The Order of Release* and sub-titled *1746*. (Millais painted another picture called *The Ransom* in 1862.) It was evidently almost three months before that Millais had decided to use Effie as a model, for G. P. Boyce in his diary writes: 'January 6th 1853. To Rossetti's. Met there W. Holman Hunt, J. E. Millais. . . . Millais somewhat egotistical and little real, his attention being easily distracted. He jerked out some good remarks. Spoke highly of Ruskin as a friend of Art; said that Mrs R. was sitting for one of his pictures.' (*The Old Water-Colour Society Club*, 19th Annual Volume, 1941, p. 17.)

foxglove, fircones, birdsnest and old wood contrasting with the splendid Orange Satin and black dress of the Woman—the second as a painting of expression and of human sympathy and incident. They are perfectly different and will each have their admirers. My head you would know anywhere. In fact it is exactly like,* but as Millais truly says, and I felt, he has not refined the face in this picture as he wished me to look the character. It looks a little stronger than I do but it looks very well indeed and is precisely what he wanted. Next year he is going to paint another picture on purpose to put my face in quite another position and under other influences to refine as well as to paint an equally good likeness—but this is really absurdly like; any body who has ever seen me once would remember it was somebody they know. The man† who has fallen on my shoulder with his head buried is very grand. His arm is wounded and over it hangs the undress Highland jacket of Gray—a Kilt of Gordon Tartan and purple stockings with shoes. I have a purple woolen gown tucked up showing my bare feet and a sort of upper petticot of blue thrown over my head and enveloping the child, a little golden haired thing in Drummond Tartan, who has fallen asleep from fatigue after walking so far, primroses and bluebells it had picked by the way tumbling out of its hand. A splendid Highland Dog, black and Tan, is jumping up on his master. I am holding out the note of release to the Jailor who is in the Doorway. So you see the picture is quite Jacobite and after my own heart which will amuse Papa. I think they will both encrease his fame.

All this time John had been working intensely on *The Stones of Venice* and now at last the book was finished. The second volume came out in July, and the third, held up by the index, in October. He was in need of rest and relaxation and he and Effie planned to go into London in May for a few weeks and then for a tour of the Highlands. It was this tour which turned into the fateful stay at Glenfinlas, in the Trossachs, where Millais began his portrait of

* The only difference was that in the picture her hair was painted black to contrast with the fair hair of the child whereas in reality it was auburn.

† This was a professional model called Westall who had deserted from the Army. (Millais, Vol. I, p. 184.)

Ruskin—a portrait which perhaps has as much drama behind the painting of it as any picture in history.

In Effie's next letter to her mother of March 31 she outlines the tour as it was originally planned:

I have to thank you for three kind letters. It is impossible for me to expatiate on their various topics as I am very busy and have Lady Trevelyan* in the house for a few days . . . You will wonder at my being so busy but you know I have always a great deal of writing and as I have no gardener and don't want the expence as long as I can do without it, Phemy [the temporary Scotch cook] and I in this fine weather are putting it tidy. I find her a very nice help. I would be very much obliged for some Lily of the Valley if you could spare some now. Then I have had no clothes all this winter and feel particularly dirty and shabby and I must begin to get my things in order as John is going to take a very extensive tour this year for the two principal purposes he says of seeing Turners and Missals and secondly to cut Railroads [i.e. not to travel by them but by carriage]. I am sure you will be amused when you hear our plan but I think it will be very nice and you will quite approve. His Book is now in the press and by the end of April all the trouble of it will be out of his hands. All May he says he is going out into *Society* and make as many acquaintances as he can and know everybody who has either *Turners or Missals* and get invited to their houses. Then in the beginning of June he goes to Oxford in a *carriage* where he reads a paper on "the Uses of Gothic" which he has been asked to do, then we proceed Northwards always with the carriage, stopping at any

---

* A very old friend of John's and one of his greatest admirers. Born in 1816 Pauline Jermyn, she had married in 1835 Sir Walter Trevelyan, Bt, the naturalist. She was herself a botanist and an artist and wrote stories and reviews for the *Scotsman*. Effie had met her first when staying at Denmark Hill in 1847 and had described her as a 'nice little woman, very quiet and rather pretty'. Effie had met her again while staying in Edinburgh just before her marriage to John when the latter wrote to her that he knew no one whose friendship he more desired for her. He valued Lady Trevelyan especially for her liveliness and wit. She had recently been ill under Dr Simpson's care in Edinburgh so she and Effie had the great bond of a doctor in common; moreover she had no children.

friends, Lady Trevelyan's for instance and Mr Fawkes.* Then we shall come on to you and stay some time or else go on after two or three days to "John o Groats" house† and stay some time with you in returning. Is not John coming out!! . . . John first proposed my going to you alone and his taking his Father and Mother to Switzerland for a couple of months and then coming to Perth for some time to bring me home, but they refused as Mr R has made some arrangement with the Spanish people [the Domecqs] about the wine trade and he and Mrs R go to Paris for a month to see them—so John began proposing the other plan which luckily for me I think he will carry out as he seems quite delighted with his idea of cutting the Railroads and travelling the old way in a chariot.

And a fortnight later, on April 15:

I have not written to you for some days, I have been so unwell lately and all the strength I have I have kept for the present demands on my time. It is a great pity, is it not, and indeed could I get on without saying anything I would only be too happy. I almost fear that if my weakness continues that much as I should enjoy going out in town in May I shall be able for very little. I went to Mrs Buckland's‡ to dinner on Wednesday and felt so unwell that when I got home at midnight I hardly know how I got to bed and in consequence was unable to dine at Lady James's§ yesterday where John went and had a very agreeable party . . . John enjoyed himself very much so I shall, I think, just struggle on and go into town as I might be a little better and I would be too glad to get John out a little

* Francis Fawkes, who had a famous collection of Turners inherited from his father, one of Turner's first patrons. He lived at Farnley Hall near Leeds. The Trevelyans lived at Wallington, Morpeth, Northumberland.

† Even then there was nothing but a mound left of the house at John o'Groats with its legendary octagonal table built by John de Groat so that the representatives of eight families could all sit at the head of it. Before the present hotel was built in 1875, visitors stayed at the inn at Huna a mile away which possessed a famous visitors' book.

‡ Wife of William Buckland, Dean of Westminster from 1845 to 1856.

§ Wife of Sir Walter James who was created Lord Northbourne in 1884. He had been at Christ Church with John.

and everyone seems anxious we should go in [to London] for the month of May. It is not of much consequence whether I go out or not to parties but I think it would be right to encourage John to go as much as possible and when the moment came I would excuse myself if unable. You know I have no faith in Doctors and I know they would only order me change of air. I only complain of weakness and pains in my bones but it is sad sometimes to pass days without doing a single thing of use, and these last weeks I have never been down stairs till eleven and in bed at $9\frac{1}{2}$—so wearied. I think your Pills did me good. My spirits are very cheerful and I look so pink and white that when I told Mr Cheney* I was unable to do anything he said, 'you know with these spirits and that colour nobody will ever believe you.'

Mr and Mrs R seem to be aware in spite of themselves that I am not well and Mrs R says it is a good thing if I do feel ill that in losing my strength I don't lose my looks, and Mr R who really is without exception the most extraordinary man alive, on my marriage day, the 10th,† kept hitting [*sic*] disagreeable things at me all dinner time and was in a very bad humour, but as I suppose I was too careful or too weak to resent anything anybody might have said, on the Monday when at Liverpool in the Inn he sat down by his *own account* (for the letter is unique and if I could only send it for your inspection I think my father and you would think it as extraordinary a production as I did) he said he had taken pen in hand to John to expatiate on my perfections of appearance and manner, that in his Life he had never seen anything so perfect as my *attitude* as I lay on the sofa the night before and that no wonder Millais etc, etc, but it sickens me to write such nonsense as I could spare such writing and excuse it from a fool but from Mr R it

* Edward Cheney (1803–84), the second of three very rich bachelor brothers who lived at Badger Hall, Shifnal, in Shropshire and at 4 Audley Square in London. They were Rawdon Brown's best friends. The Ruskins had seen a good deal of Edward in Venice where he had had a house for many years. In June, 1852, he had sold it and removed his valuable collection to England.

† The fifth anniversary of April 10, 1848, when, a month before her twentieth birthday, she had been married to Ruskin in the drawing-room at Bowerswell.

sounded, to say the least, I thought, unatural and almost suspicious.[10]

For the first time a suspicion was forming in Effie's mind that Mr Ruskin was plotting to get her into 'a scrape' as she afterwards expressed it—that by flatteringly drawing her attention to Millais's interest in her and admiration for her she might come to reciprocate it and commit some indiscretion. There is little doubt that Mr Ruskin had hoped for a long time that she would behave in some way to lower herself in John's eyes and in the eyes of the world even if she did not go as far as to give them evidence for divorce.

# A LONDON SEASON

✷

Effie's next letter to her mother was written on April 21, six days after the previous one:

I am a little better but so weak a drive into Town finishes me and after being in yesterday I passed a sleepless night but I feel tolerably today . . . I went in yesterday to meet Lady Trevelyan at Claudet's for she wished a picture of Miss Stewart Mackenzie* and me together on the stereoscope.† I can't tell you the times he tried. I should think they did us 14 times it was so difficult to get Louisa to look pleased and as she is very handsome it was important and provoking for me as I was always right and wanted away but I stood it out as Lady T had asked us . . . I am like you getting my things ready for the summer. All materials are very dear and much gold on silk is being used. I saw all Miss Rutherford's‡ fashions yesterday but I thought I could invent much prettier things than any I saw. The bonnets are all absurdly small and off the head.§ John thinks now of not going to Oxford as he wants rest and has not time to prepare a Lecture. I think he is very wise as for Oxford he ought to be perfectly got up. Nothing more can be heard of

* Louisa Mackenzie, who was a year older than Effie, was the daughter of the Rt Hon. J. A. Stewart Mackenzie. Her mother had been the widow of the great Admiral Hood. In 1858, Louisa married Lord Ashburton as his second wife.

† Claudet, whose studio was at 107 Regent Street, was the first to apply photography to the stereoscope in 1851. The picture had to be taken with two cameras set up side by side as the twin-lens camera had not yet been invented. In 1853 he patented a folding pocket-stereoscope.

‡ Grace Rutherford, who, with her sister Janet, was in business as a dressmaker at 56 Pall Mall. She was a very old friend of Mrs Gray's family, the Jamesons.

§ *Punch* that summer was full of jokes about the smallness of ladies' bonnets whereas by the following year they had been superseded by equally risible mushroom hats.

44

Millais' picture till the 2nd of May when the Exhibition opens. Then I will send you all the criticisms.

It was evidently no secret that Effie was the model for Millais's picture, for Richard Ford wrote on the bottom of an invitation to the Ruskins to dinner on April 24: 'Mrs Ford\* wants an autograph of *Millais*. I hear his picture of you is ravishing.'†

On May 3 Effie was writing excitedly to her mother: 'Millais' picture is talked of in a way to make every other Academician frantic. It is hardly possible to approach it for the rows of bonnets. I sent in Phemy and Crawley last night and Crawley said they could hardly get to it and everybody was saying, Have you seen Millais' Picture?'

The Private View of the Exhibition, which was then held in the east wing of the National Gallery, had been on Friday, April 29, and Effie had attended it although she does not mention the fact. On Saturday, the art critic of *The Times*, very much to his own declared surprise, found himself praising Millais. He wrote off *The Proscribed Royalist* as being as bad as anything Millais had ever done but said of *The Order of Release* that 'A more beautiful and finished work of art has seldom graced the walls of the Academy.'

The May 7 issue of the *Illustrated London News* confirmed Effie's statement that Crawley and Phemy had not been able to get near the picture. After praising it lavishly, the reviewer declared that Millais had 'a larger crowd of admirers in his little corner in the Middle Room than all the Academicians put together'. It was reviewed again in more detail in the next issue and only one objection was made to it, that the dog should be 'participating on equal terms with the happiness of his master and mistress'. The dog's red tongue was obtrusive; it would be better if he were lying quietly at the feet of his master.

It was left to *Blackwood's Magazine* to attack Millais with all the old spirit. In the number for July, 1853, in a long anonymous

---

\* His third wife, whom he had married in 1851, a sister of Sir William Molesworth, Bt.

† Effie was afterwards criticised in some quarters for sitting as a model. A friend of Mr Ruskin's declared that 'the woman who was made an Academy Model could not be a virtuous woman'. (Letter from Mr Ruskin to his wife, December 15, 1854. Bembridge.)

article, 'The Fine Arts and Public Taste', two whole pages are given to *The Order of Release*. It is the figure of the woman against whom the attack is chiefly directed: 'Her face is plain to a degree; and if it be true that he had a certain model this is really inexcusable . . . The face far from pale is blotched with red, and the shadows stippled with bilious brownish green. Instead of the eye dimmed even with a tear it looks defiance . . . Instead of tenderness she is the hardest looking creature you can imagine . . . A friend of ours said aloud, "I would ràther remain in prison all my life, or even be hanged, than go out of prison to live with that woman." '*

Effie had more to say about the picture in her next letter. They had now moved to 6 Charles Street, Berkeley Square,† and Effie's brother George had come to London to pay them a visit. John had by this time decided to settle somewhere in the Highlands instead of making a tour, and Effie had asked her father to find accommodation for them. It was probably already decided that Millais should go with them.

6 Charles Street, 8th May

Dearest Mama

Thank you for your kind birthday letter [her twenty-fifth birthday on May 7], also a nice one from Papa. We are much obliged to him and will think over the place he proposes‡ which I should like very much and would save immense trouble and inconvenience I think . . . It is very kind of Papa letting George stay and I think he will be amused with all his gossip when he returns. In the evening I dined at Mrs Marlay's§ who was so kind as to make a very nice dinner for my Birthday.

* This article was written by the Rev. John Eagles (1783–1855), author and artist. The picture was sold by Millais to Joseph Arden for £400; in 1878 it was bought by James Renton for £2,835, and at the sale of his collection after his death Sir Henry Tate bought it for 5,000 guineas in 1898 for the Tate Gallery where it still is.

† At that time there were eight families living at No. 6 Charles Street, so it was evidently an apartment house.

‡ Dalnacardoch in Perthshire on the River Garry. There was an inn there in which Prince Charles Edward had spent the night in 1745 and this was where Mr Gray had suggested they should stay.

§ Widow of Lt-Col George Marlay. She lived at 14 Cavendish Square. Effie had got to know her through her son, Brinsley, whom she had met in Venice. Her only daughter was married to Lord John Manners.

Mr Stirling Keir* was there and very pleasant and kind, talked much of my picture but said many pretty little compliments to the effect that it was like, but he should not call it a portrait of me. I said neither he [Millais] did. Then he said it was admirable . . . They all very politely drank my health after dinner. A number of people and some very pretty girls came in the evening and John said he enjoyed himself very much.

Today Lord Lansdowne and Mr Stirling paid me long visits. The former had gone to Herne Hill on Friday and found we had just left and come here. Today I interested him much in "Millais" who I hope he will now know and ask to his house.† He said he must come and dine with him in a few days. Mr Stirling I also like much. He is very amiable, I think. I wish very much George had been here to have presented him. He says he is preparing a 3rd edition of Charles V . . . We were laughing over Carlyle who is in an immense rage at the *fuss* that is being made over Mrs B. Stowe. Really yesterday they said it was just like a levee day at St James the rows of carriages going to Stafford House.‡ I quite forgot to ask Lord Lansdowne about her but those who have seen her seem pleased with her face and expression. The Prints of her are very ugly . . . I feel much better. Lady Trevelyan said today it was a pleasure to see me, I was like a different creature. I have taken to drinking Portwine these last three days and have not coughed once.

* William Stirling (1818–78) of Keir House, Dunblane, was M.P. for Perthshire from 1852 to 1868. In 1852 he had published *The Cloister Life of Charles V*. In 1865 he succeeded his uncle, Sir John Maxwell, Bt, and assumed the additional surname of Maxwell. He was still a bachelor. In 1877 he married as his second wife the notorious Caroline Norton on her death-bed. He was already in love with her by 1853.

† Effie had met the 3rd Marquess of Lansdowne (1780–1863) soon after her marriage and had been invited several times to Lansdowne House. He was a great admirer of hers. He was a trustee of the National Gallery and a collector of pictures. The last picture he ever bought, in 1862, was a little portrait of Effie by Millais entitled *The Music Mistress*, now owned by his descendant, Viscountess Mersey.

‡ *Uncle Tom's Cabin*, published in 1852, had had a world-wide influence. Harriet Beecher Stowe (1811–96) was now on a tour of Europe with her brother, the Rev. Henry Ward Beecher. On May 7, an afternoon reception had been given for her by the Duchess of Sutherland at Stafford House to welcome her on behalf of the abolitionists of Great Britain and Ireland.

It seems from the above letter that Effie had recovered her health as soon as she got to London but by the time she wrote again on May 14 she had had a relapse:

I have not been able to answer your letter before. I have been too weak in the mornings and had too many visitors in the afternoons not to find myself beyond writing in the Evening. Tonight I am all alone and send you a line. George has gone to hear "Rigoletto" and John is at that eternal Denmark Hill. I got him to go however to Lady Lewis's* last night by himself and he stayed half an hour, actually making no mistake about the people of the house, but Col. Hamilton told me today that he saw him getting away again as fast as ever he could. My little place here is very comfortable and George seems very happy and gay ... We have lots of invitations and everybody is kind in returning the mere announcement of one being in town by cards ... Mr Rogers has had Mrs Stowe to breakfast and says she is the most modest creature he ever saw, and that her countenance is quite beautiful from its excessive humility. She seems popular and not to have said or done anything to make herself remarkable. She and Table-moving† seem to form the chief subjects of conversation.

Four days later she reported that she had had a try at the moving tables at Lady Glasgow's (widow of the 4th Earl of Glasgow). 'We were all very honest and the tables would not move an inch. I begin to think it humbug for I have twice tried it now fairly with sensible people and it has failed.'

On May 21 she was writing to her mother again:

George has gone out to Denmark Hill to dine with John but I could not as the east wind puts me back again into a wretched condition. I had a violent headache yesterday with it by merely trying to take a quiet little walk in the Park, but after tea I

* Wife of Sir Frankland Lewis, Bt. They lived at 21 Grafton Street. Both Sir Frankland and Lady Lewis wrote very sympathetic letters to Effie after she left John.

† The craze for table-turning had come over from Germany.

went to Mrs Monckton Milnes* who were kind enough to send us a card and as I did not know her I thought it polite to go. Every thing was so beautiful in the house, and such lovely taste and so many gay people that I regretted much that not having previously known Mrs Milnes I could not take George as it was just a party he would have enjoyed. Millais and Hunt were there and I had the good fortune to be chattering with Lord Lansdowne and Chichester Fortescue† when Millais passed so I presented him to them both. Almost everybody I knew was there so it was very pleasant . . . Will Papa be able to send me some particulars of the Inn at Dalnacardoch? John thinks it will do capitally and thinks it of great importance that we should get the permission of the Duke [of Atholl] to fish and walk on his premises.

For some unexplained reason Dalnacardoch fell through. Effie wrote about it to her father in her next letter of May 30:

Many thanks for taking so much trouble for us which I fear is not yet over. I am very sorry that we cannot get to Dalnacardoch but it cannot be helped. As far as I can understand John, we shall want our rooms for the first week in July, and he intends to be all the time in one place and remain until the weather breaks as he will like to be as long in the company of Millais and, I hope, Hunt, who, with Millais' Brother, will I hope form our party. The Edinburgh people [the Philosophical Institution] want John to give some Lectures there in November and if the season proves fine.I would try and keep him all the

* *Née* Annabel Crewe, she had married Richard Monckton Milnes (afterwards Lord Houghton) in 1851. They lived at 16 Upper Brook Street where they did a great deal of entertaining.

† Chichester Fortescue (1823–94) was Liberal M.P. for Louth. He married in 1863 the fascinating Lady Waldegrave with whom he had been in love for years. His sister, Harriet, stayed with Effie at Charles Street for a week in June. Harriet tried to interest her brother in Ruskin's books 'but he was only interested in the pretty little Mrs Ruskin'. (*Strawberry Fair* by Osbert Wyndham Hewett, p. 79. Murray, 1956.) Mr Hewett on p. 95 of this book writes most unfairly that Effie enjoyed confiding her woes to Fortescue 'in the elegant house she had made her husband take for her in Charles Street'. We know that it was only an apartment and that it was John's own idea to go to London.

time in the North. But of course the Ruskins will try to prevent that if they can. George will I trust reach home safely on Friday ... Lord Denbigh wants us down to the Country for a week. Lord Feilding has arrived from Naples in great distress for the loss of his Wife and he wants us to be with him, but I'm sure John won't go; he does not understand that sort of thing and not knowing what to say he would fall ill in a couple of days.*[1]

Mr Gray suggested other accommodation for them—a house this time, at Dalreach on the River Tummel, south of Dalnacardoch, and on June 13 Effie asked her mother to take it for them. On the way there they were going to spend a week with Sir Walter and Lady Trevelyan at Wallington near Morpeth, Northumberland. Crawley was going with them and Effie intended to engage a cook and a maid in Perth although her new Scotch cook, Robina, had only just arrived at Herne Hill from the Highlands; but it would be cheaper, she told her mother, to engage temporaries on the spot than to pay her own maids' fares to Scotland.

On Sunday, June 19, John and Effie left Charles Street and returned to Herne Hill for a couple of days just to pack up. The next day Effie wrote to Rawdon Brown:

I am much better and if the warm weather would continue I think I would get strong. You may be sure that so long a visit as we shall probably make in Scotland makes me extremely happy. Papa has taken a nice place for us on The Tummel where for the next two months I fancy John and the two Millais and Holman Hunt will be very busy sketching and walking over the Mountains and I shall occupy myself in trying to make them all as comfortable as I can, for we shall not have a very extensive establishment and there seems no certainty of any thing to eat but Trout out of the Tummel or the Garry,

* It was Lord Feilding who had tried to convert John to 'Romanism'. His wife, Louisa, daughter of David and Lady Emma Pennant (a sister of Lord Cardigan who was to become famous in the Crimean War), had died in Naples on May 1 at the age of twenty-four. They had been married in 1846 and had no children. Lord Feilding married again in 1857 and had a family of six. His father, the Earl of Denbigh, had not spoken to him since his conversion, so the death of his wife had evidently brought about a reconciliation.

but it would amuse you to hear the Pre-Raphaelites and John talk. They seem to think that they will have everything just for the asking and laugh at me for preparing a great hamper of sherry and tea and sugar which I expect they will be extremely glad to partake of in case of returning home any day wet through with Scotch mist. If you are so kind as to let me hear how you are passing your Autumn, always direct your letters here as it will be the most sure place. When the artists leave us we shall go on a tour and pay some visits into the far North and if the season is not very severe I hope John will stay to deliver some Lectures to the Edinburgh Institution as they have long asked him to do so and he has had other work in hand. I have merely time now to close the shutters and lock up the rooms till, I hope, Christmas.

In a letter to her mother of this same date, June 20, but evidently written later in the day, Effie told her that Holman Hunt would not be going with them after all but would be joining them later. In the event he did not go at all. Ever since he was a boy he had been determined to go to the Holy Land to paint and nothing but lack of money had prevented him from going before. He had now at last almost finished his most ambitious picture to date, *The Light of the World*, and was only waiting to sell it before setting out for Syria. Had he gone with the Ruskins to the Highlands it is quite possible that his puritanical influence on Millais would have changed the course of all their lives.

'Millais is getting quite blasé,' Effie ended her letter, 'and says he has had enough of London and that the sight of a dress Coat is to him now the most horrid thing he could see. He is so extremely handsome, besides his talents, that you may fancy how he is run after.' And then, as if she might have sounded too partial, she added, 'I think you will like William Millais also very much and Papa will be quite enchanted with his voice.'

No doubt at this stage she imagined that her parents, who were now at St Andrews, where they always went for their summer holiday, would meet the Millais brothers after the visit to Dalreach.

# TO THE HIGHLANDS

❊

And then at the last moment they changed their plans again. This is only known from a note from George Gray written from Perth to his mother at St Andrews: 'Dalreach is all up—John wrote me a note to stop all arrangements'. Why John decided not to go to Dalreach after all is never made clear. The plan was still to go to Wallington, near Morpeth, and then, apparently, to drive to Callander via Edinburgh and from there find a suitable place to stay.

In spite of John's desire to cut the railways, they must have gone to Northumberland by train because they did not leave Herne Hill until June 21 yet arrived at Wallington on the 22nd. Presumably it was in Northumberland that they hired the carriage in which they afterwards drove to Edinburgh, and presumably again the two Millais brothers travelled with them by train to Morpeth which was served by the railway. When they left Wallington a week later, it was by carriage and pair with Sir Walter Trevelyan accompanying them nine miles across the moor in his dog-cart. A sketch by William Millais shows Sir Walter, Effie and Miss Mackenzie in the dog-cart, Millais standing beside it, Ruskin inside the carriage and William Millais on the box.* From this sketch it has been assumed by many writers that a Miss Mackenzie, a mysterious friend of Effie's, never identified, went with them to the Trossachs. This is not the case. The original party at Glenfinlas consisted of only the two Millais brothers, John and Effie and their servant Crawley. Miss Mackenzie was almost certainly Louisa Stewart Mackenzie, afterwards Lady Ashburton, the girl with whom Effie had been photographed for a stereoscopic picture for Lady Trevelyan. She must have been staying at Wallington and would have returned there with Sir Walter in the dog-cart.

* This sketch was sent to the wife of William's half brother, Emily Hodgkinson, for her album. William recounts that the postillion was drunk and that he had to take the reins (Millais, Vol. I, p. 196), a fact which neither Ruskin nor Millais mentions.

During the six months they were away from London there are only six letters in all from Effie, two to her mother and four to Rawdon Brown. Effie must have written home with her usual regularity, so why have these letters not been preserved? Did Mrs Gray destroy them because they showed that Effie was falling in love with Millais? Was she in love with him before they left London? Was he already in love with her then, or did love come gradually to

them both only after they were thrown so closely together at Glenfinlas? All we know for certain is that the whole party started out on this Highland adventure in the highest possible spirits, delighted with themselves and with each other and with the prospect of spending several weeks in each other's company.

When the party broke up fifteen weeks later, irrevocable changes had taken place in three lives. Ruskin, who wrote home every day to his father, seems to have been unaware of the growing feeling between his wife and Millais and to have taken Millais's state of mind at its face value: misery that Holman Hunt was so soon to go

off to Syria and that he was finding it difficult to work in the perpetual rain. From Millais's own letters to Hunt, his growing despair
is revealed.

From an unpublished extract in the *Autobiographical Notes* of
William Bell Scott, the artist, it appears that Millais and Effie were
already obviously in love by the time they stayed at Wallington, but
there is no corroboration of this and as the notes were written from
hearsay many years after the visit they have merely the interest of
gossip.[1]

Ruskin wrote two letters to his father from Wallington ('the most
beautiful place possible' as he called it—'a large old 17th century
stone house in an old English terraced garden') but he best described the visit in a letter written after they had left:

Jedburgh. Wednesday Evening [June 29, 1853]
My Dearest Father
I have been sending you very shabby letters lately. I must
really tell you something about our proceedings—We left Wallington this morning at eleven o clock—to the great grief of our
host and hostess as we very plainly saw—indeed we had been
very happy with them and they with us—and Millais kept
drawing all the while he was there—he could not be kept from
it—first he made a sketch of me for Lady Trevelyan—like me—
but not pleasing, neither I nor Lady Trevelyan liked it except
as a drawing: but she was very proud of it nevertheless, then he
drew Sir Walter for her, most beautifully—as lovely a portrait
and as like as possible—I never saw a finer thing—she was in
great raptures with this, and then he drew Effie for her—and
was so pleased with the drawing that he kept it for himself and
did another for her—but he does not quite satisfy us yet with
Effie. I made a sketch of a hawthorn bush for her—and she
really therefore has some cause to be proud of our visit—She
and Sir Walter are two of the most perfect people I have ever
met with—and Sir Walter opens out as one knows him, every
day more brightly. Lady T kept us laughing all day long . . .
We left them to day in the beginnings of a piece of renovation
and alteration which they put off till now that they might receive us in their old house—Sir Walter drove Effie and Everett*

* From this time onwards Millais was usually called Everett by both

Millais nine miles in his dog cart—before our travelling vehicle —William Millais and I therein—in a tremendous north west gale over the moors—Sir Walter drove through it all hatless— his hair driving back from his fine forehead as if it would be torn away. I kept inside the carriage—not liking such rough weather—We bid him goodbye within four miles of Otterburn, and drove on and lunched at a quiet and clean little roadside inn on the moors—then on over Carterfell—the pass of the Alps between Scotland and England where we had a glorious view towards Jedburgh and Melrose—and so down the sweet valley of Jedburgh in the afternoon—arriving here in a state of great enthusiasm—culminating on being furnished with such a tea as you could not have beaten at Denmark Hill—new laid eggs and fresh butter—just churned, like yours*—and heather honey—and bread, the best I ever tasted . . .

Dearest love to my mother

Ever my dearest Father

your most aff*e* Son

J. Ruskin[2]

Millais had written to Holman Hunt from Wallington the day before: 'Today I have been drawing Mrs Ruskin who is the sweetest creature that ever lived; she is the most pleasant companion one could wish. Ruskin is benign and kind. I wish you were here with us, you would like it.' He was suffering terribly, though, from midge bites, and complained that his hands, arms, legs and face looked as if he were just recovering from smallpox. The midges continued to torment him the whole time he was in Scotland.

They spent Wednesday night at Jedburgh and reached Edinburgh on the evening of Thursday, June 30, having dined at Melrose. ('We have been very merry over our dinner of Tweed trout,' Ruskin wrote from there.) They took the railway from Melrose to Edinburgh and either put their carriage with the luggage in it on a truck at the back of the train, as was the common practice in those days, or left it there and hired another in Edinburgh. We know from a letter of John's of

---

Ruskin and Effie, no doubt to distinguish him from John. He had never been called Everett before, but either Johnnie or Jack.

* Mr Ruskin kept three cows on his small farm at Denmark Hill.

August 6 that he enjoyed the posting to Melrose exceedingly although
subjected to considerable inconvenience from the smallness of the
carriage.

They stayed in Edinburgh for only two nights but Effie wrote from
there to Rawdon Brown and to her mother:

Edinburgh [July 1]

Dear Mr Brown

. . . We arrived here late last night from Sir W. Trevelyan's
in Northumberland where we have spent the last week very
happily. The Country is so delightful after London and I was
so happy running into the woods and down the Trout streams
without a Bonnet or walking the Poney over the bleak Border
Moors to a Mountain Tarn they have where hundreds of young
sea-gulls were just beginning to fly, a curious sight. Then I had
such charming ripe Figs and Grapes out of the Hothouses
which put me in mind of Venice. John and the two Millais
sketched a great deal and then we spent two days coming here.
We posted through the Borders to see the Valley of Jed and
Melrose, the last a complete take in. Jedburgh Abbey is very
grand and characteristic but the latter is a commonplace ruin.
By the way, about the Engraving from the Release you shall
surely have it. I asked Mr Millais a little ago [*sic*] about it.
He says that Graves is to engrave it the moment the Exhibition
closes and that in a year and a half you shall have it whenever
it is finished.* I should not wonder if I brought it myself for
to my great joy, I heard John and Mr Millais talking yesterday
about some plan for preserving all the Tintorettos and saying
they should like to go to Switzerland next year and then to
Venice. John has put a very nice little bit in his book about
your work† which I enclose.

* *The Order of Release* was not engraved until 1856 when a mezzotint was
made by Samuel Cousins, R.A., and printed by Henry Graves & Co.
This was the first of Millais's pictures engraved by Cousins and the beginning of an association of almost thirty years.

† In *The Stones of Venice*, Vol. III, Appendix 9. It is indeed a nice little bit
which for over a century has drawn attention to an otherwise forgotten
book.

And the next day, Saturday, July 2, she wrote to her mother who was still at St Andrews, although her father had returned to Perth:

Thanks for your two nice letters which I have not had a moment to answer before we go this morning to Stirling where I have asked Papa to come and take an early dinner with us before we go to Callander where we shall remain a few days I suppose. On the whole we have had fine enough weather and the Millais are enchanted with Edinburgh. I have been very fortunate about Simpson [her doctor]. He came to me yesterday and again today, and spent last evening at Andrew's* with us. He says that I am just in the same state as before but rather worse—the throat much swollen and the whole mucous membrane in a state of irritation. He says that I am to eat everything I like and to take some pills, to rub myself all over with olive oil every night which is to fatten me and when I am poorly to take Chloroform Pills instead of the liquid. He hopes to see me again when I return. I made him look at Millais who I find has the same symptoms and he said I was right and bid me look into his throat which is in the same state as mine. He says I am to feed him with my pills.† I never saw such a dear kind man as he is. He says if we want fishing anywhere in the Highlands he will get it from any body without the least trouble . . . We had a charming little party at Andrew's last night . . . William Millais sang and delighted them all.

A line from John to his father written on this same Saturday morning told him that they were leaving Edinburgh at half-past

* Andrew Jameson, Mrs Gray's elder brother. He was an advocate and lived at Greenhill Gardens.

† Effie had for years been troubled with her throat. It is quite possible that she had septic tonsils which were poisoning her whole system and that Millais too was suffering from inflamed tonsils which might have accounted for some of his ailments. At this time no safe method of removing tonsils, such as that later developed by Morell Mackenzie, was obtainable, and surgeons were increasingly realising the dangers of the old method of tonsillectomy, a partial guillotine which was liable to cause fatal post-operative haemorrhage. Dr Simpson's chloroform pills would be regarded by modern throat specialists as the best treatment to relieve pain then available, the only other alternative to surgery being mint tea, hot fomentations to the throat and rest.

eleven. As they got to Brig o' Turk that night, a distance of sixty miles, they must have taken the train as far as Stirling (thirty-six miles) although we know that they drove the rest of the way. It took an hour and a half from Edinburgh to Stirling in a fast train; they would have got there about one o'clock which would have fitted in with Effie's 'early dinner', for at Herne Hill dinner was at 1.30.* Mr Gray did come from Perth and spent about an hour with them. Stirling was on the direct railway line between Perth and Edinburgh.

John wrote again to his father in the afternoon from Doune, ten miles from Stirling: 'We have just dined at Stirling, drove on to Dunblane [six miles] and saw the most lovely abbey there, far the finest thing I have seen in Scotland†—We are feeding our horses here and going on to the Brig of Turk where there is a new Inn and where I hope we shall have a happy Sunday. I shall ask for letters at Callander as I pass and post this ... It is a lovely afternoon and William Millais is half beside himself with delight and all of us very happy.'[3]

They intended staying only one night at Brig o' Turk. As it happened they stayed nearly four months. A letter from Millais to Holman Hunt, written on the Sunday, explains their reason for staying:

New Trossachs Inn by Callander
North Britain, or Stirlingshire.
[July 3]

My Dear Holman,

This is Sunday night, we have been to the kirk to-day, walked to the Trossachs, which is mentioned by Scott in the Lady of the Lake, where the king in hunting is lost, have fixed

---

* At Charles Street they had dined at five, and no doubt when Effie gave dinner-parties at Herne Hill the meal was at this later hour. Mr Ruskin in his diary mentions guests coming to luncheon as well as to dinner at Denmark Hill but Effie never mentions luncheon at Herne Hill. At Denmark Hill, dinner guests were invited at six except on Sundays when dinner was at 4.30.

† In this letter there is a sketch of Dunblane Abbey. Ruskin also made a lovely drawing of the oval window in the centre of the west end which he used to illustrate his first Edinburgh lecture. (Reproduced in *Works*, Vol. 12, Plate IV.)

upon a subject for painting, and I have fatigued my limbs and returned with a dreadful headache from which I have partly recovered—You would go mad if you saw some of this scenery it is so fine.

Yesterday Mrs Ruskin, William and myself went over a ruined Castle (the fort of Doune). I never saw anything so beautiful. Ruskin did not accompany us as he has sprained his ankle. During the day we saw Stirling, such a place, the view from the castle is most wonderful—We are likely to stay here some little time as I am going to paint Ruskin's portrait by one of these rocky streams. This year I am going in some measure to idle, as I feel quite done up . . . Although this place is so beautiful and William is with me I feel very lonely and miserable; there is something depressing about these far stretching mountains, everything looks wild and melancholy and one cannot help feeling you are very far from your other friends. The Ruskins *are most perfect people*, always anxious and ready to sacrifice their interest in our behalf. She is the most delightful unselfish kind hearted creature I ever knew, it is impossible to help liking her—he is gentle and forbearing. I have lost all my old liking for letter writing. I cannot express myself otherwise than commonly. It has been raining almost the whole of the day. I hope tomorrow it will be fine as I long to be painting. I am getting restless for work—William sends his love and I am sure the Ruskins would desire remembrances if they were here but they have gone to bed, where I am also going.

Goodnight
Affectionately yours
John E. Millais

Ruskin did not tell his father that he had sprained his ankle, for fear, no doubt, of worrying him, but he wrote to him on this same Sunday, July 3, after describing the scenery, 'Millais however has been more struck by the castle of Doune than anything and is determined to paint Effie at one of its windows—inside—showing beyond the window the windings of the river and Stirling castle. He is going to paint *me* among some rocks—in a companion picture. I thought you would be glad to know he is going to do something for

you,* though he does not seem up to a *composition*. Address still to
Callander as I know not how long we shall stay here.'⁴
   And the next day:

   Another pouring wet day but we went out for an hour nevertheless to look for a subject and found plenty quite to Millais'
mind beside the stream that runs through Glenfinlas—we are
going out tomorrow, if possible, to get a glance of it in sunshine
—and then he will fix—but he has nearly resolved to paint me
beside the stream, and Effie at Doune castle—two companion
pictures—and he is in high spirits about them because he says
they will give him no trouble and be a rest to him, and yet be
full of interest—only he says everybody will be plagueing him
to do their portraits in the same way. The pictures will be
simply called "Glen Finlas" and "Doune Castle". We are all
fatter and rosier than we were, already, and if we can get a
little sunshine we shall pass from rosy to brown with all speed.⁵

   And on the 5th:

   We have had another pouring day but got out in the afternoon and Millais and Effie and I have been building a pier
for three hours into Loch Achray—as I used to do at Winder-
mere, with much success and satisfaction.

   And the 6th:

   I shall soon be able to give you a more accurate address for
Millais has fixed on his place—a lovely piece of worn rock, with
foaming water, and weeds, and moss, and a noble overhanging
bank of dark crag—and I am to be standing looking quietly
down the stream—just the sort of thing I used to do for hours
together—he is very happy at the idea of doing it and I think
you will be proud of the picture—and we shall have the two
most wonderful torrents in the world, Turner's St Gothard—

   * Mr Ruskin had evidently written to John the day after he left London
suggesting that Millais should paint something for him, for John had
replied from Wallington on June 23: 'I will mention subject to Millais
when I have an opportunity—he seems inclined to do something.'

and Millais' Glenfinlas. He is going to take the utmost possible
pains with it—and says he can paint rocks and water better
than anything else—I am sure the foam of the torrent will be
something quite new in art.[6]

On this same day Millais wrote to his great friend Charles
Collins, an artist who had been with him at the Academy Schools,
and younger brother of Wilkie Collins the novelist: 'Ruskin and I
myself have just returned from a glorious walk along a rocky river
near here and we have found a splendid simple background for a
small portrait I am going to paint of him. I feel much too seedy to
think of painting other than something quite simple so that this will
be delightful. He is such a good fellow and pleasant companion . . . I
am going to paint him looking over the edge of a steep waterfall—he
looks so sweet and benign standing calmly looking into the turbulent
sluice beneath.'[7]

And so the celebrated portrait of Ruskin at Glenfinlas was
planned.

# GLENFINLAS

❈

Brig o' Turk has not changed much since Ruskin's day. It is still a tiny hamlet. The cottage roofs are tiled where once they were thatched, but the only other concessions to modernity are telegraph poles, a petrol pump and an ugly tin hut where high teas are served to tourists. The hotel where the Ruskins first stayed was burnt down at the end of the century—purposely, tradition has it, for the insurance money—and the stable which belonged to it is now a private house called Burnt Inn. The present owner has kept the old inn sign in his loft: TROSSACHS NEW HOTEL it reads in white letters on a long blue board. The schoolmaster's house, to which they moved after a week at the inn, was rebuilt in 1875, but that it is still on the same site is unmistakably shown from drawings in two of Ruskin's letters.[1]

As for the Glen itself (Glen Finglas as it is called today), there is now a dam at the top of the stream (making a reservoir on the moor) where there used to be a seventy-foot waterfall. Consequently there is so much less water in the stream that it is impossible to identify the exact spot chosen by Millais for Ruskin's portrait. Ruskin while he was there frequently saw 'small salmon trout leaping like little dolphins among the spray', and in September he sent his father a salmon pulled out of eight feet of water just below the place where Millais was painting him.* Now the water is no more than about a foot deep in any place.

The atmosphere is still so much the same, though, that anywhere within half a mile might be the chosen spot, and almost every rock might be the piece of gneiss which Ruskin himself painted[2] while

---

* Millais confirmed this in a letter to his sporting friend John Leech, the *Punch* cartoonist. 'Fishing here is not so good as angling for Bream in the London docks,' he wrote. 'Salmon are occasionally speared but very rarely caught with hook and line. A fish of about 12 pounds was taken out of a pool close to where I am painting a background of a portrait I am about.' (Letter of September 27, 1853; Sir Ralph Millais's Collection.)

Millais painted him—and there are several places where it is easy
to imagine the party having their dinner on the rocks. The little kirk
is still there which they attended on the Sunday morning after their
arrival, about a mile and a half away, enchantingly situated on the

*Ruskin's sketch of the schoolmaster's cottage in his letter to his father of
September 30, 1853. The door on the left was used by the Ruskins, and the
two windows on the right of that door were those of their sitting-room. The
school barn was on the extreme left.*

edge of Loch Achray. Above all, evoking the atmosphere more than
anything, there is still the rain that raineth every day.

Is Ruskin remembered at Brig o' Turk today? Oh, yes. The wrong
house is pointed out to the visitor: 'That's it over there,' a better
informed inhabitant affirms, 'and that's the window Ruskin jumped

out of when he ran away with someone's wife—I can't remember just whose at the moment.'

Ruskin was fully occupied the whole time he was at Glenfinlas—for the first weeks in compiling the eighty-page index for *The Stones*\* and then with preparing the lectures he gave in November to the Philosophical Institution in Edinburgh. His daily letters to his father are almost entirely filled with details of these matters and, therefore, seldom illustrative of this story. Nevertheless he gives occasional glimpses of their daily life:

Friday, 8th July

We have been out all day again sitting on the rocks—painting and singing and fishing. William Millais catches us a dish of trout always for breakfast and we have a picnic dinner on the rocks beside the stream. Millais himself is doing a bit for practice . . . beautiful thing it will be when done—and mine will be begun I hope early next week.

10th July

I have your note expressing satisfaction over our portrait plan: I believe indeed that these two pictures will be very interesting and they will not cost Millais much trouble—we are making him walk and fish a great deal and we hope to bring him back quite strong. I enjoy the Highlands more than I did—for I expected less—and found more . . . I have introduced Millais to George Herbert to night and he is in a state of great delight. I could not get him to read the Lady of the Lake at all.

14th July

Wet weather again—but Millais has painted a beautiful study of Effie with foxgloves in her hair† and I think he will do the castle of Doune superbly.

* Mr Ruskin had written on June 28 to his old friend William Harrison, 'I wish he [John] had stayed to finish his Book in place of having parcel sent after him as big as portmanteau.' (Morgan.)

† This little picture, reproduced on p. 34, is mentioned several times hereafter. It was copied by John and Effie and signed with a monogram of their joint initials. The copy is reproduced in James, p. 120

Although the food was excellent and they were very comfortable at the inn with a wood fire burning in the evenings in their own sitting-room, where Effie and Millais blew bubbles together and where they all played Battledore and Shuttlecock when it was wet, it was extremely expensive, the inns having to rely on what they could get from the tourists in the three months of the holiday season.[3] On July 9, therefore, they all, with the exception of William, who remained at the inn, moved to the house of the schoolmaster, a white-washed thatched bungalow, about four hundred yards from the hotel, nearer the stream and at the foot of Ben Ledi. Effie's next letter to her mother—the only one written to her from Glenfinlas to survive—tells of their new living conditions:

care of Mr Alex Stewart
Teacher
Bridge of Turk
near Callander
Sunday, 10th July 1853

I am wearying very much to hear from some of you and now as we are settled here for I hope some weeks I trust you will write to me whenever you can and have time, because a letter will be quite an event. The Millais make all their letters common property and get very nice letters from their home.\* John has letters every day from his Father but it never occurs to him to mention what are in them, but I have a suspicion that the old people are at Dover† where I suppose they are happy enough. Crawley thinks Mrs Ruskin would be awfully horrified if she saw our dwelling. We are however as happy and comfortable as any people could desire, being now in the school-master's cottage where we each pay £1 a week including everything instead of £13 which we paid the week we lived at the Hotel which however is an excellent one and very nice people. We are just about 3 minutes walk from it and came in here yesterday. We are so much out of doors that we are not so

---

\* Millais had written to Collins on the 6th: 'Mrs Ruskin is ill to day in bed. I sent her your letter to amuse her.'

† They were at Folkestone. They moved on to Dover and then to Tunbridge Wells, and were home by August 10. They did not go to Paris as had been their intention. See p. 41.

dependent on indoor comforts but our parlour is nice enough.
Crawley I fancy sleeps among the Peats but is charmed wherever
his bedroom is. John Millais and I have each two little dens

*Effie, William (fishing) and Millais.*

were we have room to sleep and turn in but no place whatever
to put anything in,* there being no drawers, but I have estab-
lished a file of nails from which my clothes hang and John
sleeps on the Sofa in the Parlour. At the other end is the day

* Ruskin described Effie's 'den' in a letter to Mary Russell Mitford as
'a little cupboard . . . to sleep and dress in, some five feet broad by seven
long'. (August 17. Yale.)

School and at the Kitchen end a nice large room where the clergyman lives, an excellent Preacher who however is not here today as it is the sacrament at Callander. I think we shall do very well and the Cooking is excellent and the people [Mr and Mrs Stewart] a very respectable old pair.

I have made myself a rough Linsey wolsey dress which I could not do without. With a nice Jacket and large brown wide awake* I am quite independent of weather and sit out all day on the rocks and then wander away towards evening with the Millais who fish up the trout streams, and we generally come into tea about half past eight with a pretty large dish of trout for breakfast next day. John [Ruskin] and William Millais take off their shoes and stockings and wade about the Torrent beds with great Poles in their hands—they put Everett and me into fits of laughter, they are so like Tyrolese Tourists or American Scouts or Cochines [Chinamen] and do look so ridiculous, their Legs so tremendously white and so frightened where they put their feet. Yesterday William lost a valuable pair of Boots whilst spluttering across a deep place. Fortunately John had taken an extra pair and he got them on. You will be sorry to leave St Andrews. Tell me how we could have some Peas and Strawberries sent to us. The gentlemen are groaning sadly over the summer passing without tasting either one or other. I suppose I might write to Mrs Davidson [the cook at Bowerswell] and she would send some just to try. My dearest love to all.

On this same day, Millais described his room at the cottage in a letter to Mrs William Collins, Charles's mother, whom he often referred to as his second mother. He was evidently writing this letter at the same time as Effie was writing hers:

Today is Sunday the 10th of July, and at this moment we are all lazy from having clambered up a mountain† before dinner

---

* In the many sketches Millais made of Effie at Glenfinlas she is always wearing this dress, hat and jacket out of doors. Linsey-Woolsey was a rather rough material made of mixed wool and cotton.

† It is known from Ruskin's letter to his father of July 10 (wrongly dated 'Sunday, the 7th') that the mountain they climbed that day was Ben Ledi. Millais made a sketch of this climb which shows Ruskin and William

and eaten considerably. Ruskin is reading Wordsworth, Mrs R
is writing and William is lying on the sofa . . . Every day that
is fine we go to paint at a rocky waterfall and take our dinner
with us. Mrs Ruskin brings her work and her husband draws
with us, nothing could be more delightful . . . This new residence is the funniest thing you ever saw, my bedroom is not
much larger than a snuffbox. I can open the window, shut the
door and *shave* all without getting out of bed.*

He then went on to describe the incident about William losing his
boots, after which he continued, 'I am painting at present a fall
about a mile from this house until a canvas shall come whereon I
intend to paint a portrait of Ruskin looking into the depths of a whirl-
pool, standing upon a crag. I have come here principally to get
strong, so that I will not work too much like other years. You really
have cause to be jealous of Mrs Ruskin for a more delightful creature
never breathed. If I could meet with her . . .' Tantalisingly the letter
breaks off at this point and the rest of it is missing.

A week later he wrote to Collins, 'The last three days I have been
painting Mrs Ruskin who sits like a real model, so that I have not
lost time.'

There is little doubt that this picture of Effie, painted while
Millais was waiting for his canvas to arrive, is the one reproduced
on p. 83. It is very small (only twelve and half by ten and a half
inches) but perfectly finished. Effie's dress, jacket and wideawake hat
are all brown, her scarf a bright green and her piece of needlework
red. It is a much lighter picture than the portrait of Ruskin, and is
painted lower down the stream, showing the rocks on which they sat
to have their dinner.

Ruskin, in a letter to his father of July 17, confirmed how cheap it
was living at the schoolmaster's: 'I shall economise here—our board
and lodging, both excellent, being £1 each per person per week;—
the Millais of course pay for themselves so Effie, I and Crawley live
including extras—for £14 a month—and we are more comfortable
than at an Inn—so that I see we can live quite in luxury in the

---

walking on ahead while Millais himself, with Effie clinging to his arm,
brings up the rear.

* See illustration p. 82.

Highlands for 200 a year: I would fifty times rather live in this cottage than in Grosvenor House.'

On this same day Millais was writing to Hunt:

Sunday                         At Mr Stewart's, Teacher,
[July 17]                             Bridge of Turk

The last four days we have had incessant rain, swelling the streams into torrents. This afternoon we all walked to see some of the principal waterfalls which in colour resemble XXX stout; the roads are deeper in water than the Wandle so we were walking ankle deep. The dreariness of mountainous country in wet weather is beyond everything. I have employed myself painting little studies of Mrs Ruskin whilst poor William has given way to whisky and execration . . . The greatest change which has occurred since I left Town is the increased growth of my whiskers—they are now so perceptible that Mrs Ruskin in drawing my profile (*without comment from me*) positively pencilled them a-down my cheek. To-night I mean to sacrifice them to the razor—Although my life here is quite novel yet I don't know what to write about—Having the acquaintance of Mrs Ruskin is a blessing. Her husband is a good fellow but not of our kind, his soul is always with the clouds and out of reach of ordinary mortals—I mean that he theorises about the vastness of space and looks at a lovely little stream in practical contempt. I have had a canvass and box made at Edinboro' to paint his portrait looking over a waterfall.* I think it will be fine as it quite suits his character and the background of the foaming water, rocks, and clasping roots look splendid behind his placid figure. I intend painting a companion of his wife at Doune Castle where we stopped on our road here. It is a ruin and I am going to paint her at a window overlooking a river and distant mountains with a view of Stirling Castle.

Copies of the second volume of *The Stones* had arrived by this time and Ruskin wrote to his father on Tuesday, July 19, to tell him to whom to send presentation copies of the book: 'I should like both the volumes bound in *dark green*, strongly, for Millais, who has been

* The canvas in fact had not yet arrived.

making me innumerable presents of little sketches and a beautiful one of a painting of Effie with foxgloves in her hair—worth at least £50. I should like the books done with silk inside . . . Millais will be a good long time painting these two pictures, so you must not be in a great hurry for us back. The rocks in the torrent will take a long time. The pictures are to be companions this shape [here is a sketch of a lunette window showing Doune Castle] 24 inches broad by 28 high. This is the first fine day we have had for a week—and we hope the canvass will arrive today or tomorrow so that my picture may be begun without loss of time.'

The picture of Effie at Doune Castle was never painted. The portrait of Ruskin is, however, of the lunette shape sketched by him in this letter, and is exactly the size he stated. The lunette shape of the picture was almost certainly inspired by the window in the castle at Doune.

On Sunday, July 24, he told his father that Millais had received his canvas from Edinburgh but as it was not white enough he had sent for another to London.* They had been there three weeks and the portrait was not yet begun.

On this same day, the 24th, Millais was writing to Hunt:

This Sunday morning I am hors de combat having met with two severe misfortunes—first when bathing, in ducking my head I struck my forehead and nose against a rock at the bottom. The blow was so violent that I thought the outline was gone forever, it bled awfully, streaming all down my nakedness. The first kind remark Will, in his immediate manner, made was you have broken your nose. I felt so weak from loss of blood that Ruskin hurried home for whisky, which bettered me. The afternoon of the same day I was making a bridge of stones for Mrs Ruskin to cross the stream when my left-hand thumb was somehow crushed between, and I find it so much hurt that I must lose the nail. The pain kept me awake all last night listening to an howling tempest—I lighted the candle not being able to stand the suffering lying down any longer and tried to read

* A white canvas, or a white painted ground, was one of the distinguishing characteristics of Pre-Raphaelite painting and a great break-away from the dark brown ground of the 'antique' school. The fumes of white lead accounted for the terrible headaches the Pre-Raphaelites suffered from! (Hunt, Vol. I, p. 229.)

In Memoriam.* My hand is now poulticed and I am a little eased.

I am almost glad to hear the weather is so bad in the south, for here it is past remark—the horror of this climate is, you start off in the morning (which is fine) of course expecting a continuance after a months pelting, but no such thing, directly the palette is in readiness clouds come over and down it comes again. I am teaching Mrs Ruskin drawing and it is wonderful how well she gets on. She will beat Lady Waterford† whose acquaintance I made in Town before I left.

Millais's accidents had taken place on the Saturday. Effie later mentioned in her diary how accident-prone he was. On his cheeks when he was cold could be seen 'slight furrows of what must have been serious hurts in childhood'. She then went on to describe his two accidents at Glenfinlas. After the last one, when his thumb was crushed, 'he got quite pale', she wrote, 'and I led him home as best I could. He lent on me all the way and it was dreadful pain between his nose and thumb. He got into a perfect fever and it was long before he had his right use of it [his left thumb]. At last the nail began to come off and had he not been in such an irritable unhappy state of mind at the time and constantly pulled it about in nervous unrest it would soon have got well. I have a drawing of myself cutting his Hair at that time in the little Cottage where he has traced the bar across his nose and I think also his wounded thumb.'‡[4]

A month later Millais again described the accident to his nose in detail in a letter to John Leech. He was evidently seriously concerned at the time that his nose had been broken and his beauty spoilt. There is no doubt that he was extremely conscious of his good looks and proud of them. 'No painter,' he once said, 'can draw who is not well proportioned. A man always reproduces himself.'[5] Certainly in every sketch he made at Glenfinlas he included himself.

* Millais had first read *In Memoriam* in October, 1851, and noted in his diary that it had produced 'a refining melancholy'. He 'venerated Tennyson'. (Millais, Vol. I, p. 127.)

† Louisa, younger daughter of Lord Stuart de Rothsay, had married the 3rd Marquess of Waterford in 1842. She was one of the best amateur artists of her day as well as a great beauty.

‡ This drawing is reproduced on p. 98.

Ruskin made no mention of Millais's accidents in his letters home. One cannot help feeling, though, that if Millais had injured his right hand instead of his left and been prevented thereby from painting, Ruskin would have taken some notice of it—or possibly he did not want his father, who was a terrible fusser, to know that their seemingly innocuous pursuit of building bridges could be dangerous. He commented on Effie's drawing, however: 'You ask how Effie is employed—Millais has taught her to draw portraits—and she has done wonderful things already of us all—and works hard all day nearly—she is so pleased at finding that she has this power. Then we play battledore and shuttlecock—go out to get wet—and come in and hang up our clothes—and the days are all too short.'

Millais and Ruskin had tremendous combats at Battledore and Shuttlecock. Millais took three pages to describe to Collins one such battle, 'hitting with such rapidity that we hit each other before being able to parry like fencing'. He referred to Ruskin as 'the Herne Hill Gamecock' and to himself as 'the Jersey Stunner'. Only the announcement of 'grub' by Crawley saved the Gamecock from defeat on this occasion. Perhaps Ruskin hoped that the game would use up some of Millais's superfluous energy, for he had ended his letter to his father on July 24: 'Millais is a very interesting study. I don't know how to manage him, his mind is so *terribly* active—so full of invention that he can hardly stay quiet a moment without sketching, either ideas or reminiscences—and keeps himself awake all night planning pictures. He cannot go on this way. I must get Acland to lecture him.'[6]

Dr Henry Acland, who was now to join their party, had been a senior undergraduate at Christ Church, Oxford, when John was a freshman. They became lifelong friends. Acland lived and practised in Oxford, but being on holiday in Edinburgh it was easy for him to slip over for a few days to Glenfinlas where he stayed with William Millais at the inn. He arrived on Monday, July 25, two days after Millais's accidents, and John went in the carriage to Dunblane to meet him, and reported to his father before setting out that Millais was very glad he was coming as he thought his head a very noble one and wanted to make a study of it. Millais had met Acland once before while staying at Oxford with Thomas Combe, the manager of the Clarendon Press, one of his and Holman Hunt's first patrons.

We now have a letter from Effie to Rawdon Brown in which she mentions Dr Acland's visit. This letter was written on July 27, and the first part of it was all about the proposed binding of Brown's book, *Giustinian at the Court of Henry VIII*. Then, after telling him that her mother was having some preserves made to send to him in Venice, she continued:

You would be amused how the creature comforts are relished by the gentlemen of the party, now reinforced by the addition of Dr Acland, a friend of John's and very clever at all sorts of things with hard names. As you predicted the Sherry and tea are very much appreciated but these delicacies only made the Artist group long for more such as this. At Breakfast, Everett Millais says to his Brother, "Well, William, there's nothing but rain here and the summer is passing and we have not had a single strawberry." "Yes," replied William, "but only think of the Lamb without mint sauce or vegetables. I suppose the peas are ready here about Christmas," therefore I was ordered to open communication with a Greengrocer at Stirling for the supply of the Artistic table. These are the gentlemen who actually live on Hotchpotch, fruit Tarts, broiled Trout for tea and the richest cream, milk, eggs, every thing of the very best—but who [talk?] in an ideal manner of the necessity of living on Beef sandwiches which they make a resolution every second morning to dine upon with nothing for their drink but the Torrent water.

The rain is really dreadful but as it is the same all over England I still hold up my head. We are obliged to have recourse to Battledore and Shuttlecock in a Barn place redolent of Peat reek and where a school of Gaelic bairns is held every morning. John reads aloud to us in the evening Guy Mannering and we all get on very happily and, what is curious, never catch cold from the frequent soakings we get in the course of the day . . . I am much better and Dr Acland says I am to be out in the open air as much as possible but I am really much stronger.

Ten days later Millais was reporting to Collins, 'We have had our dinner on the rocks . . . we had roast lamb and peas, afterwards blackcurrent pudding, cream and champagne, each of us resting our plates uncomfortably on our knees seated on pitiless summits of small Mont Blancs.' So Effie's efforts to supply summer fare for the 'Artistic table' were evidently successful.

# RUSKIN'S PORTRAIT BEGUN

✳

At last, on Thursday, July 28, Ruskin was able to write to his father, 'you will be delighted to hear that my portrait is verily *begun* to day and a most exquisite piece of leafage done already, close to the head —the finest thing I ever saw him do—he is on his highest mettle . . . We have had a glorious day to day, fine weather, and Henry Acland went up the Glen with us and saw the portrait begun to his great delight—he says it is in every way perfect both for me and Millais.'* And on Friday: 'Picture goes on beautifully.'

But by the 30th the rain had started again. 'Rain all yesterday, rain again to day,' Millais complained to Hunt. 'It is truly disgusting . . . I have begun a portrait of Ruskin out of doors but have not done more than two inches of work. I have trotted out at five in the morning so determined was I for getting on but have been miserably damped in body and spirit . . . I cannot help in my letters referring to the wet as that prevents our doing anything but grumble indoors . . . My nose and thumb are getting well. Almost the whole day we play battledore and shuttlecock.'

Acland left on August 1 and the day after his departure Ruskin was writing to his father: 'I have to day two delightful letters— announcing your pleasure at the beginning of the picture, which is now really going on . . . Millais is chattering at such a rate—designing costumes—helmets with crests of animals, and necklaces of flowers, that I hardly know what I am writing . . . We are all getting stronger and better every day.'

* On this same day Millais made a pencil sketch for the drawing which is now at the Ashmolean Museum, Oxford. It is on a piece of pale blue drawing paper measuring eight inches by five. The face is not Ruskin's— it is of a younger man, probably imaginary—but the pose is identical to that of the finished picture and the figure is holding Ruskin's hat and stick. On the back of the sketch is written in Dr Acland's writing: 'The first sketch of J. E. Millais—Picture of John Ruskin/done in the bed of the stream at B. of Turk/Thursday July 28th 1853.'

Because Acland was in at the birth of the Ruskin portrait, some of Ruskin's biographers have assumed that the idea for it originated with him; but Millais himself even robbed him of the pleasure of being there when it was begun. 'Dr Acland has been staying here for a few days,' he wrote to Thomas Combe on August 4. 'What an

*One of Millais's sketches done at this time shows Effie wearing flower bells round her neck, wheat in her hair, a lizard bracelet up her arm and a pineapple and squirrel emblazoned on her breast.*

amiable man he is! He left us on Monday [August 1] and I have taken his room at the inn because of the fine view its window affords. I was determined to bring back something, so on the very afternoon of his departure I began a new picture. Oh that I had tried this bate before with the sun, for I had barely sketched in my work before the sun, with British effulgence, burst out upon the rocky hills.'[1]

This is very confusing, especially as Millais had told Collins as well as Hunt on July 30 that he had begun Ruskin's portrait although he had not done more than two inches. One can only conclude that he did not consider those two inches, that 'exquisite piece of leafage', a real start to the picture at all.[2]

Anyway, by August 4 he was writing to Collins: 'Yesterday we had very fine weather and likewise today. I have painted away like a Baiter. Ruskin sits alongside of me, Mrs Ruskin reads Dante to me, and William sits afar off with Crawley (Ruskin's man servant) who angles for small trouts with a worm.'

Ruskin also was writing to his father on the 4th:

The Amontillado will serve us a long time as we take very little wine—we dine always out of doors now the fine weather has come—on the rocks where Everett is painting me and dip our glasses in the stream. We had a glorious day to day, quite quiet and fine—and I think the picture will be peculiarly beautiful because there is no *sun* in it; all dark rocks with plants hanging down over them and the foaming water below—and Everett paints so brightly that he cannot possibly have too quiet a subject. I am drawing part of the rocks close to him and Effie reads to us, or draws separate plants and flowers for practice—William Millais is at work higher up the stream: Nothing can surpass the beauty of this place, the rocks are so various in form and the vegetation so lovely and the water so bright and brown.

And on Tuesday, August 9:.

I fear it will be a good while yet before I can be back as Everett does not do above an inch of picture each day but he is doing it *beautifully* and the weather is now highly favourable —windless and mild and dry.

And on the 12th:

I am very idle at present getting up marvellously late in the morning—chiefly because Millais picture is an afternoon subject so that he paints late—and as the exercise is best *after* painting we don't get in to tea till ½ past eight nor to bed till ½ past 10 and we never get up till we feel inclined so I am getting as complete a rest as ever I had in my life. By way of exercise we are digging a new channel for the Glenfinlas stream through a bank of shingle which has buried its course and thrown it aside into meadow land and dividing it into branches so that we may build a bridge over it or rather a series of convenient stepping stones.

Everything seemed to please Ruskin about this holiday and he was in high spirits the whole time they were there. Not so Millais who became terribly despondent when he heard that Hunt was shortly to set out for the Holy Land. He was now back at the schoolmaster's house and wrote to Hunt from there on Sunday, August 14:

William has received a letter from Mr Combe in which he speaks of your paying a farewell visit at Oxford previous to your Syrian voyage, as though you were going off in a fortnight's time. Is this true? If so, you are only fit to be potted like ships' provision for such a determination. I should like to get back before you start so let me know something about your intention—William returns to Town on Wednesday next [August 17] and I shall probably stay here until November when Ruskin intends delivering some lectures on Art and Architecture in Edinboro'. I am getting on but slowly here with his portrait although the weather is now splendid. I feel very tired this year and low spirited, I don't receive gratification scarcely from anything. The only pleasure is teaching Mrs Ruskin drawing, she is such a delightful creature and gets on in a manner reflecting great disgrace on me for having been so long before painting as I do now. She has drawn and painted some flowers in oil (the first time she has ever touched a brush) almost as well as I could do them myself. If it was not for her being such a captivating person I should feel disgusted with such aptitude. To day we have had a delightful walk up a glen to a waterfall where Will and myself had a bathe under the shower of water, which falls *seventy feet.* Will underwent the lashing bravely which was almost as severe as a soldiers whipping. I of course kept my delicate person from such treatment and meekly sat in a pool looking on at the swimmer's evolutions . . . We are so short of room here that Ruskin is obliged to have his bed made in our only sitting room. He is sleepily looking over an illuminated

missal so that I cannot keep him up later, and I have no room in my compartment for a flat candlestick to stand much more than a sheet of paper. I am obliged to put the candle in the washhand basin—Good night, write when you can for it is almost my only pleasure.

On this same day he wrote to Collins:

William leaves us next Wednesday morning, Mrs Ruskin accompanying him to Perth, where her relatives (Father and mother) live, where he will stay for two days and then hurry home to resume the severe tutor. It will be a loss as four is much better than three and he is always healthy and happy. Mrs Ruskin returns to us the following Monday [August 22]. Every evening I take a walk with her, and leave Will and Ruskin to labour with spade and pickaxe at making a canal across a bed of stones which has formed on the banks of the river and which obliges the stream to writhe away from its proper course—they work away with as much ardour as Australian gold finders, or seekers.

In fact William and Effie did not leave until Thursday, the 18th. On the 17th Millais was writing to Hunt:

I am very anxious to know if you are really going to Syria immediately—as I should be so very sorry for you to leave without my seeing you, particularly I should not like you to go away without my asking you a favour*—I have felt dreadfully fatigued all to day with doing nothing. As William leaves us to morrow we have sat with him all the day where he is painting to keep him company. Ruskin and myself are deep in the designing of novel architecture. He is quite delighted and astonished at my designs—he thought that we were simply capable of copying nature, and that we had no invention. Now he admits that he was awfully mistaken . . . I am writing this in my bedroom resting this scrap of paper on my thigh, which limb as you know is none of the broadest—Tell me what you are painting and have you finished the Moonlight?† Now I am going to bed to act another part in a dreamland with which I soothe myself to sleep.

* If Millais might join him in a year or two in Cairo and travel home with him. See Millais's letter of October 20, p. 98.
† This refers to *The Light of the World*.

Millais told Collins, who was interested in architecture, more about his new activity:

You will shortly hear of me in another art besides painting. Ruskin has discovered that I can design Architectural ornamentation more perfectly than any living or dead *party*. So delighted is he that in the evenings I have promised to design doors, arches, and windows for Churches etc, etc. It is the most amusing occupation and it comes quite easily and naturally to my hand . . . Ruskin is beside himself with pleasure as he has been groaning for years about the lost feeling for Architecture. When I make a design he slaps his hands together in pleasure. He draws the arches and frames the mouldings for me to fill up. The Church which will be designed *entirely by me* (excepting the ground plan) will *for certain* be executed shortly as Ruskin is mad that it should be begun as soon as the drawings are made . . . Ruskin believes now that I have almost mistaken my vocation and that I was born to restore Architecture. Please say nothing about this, as we don't wish it to become public that we are working in consort . . . I have made several drawings for the Church, amongst others a cloister on which are to be cut in stone all the vices and virtues opposed to each other. The windows I have finished represent eternal happiness and the struggle for life. To give you a notion of how they are designed (for they are unlike any other windows ever thought of) the figures form the shape of the window thus. I only make this stupid little drawing that you may understand that figures are bended into form of the porch, or window, instead of the rotten old notion of having flowers (which are naturally frail) to support walls.

Millais made a large painting of this window, over nine feet wide at the base and seven feet high. The three pairs of angels that form the stone-work all have Effie's profile. It was intended for exhibition at one of Ruskin's lectures in Edinburgh* and is painted in turpentine, which washes out like water-colour, on large sheets of grocery

* According to Millais's *Life* it was exhibited at one of the lectures but it is not mentioned in any of the reports nor is it among the illustrations

paper pasted on to strips of canvas. The stone-work is painted brown and the spaces in between green to look like glass.

'Millais has done me a beautiful design of angels,' Ruskin told his father; and later, from Edinburgh, he sent it to his father who was 'thunderstruck' by it. 'It is the most angelic Painting or Fresco I ever set eyes on,' he told John. 'This is pure sublimity.'[3] (See p. 147.)

---

to the printed lectures. It was never executed in stone because of the cost. Surprisingly, considering its size even when rolled up, Effie took it with her when she left John for good. For over eighty years it hung on the landing at Bowerswell. It now hangs on the author's staircase in Sussex.

My foot ought to be against the wall —

Millais in his bedroom in the schoolmaster's cottage. (*See p. 68.*)

*The Waterfall* painted by Millais at Glenfinlas. (*See pp. 68, 162.*)

# MILLAIS IN LOVE

❋

By the end of August, Ruskin, having finished his index, began to prepare his Edinburgh lectures. Thereafter his letters to his father are full of requests to send reference books, architectural sketches and *Liber Studiorum* until his father must have dreaded hearing from him. He seldom knew exactly where anything was and his father was obliged to look in several places, either at Herne Hill or Denmark Hill, and then, when the book or drawing was at last found, follow exact instructions as to how to pack and despatch it.

Although the lectures had been spoken of for so long (Effie had mentioned them to her mother as early as May 30) it appears from the following letter to John from his mother* that the old Ruskins had only just got to hear about them:

Denmark Hill Aug<sup>t</sup> 15<sup>th</sup> 1853

My Dear John

I am not sure whether you have read the sermon I send I think you have not—glancing over it it seems to me even more admirable than it did when I heard it preached—I never Dearest wish you to be with me because I trust you are led to be where you may get good and do good, but I see nothing more than usually beautiful in earth and sky, that I do not deeply feel you are not with me . . . Mr Gray of Perth mentions that you have some purpose of giving a course of Lectures in Edinburgh. I cannot reconcile myself to the thought of your bringing yourself personally before the world till you are some-what older and stronger prehaps superstition may have some-thing to do with it—I do not say to your father anything about it but I should I think be better satisfied if you continued to benefit the public by writing untill you are turned forty two—pray do not let anything I write about this annoy or irritate

* Mrs Ruskin's spelling and punctuation in this letter have been faithfully copied.

you, you know dearest that what you think you ought or is right to do I should be grieved be grieved [*sic*] beyond measure were any thing I write to make your task less pleasing. Your father tells you how we have read your vol*ᵉ** I rejoice and am filled with thankfulness—I would rather be your Mother than the mother of the greatest of Kings or Heros past or present, you know how all you think or feel, or say or do interests—I trust you will succeed with your river and bridge—take care of heavy weights—Your father is thank God wonderfully well and happy in his work, and I take my walks with the same untired delight as far as walking and loving nature goes but I want you to enjoy with me—My kind regards to Mr Millias I think of you always and pray for you always My love and best blessings to you both—how does Effie keep her health are your throat and eyes better ever My Dearest John

Your Affect Mother   M Ruskin[1]

Ruskin answered this in his next letter to his father:

Thursday [August 18]

I am quite losing all count of days of month, only remembering those of the week for my dates, otherwise I should forget those too—one day being here so like another. Some variety has been created to day by William Millais leaving us, his holiday being expired—Effie has taken our hostess Mrs Stewart with her by way of chaperone and they have all gone to Perth—which William leaves on Saturday for London and Effie returns here with Mrs Stewart on Monday [the 22nd]. Everett and I are left to pursue the arts by ourselves. We shall not go to Perth till the picture here is finished. It is getting on beautifully—but terribly slowly: indeed I saw as soon as it were begun that it would take two months at least—and as for the Doune castle we should have to wait for another month it being a simpler subject. I thought it impossible to get away and therefore acceded to the request of the Edinburgh people to give them four lectures in the first fortnight of November. I am not afraid of the climate as I can take as much exercise

---

* The second volume of *The Stones*.

here as I like, and rather think the Highland air must in autumn be better than that of Herne Hill—As the picture stands at present I think there is little chance of *its* being done till near November. Everett never having painted rock foreground before did not know how troublesome it was. I daresay he will merely take a sketch of Effie at Doune and stay behind us to finish the background—as it is under cover and he can have a fire lighted there: but he may not be able to do it at all, as he is not very fit for work at present—he overdid it last winter and now evidently stands in need of rest not being able to paint above four or five hours a day and not always that.

I have a beautiful letter from mama to day which I would answer to herself—but don't like to try her eyes: though by the writing of said note they seem as good as ever.* She speaks of the lectures with some wish that I should delay my appearance in public of this kind—but I do not mean at *any* time to take up the trade of a lecturer. All my real efforts will be made in writing and all that I intend to do is merely, as if in conversation—to say to these people, who are ready to listen to me—some of the simple truths about architecture and painting which may perhaps be better put in conversational than literary form. I shall however write the lectures first that I may be sure of what I have to say and send them to you to look over. At present I am resting and not troubling my head about anything. I am truly rejoiced that my mother enjoys her country walk so much as she tells me in her letter and especially obliged by the Mr Melvill sermon.† Would you be so good as to send me some more. We rather stand in need of good sermons here.[2]

It took more than this explanation to reconcile Mr Ruskin to the lectures. He was greatly displeased we gather from Ruskin's letters, not only that John should take to lecturing but that he should stay so long in Scotland and be kept from more important work. John

---

* Mrs Ruskin, who was now almost seventy-two, was said by Ruskin to have overstrained her eyes when she was young doing fine needlework. (*Works*, Vol. 36, p. xxiii.) It was also said in Perth that she had a pronounced squint.

† Henry Melvill (1798–1871), Canon of St Paul's. He had been incumbent of Camden Chapel, Camberwell, from 1829–43. He published numerous volumes of sermons.

assured him that the lectures had not delayed the writing of *Modern Painters* (the continuation of which was to be his next great work); he had no intention of writing any more until he had had a rest—the lectures were merely by the way. To mollify his father further he promised him the first chapter of the third volume of *Modern Painters* as a New Year's gift, if he remained in good health.

With Effie away, John was writing again on August 19:

> Friday evening
>
> I think there will be great amusement at Bowers Well [as it is pronounced] to night for Millais—having nothing else to do—made a sketch of the party which was to be given yesterday, from imagination, and sent it off last night. He had seen George Gray in London, as well as Sophie and Alice—and Mr Gray at Stirling for an hour, on our way here—and as he can draw any body after once seeing them there was no difficulty about *them* —but he had never seen Mrs Gray—I gave him an *account* merely of her face and expression and turn of mind—and he drew her from imagination so precisely like—hitting what *I* could not remember—the exact way the ribbons of her cap go down among the side curls, that if she had sat for it, it could not have been liker. I gave him an account of the room at Bowers Well and he drew Effie at the piano—George and the children dancing, Mr Gray looking on, standing up, and Mrs Gray on the sofa with Melville [aged five] so exactly, that I think their state of astonishment this evening will be something they will not forget in a hurry.*

Two days later, in answer to an inquiry from his father as to how much Millais's picture was going to cost, John replied, 'I *fancy* the price of the picture will be from 200 to 250 but he could not tell, himself, at present till he sees how much time it will take him: I think it best not to question him—but to let him do it as well as he

---

* Mr Ruskin asked John to send him this drawing but Effie left it at Bowerswell. When John himself was at Bowerswell in December, however, he sent it to his father. (See p. 115). One may wonder how Effie could have got home in time for the party. She would have had to drive to Dunblane, the nearest station, twenty-four miles away, but from there she could have reached Perth within an hour.

possibly can. I fear the other [Doune Castle] cannot be done at present—he is taking plenty of studies of her head and can put it into the castle at any time.'³

For Millais, who was undoubtedly in love with Effie by now, it must have been a comfort to have this perfect excuse to be forever sketching her. In a letter of his to Mrs Gray written four months later (given in full in its chronological place, p. 122) he writes that Ruskin was all for his accompanying Effie and William to Bowerswell, and returning with Effie, but that he had refused. He also says that Ruskin had appeared 'purposely to connive' at the result which had come about—i.e. that he and Effie should have fallen in love. Millais was not the only one to think this. Many people were afterwards to maintain that Ruskin had deliberately thrown Effie and Millais together in the Highlands with a view to getting rid of her. If Ruskin did have any such dishonourable intention he must have known that should his scheme succeed he would lose them *both*, and however much he may have wished to be free of Effie it is hard to believe that he wanted to lose Millais. Millais was *his* protégé, and even if he did not care for him as a man, he certainly loved his genius. On August 17 he had written about him to his old friend Miss Mitford: 'I do not know whether you have heard anything of the *Pre-Raphaelite* school of painting—or of Mr Millais—its principal representative in the public mind—but if not I must tell you that he is a youth of about four and twenty—gifted with powers of penetration into character and of pictorial invention such as assuredly have not hitherto existed in my time, and capable it seemed to me of almost everything, if his life and strength be spared.'⁴

It seems much more likely that far from wanting Effie and Millais to fall in love, Ruskin looked to Effie to help and encourage this 'youth'. He believed her influence on young men to be wholly good and he trusted absolutely in her discretion. For more than four years he had seen her surrounded by admirers, some of them obviously in love with her and more mature and attractive than Millais, yet never losing her heart or her head, and as there is no evidence (apart from Bell Scott's gossip notes) to suggest that she showed her true feelings for Millais at this time, Ruskin had no reason to think that this hysterical youth was favoured more than the others. And even if he knew, which he may well have done, that Millais was in love with Effie, it was not going to make any difference to his own friendship for him (after all he had gone on helping Clare Ford with his drawing knowing that he was in love with Effie); indeed it seemed to give him positive satisfaction when some man became infatuated with his wife, and the more he admired the man the more highly he thought of his wife for having attracted him.* He was by no means unusual in this, and if Effie's own feelings had not become involved, there seems no reason why this threesome should not have held together at least until Millais fell in love with someone else.

Ruskin made no mention of Effie's return to Glenfinlas, but he wrote on Tuesday, August 23, the day after she got back, 'The picture is going beautifully. All the *dark* rocks are done most solemn and Rembrandt like and the white water and light rocks are to come.'

Millais in the meantime had gone back once more to the New Trossachs Hotel. He was getting more and more gloomy as is shown in a letter to Hunt written on the 29th:

I sleep at this inn, now that William has left us, and have to cross a bog every night, lighted by a small girl with a big lantern. It has been raining for three days without ceasing, swelling the stream to quite a theatrical Swiss torrent. My window is now open and I can hear a melancholy hushing from Glen Finlas waterfall. To day I walked up to the place I am painting, but found it much too swollen to permit my working, the fall looks like writhing liquid amber, so immensely beautiful —sending up a steam, from which one gets wet through in a minute. It is horribly dull having to leave the cottage at night, and go up to a numbered Hotel bedchamber, and being awakened by the Boots reminding the gentleman in the next room that he desired to be called at 3 o clock in the morning, which occurs almost always. It would be quite impossible to stay here if it was not for Mrs Ruskin who is more delightful every day. She is very happy with her new occupation, painting very nearly as well from nature as I can. I don't understand how she does it but I am certain she has learnt in the month I have taught her more than I did in 6 years. Ruskin is extremely

* Effie had written to her mother from Venice: 'I am so amused with John who says he respects me much more since he finds a man so talented as Paulizza [an Austrian artillery officer] likes me.' (*Effie in Venice*, p. 143.)

funny, placidly, alternately writing and drawing throughout the day. I never heard a man contradict himself like he does. I have given up reminding him of his own remarks for he always forgets. His great hobby now is illuminated twelfth century drawings, dragons passionately biting their own persons, and bodiless fiddleplayers, and hooded jesters terminating into supple macaroni—you know the kind of thing, the colour delicately pretty. I have been reading Wordsworth carefully. I find him a true stunner. The Pedlar story of Margaret in the Excursion is perfect. I have been also reading In Memoriam to the Ruskins who are stunned with admiration—particularly the lady. I wish you could come here a little while before starting. You can't go abroad before the Turkish question* is settled and that won't be yet awhile, and now to bed. Good night.

And a few days later in an undated letter, though written after September 3 and while he was still at the inn, he wrote again to Hunt:

I congratulate you upon the prize money from Liverpool.† What sensible people there are at that place . . . I wish old boy you were here sometimes. I find it tremendously lonely. I rarely walk out as [*sic*] Ruskin as he is not a very good companion—he is not a man who respects a person more for living with them. People seem always to die when I am away from Town; no less than three friends have gone since I have been here. I wish there was a kind of Monastery that I could go to— I am beginning to be perfectly sick of life, and only find comfort in prayer. Charles Collins is completely right in his manner of living.‡ Like you I have much that I could tell you but cannot

* At this time England, France and Austria were still trying to find a settlement for the dispute between Turkey and Russia which was to result in the Crimean War the following March.

† Hunt had won that year's Liverpool Academy prize of £20 for his *Claudio and Isabella*, now at the Tate Gallery. It was awarded to him at the meeting of the Academy Council on September 3.

‡ Collins, who was a nervous little red-haired man, had become a Highchurchman while he was at Oxford and was leading a more and more ascetic life to the permanent detriment of his health. Disappointment at not being made a full member of the Pre-Raphaelite Brotherhood may have

in a letter. I destroy your letters, at least most of them I have received here that I think you would not wish to be seen . . . I am sure I don't know what else to say except it be that I am painting rocks perpetually and designing architecture. Mrs Ruskin goes on like an 'Express' with painting, and I don't sleep very well at night and am sure if my face in slightest degree told of my restlessness, and suffering, it would be lined like a Bradshaw railway map, instead of remaining as smooth and youthful as a schoolboy. Write soon again please for it is a real mercy.

Millais soon returned once more to the schoolmaster's cottage where, he told Mrs Collins, it was 'delightful to waken in the morning in my little emigrant crib, Ruskin, his lady and me, all talking whilst dressing'. One wonders why he kept on returning to the inn. Was it in an effort to try to break Effie's spell or because he could not bear to see the way in which Effie and Ruskin lived? He told Collins on September 25 that he supposed his turn for marrying would come some day. 'I confess,' he wrote, 'I should feel considerably better for a wife in Scotland. There is such a want of humanity. These chilling mountains make one love little soft, warm, breathing bodies.' Certainly Effie's little soft warm breathing body so close to him in the next cubicle was a torment as much as a joy. In deepening gloom he wrote to Hunt from the cottage:

Now that there is almost a certainty of war will you still persist in going to the East? If so I am sure you will be cut up and eaten by the Russians. I had a letter from Mrs Combe yesterday—she speaks of your departure as inevitable and seems to think that she may accompany you, which would be splendid for you as she is a wonderful person in sickness. I hear that they have bought the "Light of the World"* (not through her but

---

had something to do with this. Millais had proposed him and he had been 'cut to the quick' when Hunt and Rossetti turned him down. (Hunt, Vol 1, p. 266.) In 1860 he married Charles Dickens's second daughter, Kate, and gave up painting for writing. He died in 1873, aged forty-five, and his widow later married Carlo Perugini, the artist.

* Thomas Combe gave 400 guineas for it which enabled Hunt to set out on his journey. It is now in the Chapel of Keble College, Oxford, presented

by Collins). My dear fellow I can't tell you the depth of dull melancholy I have fallen to since I have been away. I quite hate the thought of your leaving me positively friendless (with the exception of Charley [Collins]). I do believe you will never see me again if you stay away long. I have at night dreadful wakefulness and the most miserable forebodings. I wish you would not forget your original promise that you would write for me to meet you at Cairo after the first year. I don't think I could live in London somehow when you are gone. I have not any place to go to. You will think all this very weak but I don't profess to be otherwise. I shall go with you to Oxford when you spend the promised week with them [the Combes]. I shall not be able to return before a month or six weeks but will get on with the picture as fast as possible . . . Here I am at 24 years of age sick of everything, after having won the artistic battle and certain to realise a respectable competence as long as I can use my eyes, and yet I don't believe there is a more wretched being alive than the much envied J. E. Millais. My song shall be "Oh dear what will become of me" until you write an In Memoriam upon your departed friend. Good night you runaway.

---

by Mrs Combe on the death of her husband in 1872. A replica of it, painted by Hunt in 1900, when he was seventy-three, is in St Paul's Cathedral.

# SLOW PROGRESS

One has an impression that Millais had now lost all enthusiasm for Ruskin's portrait and, indeed, for the next few weeks the picture proceeded with incredible slowness. Mr Ruskin on the other hand was evidently feeling that Millais was not getting enough return for all his work, for Ruskin wrote to assure him that Millais was resting that year and would not have made his usual income anyway, but could make it in two months' work after he got back if he wanted to. However, he did ask his father for money for himself. On September 5 he asked him to send £20 'or I may be run out before the end of the month as I have paid a good deal for the two Millais's which they partly don't know of and partly forget—and which I don't like to ask for as Everett gives me every now and then five pounds worth of pen sketches, besides the oil painting of Effie with the foxgloves.'[1] And on October 18, a week before they left Glenfinlas, 'I shall soon want some more money, about £50 as I have to pay Effie her October allowance.'*

On September 22 he sent his father a packet of Millais's sketches and asked him to take care of them but added that all the good sketches Millais had made for him were in books. And on the 28th he sent him a drawing of his own, showing how Millais was putting him into the picture with instructions that it was for his father and mother only. 'Don't show it to anyone else—except George Richmond—who has a right to see everything connected with portraiture of anybody—and of me, more than anybody† . . . Millais has put all his strength into the ash bough at the top of the picture—and the dark rocks and creepers below this. Nothing can be finer—and these are quite done. He is now at work on the stream.'

The picture was evidently intended for exhibition at the Royal

* Effie received £25 a quarter which John was often late in giving her.
† Although George Richmond was ten years older than Ruskin they had become very close friends since their first meeting in Rome in 1840. Richmond had painted three portraits of Ruskin and one of John James Ruskin.

Academy the following year for on October 7 Ruskin told his father, 'Millais has done some glorious bits of rock in the picture these last two or three days with all their lichens gleaming like frosted silver—most heavenly. He is delighted with it himself. I fear he will have no other important work in the academy as the moment he gets home he means to begin his great picture.'*

And on the 9th: 'We have only sixteen days more—for on Wednesday the 26th we mean to go to Keir to pay a visit to Mr Stirling† and thence to Edinburgh on Saturday. We shall have to leave Millais behind us as the picture will not be done for a month yet. We shall be very sorry to leave our cottage.'

And two days later: 'You will be delighted to hear ... that Millais' picture is beginning to surpass even my expectations—the lichens are coming out upon the purple rocks like silver chasing on a purple robe and the water—which I was nervous about is quite perfect—truly such as never was painted before.'

If Millais really was as delighted with the picture as Ruskin made out, he managed to conceal it from Hunt. In a letter to Hunt headed Saturday evening (probably Saturday, October 8) he told him:

Halliday is here‡ with a friend and intends staying until Tuesday when he will return to Town—he comes out in the Highland kilt and cap. I am still working hard out of doors in spite of my resolutions to the contrary. I believe that I shall kill myself for the cold and damp is intense. I have had a kind of tent made to protect me against showers, but it only serves as a tube for the wind to drive through, chafing the back of my head in a most disagreeable manner. To day I have worked

* *The Deluge* or *The Flood*, a subject Millais had had in mind since 1849. It was never in fact painted although a finished drawing was made of it. In 1870 he painted a very different picture called *The Flood*.

† William Stirling had inherited Keir House, Dunblane, from his father in 1847, and rebuilt it between 1849 and '51. Millais had also been invited but he declined the invitation in order to stay on and work.

‡ Michael Halliday (1822–69) was a pupil of Millais's. He first exhibited at the Royal Academy in 1853, and frequently thereafter, but he was never more than an amateur. After Effie left Ruskin, Halliday wrote to Hunt in the East: 'I have known the whole circumstances all along but my mouth has been closed, Millais having made a confidant of me in the agony of his mind for I had guessed nearly the whole from what I had seen in Scotland.' (May 5, 1854. Burt Collection.)

since breakfast, having my dinner brought to me on the rocks. To add to my comfort I have a stove which burns wood and peat, producing a smothering smoke not in the least warming but excessively pleasant to the nose. A melancholy accident finished to day's work. Crawley, Ruskin's servant, who carries my box, let the same fall and I find upon examination that it is irremediably broken, the cover is cracked all down the middle and the groove on one side has come entirely away. Surely there must be some way of getting a tin box instead of the wooden—the latter will be absurd in the East. I feel intensely incompetent of writing sense to night but never mind I will go on. I so long to finish this background but I fear it will take me three weeks more at least and you know how dreadfully these out of door affairs hang fire. This is a little writched [*sic*] picture not larger than your sheep of last year.* There is some falling water in it which is very perplexing. How much longer do you expect to be before starting and what are your plans? This war business seems never to end. We see papers occasionally and get more confused than ever . . . I feel half dead to night and only alive to cold and weariness. Have you read the Charles Grandison, it is splendid.† We have lots of invitations hereabouts but the picture anchors me, and I am afraid partly restrains my companions,‡ who must leave for Edinburgh in a fortnight for the lectures when, if I am not finished, I must remain alone for a time. I have done far too much for me to give in, so I will work until Xmas rather than strike. Write soon and cheer me, you know what it is.

At this point there appears a letter from Effie herself, the first for three months, in which she recounts an incident which would have

* *Strayed Sheep*, a small picture painted on commission from Hunt's larger picture, *The Hireling Shepherd*. It shows a group of sheep on Fairlight Downs.

† *The History of Sir Charles Grandison*, a novel in seven volumes by Samuel Richardson, published in 1753. Ruskin had told his father on October 3, 'Effie is reading Sir Charles Grandison and I can't help listening to it and Everett is delighted with it, more than with any book I have yet seen him open—he says it is pure pre-Raphaelitism.'

‡ The Ruskins went over twice to dine with Mr MacNaughton, a London barrister and a Highland proprietor at Inver Trossach, and had spent the night of September 24 there.

made good material for a romantic novelist. It is to Rawdon Brown
and is dated October 10:

I have been so busy lately with gilding some of John's Architectural Diagrams for Edinburgh, walking with, or reading to,
the gentlemen on the rocks and returning in the evening tired
and again reading aloud to them, John painting and Millais
lying with his head against the wall done up with his day's
painting on the rocks, miserable work as you may imagine in
this cold October weather, the wind and rain blowing through
a little tent dragged across oaken poles with a great pine wood
fire on one side and the spray from the Torrent dashing up and
keeping one cool on the other side. My voice has got quite
strong trying to make myself heard above the roaring waters,
and the same now in the glow is exquisitely lovely . . . The
roads are now lonely enough and almost impassible from mud.
As it is quite dark before we get home the holes and roots in
the bogs we step into render our boots, as they have lasted all
the summer, a triumph of our Glenfinlas [word illegible], but
the other evening you would have been sorry for me: I was
returning home with Millais and coming to a very dirty mud
bank I asked his help; it was quite dark and he told me to walk
on the edge of the grass and I thought I was getting home
nicely. He had fast hold of my arm, when my feet went from
under me and down I fell into a cold mud bath. He fell too
partly upon me but thereby served himself, but when I got
pulled up I found by my weight how much it had been added
to by my fall, and on reaching home I found myself in such a
state my frock could not be brushed for two days.

John and I go to Mr Stirling at Keir about three hours [by
carriage] from this for two or three days on the 26th. We then
go on to Edinburgh for his lectures, leaving Mr Millais here as
his Picture is not done. We then go to see my family for a week
and then home. We are to get to London as soon as possible
on account of your Book. Mr Rich* has sent us some of his
manuscript as ready for the Press and John thinks that it will
be certainly out after the New Year or at least to be ready for

* The editor at Smith, Elder who had been working for several months on
Brown's book, *Giustinian at the Court of Henry VIII*.

the Spring season. He is to compare Mr Rich's work with your manuscript and see it through the Press himself. I read all that was sent aloud after tea to John and Millais and the latter, who is no great reader but delights in being read to, says to me sometimes, like a child asking Cake, "Are you sure there's no more Giustinian in your Trunk, Mrs Ruskin?" . . . John sends you his kindest regards . . . I hope you are as well at present as yours sincerely Effie Ruskin.

# THE PARTY BREAKS UP

✳

Their time at Glenfinlas was running out and Ruskin began to be seriously concerned with Millais's condition. He wrote to his mother about him on October 16:

I wish that the country agreed with Millais as well as it does with me, but I don't know how to manage him and he does not know how to manage himself. He paints till his limbs are numb, and his back has as many aches as joints in it. He won't take exercise in the regular way, but sometimes starts and takes races of seven or eight miles if he is in the humour: sometimes won't, or can't, eat any breakfast or dinner, sometimes eats enormously without seeming to enjoy anything. Sometimes he is all excitement, sometimes depressed, sick and faint as a woman, always restless and unhappy. I think I never saw such a miserable person on the whole. He is really very ill to-night, has gone early to bed and complains of a feeling of complete faintness and lethargy, with headache. I don't know what to do with him. The faintness seems so excessive, sometimes appearing almost hysterical.[1]

The hopelessness of Millais's love seems to have completely unmanned him. Hunt's imminent departure, however, and then the news that Walter Deverell, a young painter on the fringe of the Pre-Raphaelite movement who had been a fellow student at the Academy Schools, was seriously ill, were made excuses for a misery which he poured out to Hunt in his next letter:

Thursday [October 20]

How can I assist in comforting poor Deverell? You say (at least his sister says) he would get well if he sold a picture, for that matter I will buy one to morrow if it will give him the least relief—Let me know by return of post his circumstances, whether they require *money, or anything*, as I *would gladly* give all I have in *such a good* cause, and think myself lucky for having such an opportunity of doing good service—If he felt uncomfortable at receiving support from me, tell him he must paint me a picture when he gets well, or let me have something he has already in the house* . . . Ruskin is much interested about him and if he gets well he shall never again be so unfortunate as he has hitherto been.

My dear old friend, God knows I will miss you, but I suppose you are doing right in leaving this country, which is getting more and more gloomy—relations and friends are dying so fast that I fear every fresh letter I receive contains the news of some other death—I am almost glad that I do not see your start as I believe I should groan myself into a fever—you must write continually and I will let you know anything that goes on in England. Remember also that I will proudly undertake all commissions regarding pictures you may send over. I feel so broken in spirit that I am afraid I shall have to leave home for some time. I think of visiting Spain for a little if I can persuade Collins or Phillip† to accompany me. Gower St will be insufferable now. Since I have been in Scotland the grain has been added to the scale that before was lingering in a perfect balance. All seems altered, the World less attractive than ever it was, and I feel inwardly a sense of returning wearedly home, after a day's idleness and pleasure. I don't know whether this is coherent, or whether you will understand it—As for the election [to the Academy] I don't care twopence about it. . . .

I should like to say a hundred things to you before starting, but for the life of me, I can't think of one—The desire which I expressed in a letter some time back to you, was that you permit me, in a year or two to join you at Cairo when we would return together. I would make the journey entirely for recreation and pleasure and therefore unencumbered of canvasses and galli-

* Millais and Hunt between them bought anonymously an unsold picture of Deverell's for 90 guineas. (Hunt, Vol. I, p. 361.)

† John Phillip (1817–67), R.A. 1859, had known Millais since he was a child. He had painted a portrait of him in 1841 which is reproduced in Millais, Vol. I, p. 15.

'*The Countess*' *as Barber*. Drawing by Millais showing Effie cutting his hair.
This drawing is dated the day after Millais's accidents. (*See pp. 71, 222.*)

*Highland Shelter*. Effie and Millais sheltering under the same plaid.

pots—I could easily return in time to see you off, but will rather escape such a melancholy business. In truth I don't think I should have the strength to say good bye—scarcely a night passes but what I cry like an infant over the thought that I may never see you again—I wish I had something to remember you by, and I desire that you go to Hunt and Roskell and get yourself a signet ring which you must always wear—Unless you have bought such a thing since I left London you require one for sealing your letters when you write to friends in England —I do not write to my Father or William to get you this as it is better for choosing for yourself and fitting your finger—get a *good one* and have your initials engraven thereon.*

Now I remember you have given me all Tennyson's poems so dont get anything for me as there is nothing that I have not, or am in want of—It is wonderful how with all the suffering I endure in thinking of your leaving, Deverell's illness, and the other calamities, how I still go on with my work, sitting numbed in the biting cold, twirling the little brushes upon a broken china palette, and doing about the size of a fiveshilling piece in a day . . . I am glad you have finished the background [for *The Light of the World*] at St John's Wood, how quick you have been about the picture. I wish I could be as soon done with this portrait—anything at present would be distasteful. I should like to go to sleep for a year and awake and find everything as it was when you lived in Cleveland St† when you were straitened for food, and we all went nightly to disclaim against Rubens and the Antique—Those were happy times to these. This sounds as if it came from a hoary headed, weakleged old

---

* Hunt bought a ring at Hunt and Roskell which he wore until his death. It is smaller than the usual signet ring. On a circular sardonyx, set into a circle of gold, are engraved Hunt's initials WHH ingeniously combined into a monogram with the letter M. The other way up, the monogram, even more ingeniously, turns into the letters PB. The ring is now in the possession of Hunt's granddaughter, Mrs Elizabeth Burt, who always wears it. At the top of Millais's letter is a note in red ink signed with the initials of Hunt's widow, MEHH: 'This letter must never be parted from the possessor of the Ring.'

† Near Fitzroy Square. Hunt had had his studio there when Rossetti first became his pupil, but had been evicted by his landlord in 1849 for failure to pay the rent. (Hunt, Vol. I, p. 182.)

boy at the Adelphi* but it is nevertheless my wish, but not so great a wish as that I may meet you stepping lightly down the plank, and returning to the old friend you know

Poor Jack—<br>Write by return of post

On this same day, October 20, Ruskin was writing coolly to his father about Deverell:

The enclosed letter is from Hunt—the P.RB. I begged it from Everett because it refers to one of the Pre-Raphaelites, Deverell—who has been unsuccessful and appears to be a person to whom a little kindness, in the way of a shape of rice now and then or a little sweet sherry or anything which would signify some care of him, would be a true service† . . . Everett is very fond of him and was crying about him all the morning.

But Deverell needed more than a shape of rice and a little sweet sherry: he was an orphan with a family of little brothers and sisters to support. He died of dropsy, brought on by a kidney disease, on February 2 of the following year.

Ruskin was far more concerned about Millais, and at last decided to take matters into his own hands by a personal appeal to Hunt:

20th October

My dear Hunt

I can't help writing to you to night; for here is Everett lying crying upon his bed like a child—or rather with that bitterness which is only in a mans grief—and I don't know what will become of him when you are gone—I always intended to write to you to try and dissuade you from this Syrian expedition— I suppose it is much too late now—but I think it quite wrong of you to go. I had no idea how much Everett depended on you,

* This probably refers to the Society of Arts at 18 and 19 John Street, Adelphi, which had many eminent Academicians among its members.

† Mr Ruskin visited Deverell on November 12 and reported to John next day, 'I half broke my heart yesterday by calling on Deverell—a most Gentlemanly young man in the poorest Dwelling's worst Room—a handful of fire on a Black cold day, painting to pass time without purpose or energy.' (Bembridge.)

till lately—for your own sake I wanted you not to go, but had no hope of making you abandon the thought—if I had known sooner how much Everett wanted you I should have tried. *I* can be of no use to him—he has no sympathy with me or my ways, his family do not suffice him—he has nobody to take your place—his health is wretched—and he is always miserable about something or other: and his mind is really of too much value—as I think yours is also—that the health and life of both should be endangered because you must needs go to paint the holy land—You are not fit to do it yet—your own genius is yet *quite undeveloped*—I say so the more positively because I think it a great one—and the greater it is, the longer it will take to mature. If you go to the Holy land now, you will paint things that you will be ashamed of in seven years: if you wait, to take care of Everett till he gets somebody else to take care of him, you may go then with fully ripened power, and save *him* besides. I never saw so strange a person, I could not answer for his reason if you leave him. Instead of going to Syria, I think you ought to come down here instantly: he is quite overworked—very ill—has yet a quarter of his picture to do in his distress—and we must go to Edinburgh—and leave him *quite alone*—next Wednesday. Think over all this.

Yours ever faithfully and in haste<br>J Ruskin

Don't say anything about this letter to him.[2]

This appeal may have had some effect on Hunt. Anyway, he did not leave London until the following January, 1854, although in his reminiscences he gives as the reason for the postponement of his journey a sudden commission to paint *The Awakened Conscience*. He makes no mention of Ruskin's letter but says that Ruskin, among others, tried to dissuade him from going to the East for the sake of his career.

Millais, hearing that Ruskin had written to Hunt, wrote off hurriedly next day to try to correct the impression he had made:

I have discovered that last night when I felt somewhat low spirited and otherwise weak, Ruskin wrote a letter to you in which he spoke of me in connexion with your departure. It is true I was thinking of that event most gloomily, but for all I am likely to possess I would not have you influenced by any feeling of mine in regard to your leaving—mine is purely a selfish desire to have you always within sight and not to be considered for one moment. I write this fearing that you might be moved to delay going on my account. It was Mrs Ruskin who thought it right I should know what her husband had written that told me the purport of his letter, in which I believe he speaks of my regret seriously affecting my health—I don't feel at all well but it is quite absurd that you should let that interfere with your intended journey, so have the kindness not to consider me in the matter. I have not worked on the rocks to day as it has been raining fearfully since the morning, and so swollen is the river that my tent has been washed away and a heavy iron fireplace has been thrown over by the strength of the current. Don't mention anything about my being unwell to my family as it would frighten them to death. I have had a headache all day and feel intolerably depressed, but I hope to be better soon when this background is done. I would write more but feel unable and in truth I expounded all my day in my last . . . It is such an awful night, hail, rain, thunder and lightning. Call upon my family as soon as possible as I have written some directions concerning you and tell them to send me more money—£20—I don't want as much but would rather have more than necessary with me.

It is not surprising that when Effie and John left Brig o' Turk on October 26 for the visit to Keir, Dunblane, Millais found it intolerable to stay on there alone, especially as it had rained in floods for the past five days. On Friday the 28th Ruskin wrote to his father from Keir:

I am very sorry to say that Everett has been forced to give up for this season—he must paint in the figure and come back in March to finish the background—He held on as long as he could—but was really so ill when we left that I sent Crawley back yesterday [in the carriage presumably] with positive orders to stay with him in case he should be laid up, as I could easily manage to get another temporary servant in Edinburgh—but it had poured all yesterday, and was raining when Crawley arrived and all the country flooded—and Everett thought it more rational to give in as he is already seriously ill. He has gone to Edinburgh in great disgust with everything and I suppose will go straight up to London to try to make up for lost time. I shall hear from him today I suppose. Crawley saw him to the Dunblane station and came back here last night.[3]

But Millais waited for them in Edinburgh and on the 29th was writing to Hunt his last letter of this year, 1853:

Gibbs Royal Hotel [Princes Street],
Edinburgh

If you have no objection I will gladly join you at Florence next Spring as I am really dreadfully unwell, scarcely a day without headache—it is no use taking medicine as that only weakens me. The Ruskins have been staying these last three days at Mr Stirling's place, Keir, and I expect them here every minute. I see there is a letter to him from you, I suppose in answer to the one he wrote you about going to the East and regarding myself. How glad I am for myself that you are for the present prevented from going to Africa although I expect you will leave me in Italy directly the war question is settled. The day before yesterday I left Brig o' Turk and came away to this Hotel—so awfully respectable and solitary—nothing to do but walking up and down a kind of Regent St in a foggy London rain, with no other entertainment within doors but the Times newspaper. This day is all sunshine and somehow very oppressive but I believe I am so sick that all weather is miserable . . . I must stay here until they send me some money . . . I feel so horribly impatient to do something. Quiet is never rest to me as the whole time I remain doing nothing I feel under the lash of some demon. I can understand so well your desire to get away into new scenes, it is the only thing left for us. I am sure we would get on so delightfully together as we have heretofore . . . I have sent home the picture of Ruskin for the weather was terrible and would have killed me outright, so I intend coming for a week or so in March when it is dry, although colder than now. I have a headache coming on from writing this. I don't know how I am to employ my time here for I cannot go out I feel so tired and there is nothing to occupy me indoors. I so long to see your old familiar face again and hope you will not leave before I return . . . The Ruskins will not be here until 3 now so I will try and make my legs carry a little way . . .

The Ruskins have just come and if you will wait for a week I will join you and go to Paris as I want some trip to amuse me.

'Millais is still here,' Ruskin wrote on their arrival in Edinburgh, 'but I don't think he will stay long as he seems quite unsettled by his disappointment with his picture.'

Mr Ruskin was most annoyed that Millais had abandoned the picture, but after Ruskin had written eloquently to defend him, Mr Ruskin became what John called 'at summer heat' with him again.

Millais stayed on in Edinburgh until November 10, but we do not know whether it was lack of money that kept him there or the difficulty of tearing himself away from Effie. He arrived home in time to hear the results of the Royal Academy election. Although he had told Hunt in his letter of October 20 that he did not care twopence about the election, he was in a state of great excitement on the day the results were to be made known. He and his brother William with Wilkie and Charles Collins spent the day together walking impatiently in the country at Hendon. On their return they went straight to the Academy to be greeted with the news that Everett had been elected an Associate.[4]

# EDINBURGH

❀

On the last day of October Ruskin, in Edinburgh, received a melancholy letter from his father deploring his long absence. He wrote back by return: 'You must not get impatient for you know how we are to have a nice time in Switzerland together and so I must really let Effie see a little of her people as she has stayed so quietly at the Trossachs.'[1] This is the first mention of the proposed tour in the following spring which had evidently been discussed before John left London.

The lectures were to be on Tuesday, November 1 (Architecture); Friday, the 4th (Decoration); Tuesday, the 8th (Turner and his Works), and Friday, the 11th (Pre-Raphaelitism). Ruskin received 20 guineas for the course. On the 12th he intended going to Bowerswell for a week or ten days and then making his way slowly homewards, paying some visits en route but arriving at Herne Hill well before Christmas.

Sir Walter and Lady Trevelyan as well as other friends came to Edinburgh especially to hear the lectures which were held in the hall of the Philosophical Institution at 4 Queen Street. Over a thousand people attended each lecture and, as there was not room for them all in the hall, the overflow was obliged to stand in the lobbies.

'Everything went off capitally and I was heard very well without any exertion,' John wrote off to his father the morning after the first lecture. Mr and Mrs Gray were there to hear their son-in-law and the following letter from Mr Ruskin shows that good relations still existed between the two families:

London 3 Novr 1853

My dear Mrs Gray

I do not pass an hour without returning Mrs Ruskin's and my own sincere thanks for your kind and considerate letter of yesterday—I had a line directly from John but next came your full account of the Lecture and the sympathy you so kindly show in our feelings is very deeply felt by us and gratefully acknowledged—I had heard John's fluent powers tried at Oxford but never in such an assemblage—His Mother and I would have gladly traversed the 400 miles and remained all the fortnight at Edinburgh but our feelings would have been agitated and John knowing our anxiety might have been disturbed himself—so we determined to hear not him but *of* him and a better reporter he never had than yourself—I am very glad you and Mr Gray were present, and I am rather proud that my son has made no [word obliterated] despicable figure in my native place and that he was probably heard by many of his Fathers early friends . . . I am sorry that Effie is not so well at Edinburgh. The excitement and Bustle will be considerable but soon over and they may both rest at Perth after it.

John as well as Effie soon became ill in Edinburgh, and on the Sunday after his second lecture he wrote to his father most revealingly about his health and state of mind:

I have not said anything lately of the affection of my throat —because it neither gets worse nor better . . . I have heard much from different people . . . of a Mr Beveridge,* who has for twenty years been effecting singular cures by friction of the surface—and rose from the ranks—as Jephson† did. I have great trust in these self made men and thought I should like to see him. He said in an instant that I could take the affection away myself, by persevering friction on a particular part of the neck. I then spoke to him of the various nervous feelings I have had for some years back—more especially of the peculiar nervous headache—lasting for three or four days at a time —which plagued me a good deal even in the Highlands. All these feelings, he says, he can put an end to—if I will let him treat me like a Turk, and shampoo‡ me for an hour a day for a

* John Beveridge, of 26 London Street, described himself as a practitioner for 'synovial diseases', but he was not a qualified doctor.

† Dr Henry Jephson under whom Ruskin had twice taken a cure at Leamington. He 'had risen . . . from an apothecary's boy to be the first physician in Leamington'. (*Praeterita*, Vol. II, Chap. IV.)

‡ Then meaning massage.

month . . . What would you have me do in the matter . . . If I do not stay to be rubbed, I shall D.V. go to Perth on Saturday next [November 12] . . . If I stay here for a month, Effie will go to Perth by herself . . . In either case I shall set about the first chapter of Modern Painters directly so as to fulfil my promise of a New Years present to you.

It is curious how like your melancholy letter—received some time ago, about our staying so long away, is to the 176th letter in Sir Charles Grandison. I wish Effie could write such a one as the 177th in answer.* But I have had much to think about—in studying Everett, and myself, and Effie, on this journey, and reading Sir Charles Grandison afterwards—and then reading the world a little bit—and then Thackeray—for in "The Newcomes"—though more disgusting in the illustrations than usual—there are some pieces of wonderful truth.† The grievous thing that forces itself upon my mind—from all this—is the utter *unchangeableness* of people. All the morality of Richardson and Miss Edgeworth (and the longer I live—the more wisdom I think is concentrated in their writings) seems to have no effect upon persons who are not *born* Sir Charles's or Belindas.‡ Looking back upon myself—I find no change in myself from a boy—from a child except the natural changes wrought by age. I am exactly the same creature—in temper—

* The first-mentioned letter is from Lord G to Lady L, his daughter-in-law and sister of Sir Charles Grandison. In it he asks Lady L when she and her husband are returning from a prolonged visit in Northampton-shire and whether they have forgotten that they have a house in Grosvenor Square. Lady L replies: 'O my dear Lord! what do you mean? Are you and Lady Gertrude really angry with me? I cannot bear the serious conclusion of your letter. May you both live long and be happy! If my affectionate duty to you both will contribute to your felicity, it shall not be wanting. I was so happy here, that I know not when I should have returned to town, had you not, so kindly as to your intention, yet so severely in your expressions, admonished me. I will soon throw myself at your feet; and by the next post will fix the day on which I hope to be forgiven by you both.' If only Effie *could* have brought herself to write such a letter to her father-in-law.

† *The Newcomes*, illustrated by Richard Doyle, was being published in twenty-four monthly parts. The first part had appeared in September of this year.

‡ *Belinda* by Maria Edgeworth had been published in 1801. Mrs Ruskin had read Maria Edgeworth and Richardson aloud to Ruskin as a boy.

in likings—in weaknesses: much wiser—knowing more and thinking more: but in character precisely the same—so is Effie. When we married, I expected to change *her*—she expected to change *me*. Neither have succeeded, and both are displeased. When I came down to Scotland with Millais, I expected to do great things for him. I saw he was uneducated, little able to follow out a train of thought—proud and impatient. I thought to make him read Euclid and bring him back a meek and methodical man. I might as well have tried to make a Highland stream read Euclid, or be methodical. He, on the other hand, thought he could make me like PreRaphaelitism and Mendelssohn better than Turner and Bellini. But he has given it up, now. That is a wonderful wise old proverb, one cannot make a silk purse out of a sow's ear.[2]

He posted this part of the letter but continued it that same evening:

I was going on to say that another thing that seemed to me so mournful was the difficulty of comparing the powers of command in one person and another—I, for instance, have got tolerably methodical ways of doing things—but then I have hardly any real *warmth* of feeling, except for pictures and mountains—I don't want to do anything that I don't; I have no love of gaiety as people call it—whatever I do love I have indulged myself in—and am methodical in as far as I am so— because I am slow and progressive in my way of thinking . . . The more I see of the world the more I find the warm-feeling people liable to go wrong in a hundred ways that quiet people don't—look at Melville Jameson [Mrs Gray's brother] . . . but really there is more truth than Miss Edgeworth allows in the plea of the warmhearted group of irregularly acting people, against the coldhearted regulars.

He ended his letter by asking for some more money 'in order to get out of this fine hotel—now an exceedingly dirty and bad one—I have received I think 130 of my October allowance. I must have another 50, I fear—before I shall be able to get clear of Scotland even at the soonest.'

They were staying at the Royal Hotel, 53 Princes Street, which still exists. The proprietor was then a Mr H. M. Gibb and Ruskin was under the erroneous impression that his father supplied sherry to the house which was one of the reasons why he had decided to stay there.

The money he asked for arrived by return without question and Mr Ruskin agreed to the Beveridge treatment.

John's second lecture had been as successful as the first (he wrote that without Millais's help, though, 'it would have missed its principal *coup*'),* but the third lecture had to be postponed because of an attack of hoarseness brought on by 'excessive delight' in Holyrood Chapel where he had stayed too long, 'not drawing or standing, but running about in great exultation in the damp atmosphere'.† Mrs Ruskin evidently blamed his long absence from home for this attack, for on November 11 he was writing:

Mama allows her wishes to be a little too much fathers to her thoughts about Herne Hill—I got comparatively better there because I had quiet—the first real quiet I had had for a year or more. I always get well when I have peace and method in my life—and always ill when I have company and disturbance. But I certainly gained more at Leamington, Folkestone and Chamouni than ever I gained at home in the same time— and I hope to gain here in the same way by going into a quiet lodging and letting Effie go to Perth, so as to bring no visitors upon me. Besides, there is a great deal to be done in the world which is inconsistent with health—yet is duty. A clergyman's health is not bettered by his visits to sickbeds, nor a doctor's by his night bell—but both must submit. Perhaps for *my health*, it might be better that I should declare at once I wanted to be a Protestant monk: separate from my wife and go and live in that hermitage above Sion which I have always rather envied.‡

* A beautiful drawing of a tiger's head drawn by Millais from life in the Edinburgh Zoo (there was no lion in the zoo) compared with a distorted lion's head on a neo-Greek building. (Both reproduced in *Works*, Vol. 12, Plate IX.)

† Ruskin to his father. Letter of November 11.

‡ In 1870, in answer to an appeal from Mrs La Touche to save her daughter, Rose, from Ruskin, Effie wrote: 'He [Ruskin] once years before offered me £800 a year to allow him to retire into a monastery and retain

But then I don't think my works—though I might write more
of them would do so much good as when I bear a little with
the world—and see how Mr Stirling lives at Keir—and con-
descend to—if you will call it condescension—to talk for an
hour to a thousand people who are eager to be taught by me.
This Highland expedition—even if Millais should never finish
his picture, is no failure. I have watched him painting—have
led him to a kind of subject of which he knew nothing, and
which in future he will be always painting. I have had a wonderful opportunity of studying the character of one of the most
remarkable men of the age—and have arrived at conclusions
which fifty years of mere *reflection* would never have opened to
me—and I have no doubt whatever that the picture will be
finished in due time. Millais left us for London last night, and
will have called upon you, I suppose, before you receive this:
or at all events will call soon—he may have rather a rush of
business on his first arrival.* He is going to set to work at present
on another picture—his great one [*The Deluge*]: which is to take
him three or four years—and as soon as I return at Xmas is to
paint my portrait into his landscape so as to have it all ready
for finishing in spring.†³

On November 12, John and Effie moved to Swain's Private Hotel
at 5 Albyn Place.‡ The bill at Gibbs's had come to £40 so, as well as
the previous £50, John was obliged to ask his father for a further
£60, and for another £20 from Glasgow on the way home. The
money was immediately sent as everything always was the moment
John asked for it. It was only to the Grays that Mr Ruskin complained of the young people's excessive spending and then usually in

---

his name—that I declined. He was then under the influence of Manning.'
(Morgan; quoted in James, p. 257.)

* Millais called at Denmark Hill on November 14 and dined there on
December 7. On this last occasion he interpreted his and Ruskin's diagrams for the Edinburgh lectures to a party consisting of five other male
guests. 'What a Beauty of a Man he is,' Mr Ruskin wrote to John, 'and
high in intellect but he is very thin.' (December 8. Bembridge.)

† This shows that Millais had not as yet begun to paint Ruskin himself—
he had been wholly occupied with the background.

‡ This hotel remained in existence until 1887.

such a way as to put the blame on Effie. Mr Ruskin's chief complaint against Effie was her extravagance, and it was the most unjust.

All the same John was deeply apologetic at the amount he was getting through (the two maids left behind at Herne Hill had not had their wages paid for six months) and vowed that he would not buy any more pictures or missals unless something very exceptional came on the market. He was delighted with their new lodgings which he described as exquisitely clean and comfortable and far handsomer than Gibbs's—quite beautifully furnished. He hoped that when Effie went to Perth he would be able to economise as well as to enjoy a quiet time to himself.

He was well enough by Tuesday, November 15, to deliver his third lecture, and the next morning he reported that it had been the most successful of the three. The day after he told his father that Lady Trevelyan had said that everyone alike was delighted with it. 'She and I got into some divinity discussions,' he continued, 'until she got very angry and declared that when she read me and heard me, at a distance she thought me so wise that anybody might make an idol of me and worship me to any extent, but when she got to talk with me, I turned out only a *rag doll* after all.'[4]

In the last lecture, on November 18, on Pre-Raphaelitism, he was not quite so much at his ease although, according to his letter home, he spoke 'very vigourously and was heard all over the house'. He made up his mind to publish the lectures in book form as soon as he got back to London.

Effie went to Perth on Monday the 21st while John remained at Albyn Place until December 9 and continued with Mr Beveridge's treatments which were giving him 'a stronger and cleaner use' of his brains as well as nearly taking the skin off his throat by steady friction. On November 20 he wrote that he had really and truly begun the first chapter of the new volume. His hopes, though, of not bringing visitors upon himself were not altogether realised. He was able to refuse most of the invitations he received but could not avoid everyone who came to call. He sent his father amusing little word pictures of all the people he was obliged to see. His letters from Edinburgh at this time are perhaps the most lively and cheerful he ever wrote. He was enjoying a rare freedom: it was one of the few times when he was on his own, without either Effie or his parents.

# RETURN TO LONDON

❊

Meanwhile Effie at Bowerswell was writing to Rawdon Brown to tell him of *her* experiences in Edinburgh. This is the only letter we have of hers between October 10 and January 1, 1854. She and John wrote to each other while he remained in Edinburgh but their letters, which might have told so much, have not survived:

Bowerswell 30th November

I am very sorry to confess I have had so many reasons for a second long silence this season, but when I tell you all I have been doing and have had to do since I had the pleasure of receiving your long kind letter I am sure you will understand my silence was longer than I wished, as a letter from you is always a subject of pleasure in the house, and John always is stopped by me in whatever he happens to be engaged [in] to hear and talk over a letter from Mr Brown! He writes to me today that some more of Mr Rich's M.S. has made its appearance, so that I hope he is very steadily progressing.

We left the Highlands a month ago, with great regret and went in to Edinburgh, where we soon began to feel the effect of the town air on our health after the delightful air and quiet of the Highlands. John gave two Lectures with great success and then lost his voice for a week. Millais also turned ill and went off to London after completing some Diagrams for John's Lectures which he could not well do without, but he is very delicate and I was glad he went before the weather became frosty. My Mother was also there with my little sister Alice who I had partly to look after as my poor Mother caught a very bad feverish attack which the Docter feared would end in gastric fever—she was at an uncle's house* some distance from me, I was terribly anxious about her, and what with continual

* Andrew Jameson's at Greenhill Gardens.

letter-writing and note-sending and card-leaving on every body in and round Edinburgh who were so civil as to wish to know us and to see us at their houses, and John shut up in his own room writing his two Last Lectures—I was quite upset. I really tried dear Mr Brown to take care of myself; I did not go out to dinner once, but I had a great deal more to do than I was fit for. Every night for instance that there was a Lecture, I had to take all our own acquaintances into the Hall before it was opened to the subscribers—as the Dennistouns [see p. 114*n*] *and* all *that* set of people could not have got in unless, as they do not belong to the Philosophical Society. The place was so crowded that people were fainting and being carried out—some of these people arrived from the country, I gave them teas and suppers —but that was nothing. The talking and nervous exertion was too much for me—Simpson came and said I must go into the country for quiet and as my mother was still very unwell, and I came here as I was no longer able to remain up at all in Edinburgh but lay tossing in my bed without sleep. I am better— and when a west wind blows I am much abler to walk but I trust to get much stronger. Our planning for returning to London, is to leave this after next week, pay a visit to Lady Matilda Maxwell* at Pollok—John wants to study for a little the Missals of the Duke of Hamilton and that is close by. We then go to Glasgow College to Mrs Blackburn, who is a great friend of John's and the best Artist he knows†—I don't know if you know her. I would have very much enjoyed a couple of days with our kind friends [the Cheneys] at Badger, and they wished it, but John is not inclined. He was very much enchanted with Mr Dennistoun's pictures—He thinks it the most

* Daughter of the 7th Earl of Elgin, she had, in 1839, married Sir John Maxwell, Bt, of Pollok near Glasgow. Sir John's sister, Elizabeth, was the mother of William Stirling of Keir who succeeded Sir John in 1865 as Sir William Stirling Maxwell. It was one of those Scottish Baronetcies which can pass through the female line.

† Born Jemima Wedderburn, she was married to Hugh Blackburn, Professor of Mathematics at the University of Glasgow. She painted mostly pictures of animals, and in 1855 published *Illustrations of Scripture* depicting animals mentioned in the Bible, which Ruskin appreciatively reviewed in the *Morning Chronicle* of January 20 of that year. She was a cousin of Alexander Wedderburn, Ruskin's pupil and co-editor of the Library Edition of his Works.

interesting *early* collection he knows. I liked him—he was quiet and gentlemanly, but Mrs D.—indeed Mr Brown, I do not like to say anything against my sex, but I don't admire Mrs D.*
. . . We shall, I imagine, be home about Christmas, not later. John is in Edinburgh till Saturday when he comes here. His opinions have made a great stir there—and the Architects have met and entered into a protest against them—which amuses him. When I get home I shall be sending your jam away. Do me the favor to indulge my weakness for liking to pack up a box for you, to mention any little thing you want to make you more comfortable.

John in his letters home made no mention of Mrs Gray's illness nor of Effie's weakness, but then Effie never referred to his chronic sore throat. It was almost as if they were jealous of each other's ailments. On December 5 John answered a request from his mother to give Effie 5/- for each of her little sisters and brothers to buy a book: 'I have given Effie your message—and sent her the money. I am sure you must be wanting me back and shall be most happy to *get* back—though I am not *un*happy anywhere. As for Effie, I wish I could say that she looked forward to her house with pleasure but it is of no use to think about her.'[1]

Heartless? So it would seem until one reads part of the statement he drew up for his lawyer two days after Effie left him for good: 'Her feelings of affection towards me appeared gradually to become extinguished; and were at last replaced by a hatred so great that she told me, about the end of September or beginning of October, 1853, we being then in Scotland, that if she ever were to suffer the pains of

---

* Isabella Katherine, eldest daughter of Hon. James Wolfe Murray, Lord Cringletie (a Lord of Sessions). She had married in 1835 James Dennistoun (1803–55), author of *Memoirs of the Dukes of Urbino*, published 1851. Dennistoun had a famous collection of early Italian pictures at his Edinburgh house, 119 George Street. Ruskin had written about him to his father on November 27: 'Has a most interesting collection . . . *all* good . . . Edinburgh people don't like old Italian pictures, I *do*—and he is so grateful for my admiration that I daren't go near the house for fear of being pulled into damp rooms and not being able to get out again. He thinks because he knows old Italian that he must know modern English, and has bought a vile daub under the name of Turner. I can't venture to tell him. Wife an enthusiast in point lace—Dangerous to approach the subject.'

eternal torment, they could not be worse than going home to live at
Herne Hill with me.' If this is true—and we shall examine the whole
statement in its proper place—his remarks to his mother seem rather
mild.

He left Edinburgh on December 9 and posted to Perth, spending
a night at Dunfermline on the way and thereby allowing himself
even less time at Bowerswell. (Mr Ruskin was never happy when
John was at Bowerswell for he believed the house to be always full
of fever.) He spent only four days there and although he wrote four
times to his father he makes no mention of any of the Gray family
except to say on the evening of his arrival that they were quite well
and sent their regards. While he was there he sent his father the
sketch which Millais had made at Glenfinlas of the party at Bowerswell. Mr Ruskin's comment was '*Prodigious, prodigious, prodigious* . . . I
wonder what Millais will arrive at doing. He is the painter of the
age—greater in one way than Turner for I presume at 24—Turner
never made such pictures—Millais will be great because he is
satisfied to be small . . . Every line in this little pen and ink drawing
has soul and meaning and purpose in it.'[2] He also said that he was
returning it because it was so precious that it should always be kept
at Bowerswell. Alas, it has disappeared.

In this letter Mr Ruskin sent his love to Effie as he invariably did;
John *never* sent Effie's love to him.

On Thursday, December 15, John left Bowerswell for Glasgow to
stay with the Blackburns, still employing his old-fashioned means of
progression. Effie, travelling by train, did not join him until the
Saturday evening. Her sister, Sophie, followed two days later, and
in a letter from John to his father written on the 19th it appears for
the first time that it was their intention to bring this child of ten with
them to London: 'I found the little girls useful before in allowing me
to be more at Denmark Hill than I otherwise could have been. Effie
says she can take charge of her herself but it is sure to end in our
having a governess of some kind—I have no objection, for a month
or two—it is one of the best forms of charity if we can find a proper
person, in need of a home, and Sophia is much improved—quite
another creature from what she was, and I think I shall have
pleasure in having her in the house.'[3]

In the same letter he touched upon their plans for going to
Switzerland in the spring. Mr Ruskin had hinted that he was not

prepared to go if Effie was to be of the party. 'Mama is but half made up in mind as to Switzerland,' he had written to John on December 15. 'Go she will she says only because it is so far arranged—I scarcely see my way in it. We shall not amalgamate now—the old and young. If we go I would not think of moving till I saw Millais in exhibition.* 1st May is Monday so it opens 1 May. Please God we were well I would leave Tuesday 9 May so as to let Mama escape fatigue of people on 10 May [his birthday].'⁴

John hastened to assure him, 'I don't think there will be much difficulty in managing it so as to make you and my mother happy. Effie has a friend at one of the German (Rhine) baths—formerly Cecilia Northcote—now Mrs Bishop—staying there alone for her health—Effie would like to go and stay with her for a month or two—we could easily cross to Cologne from Calais by our old Brussels line†—now 12 hours journey only—and leave Effie wherever it is and go on into Switzerland by Schaffhausen.'⁵

This friend of Effie's was a sister of Sir Stafford Northcote, Bt, who was afterwards created Earl of Iddesleigh. Effie had met her through the Fords, her younger brother having married one of Clare Ford's sisters. Cecilia, in October, 1851, had married Dr Thomas ('Bear') Bishop, who was now practising in Naples. They had one daughter, just a year old, called after Effie who was her god-mother. Cecilia had nearly died at the birth of this child and had never since been out of pain. She was still in Naples at this time and had just received a letter from Effie saying that she would be willing to go with her in the spring to Kreuznach where Cecilia had been recommended to take a cure. She wrote to Effie immediately on receiving this letter to thank her for making the banishment she so dreaded agreeable by her companionship. 'My kind regards to Mr Ruskin,' she finished up, 'and tell him how much obliged I am to him for consenting to let you be with me.'⁶

Had Cecilia known it, the obligation was all on John's side for taking Effie off his hands. The only sacrifice he would be making was in allowing Crawley to remain with Effie, and this guarantee of a

* He meant the Glenfinlas portrait which he was evidently still hoping would be finished in time for the Royal Academy exhibition.

† On Ruskin's first journey to Switzerland with his parents in the summer of 1832, they had gone by way of Calais, Brussels, Cologne, Strasbourg and Schaffhausen. (*Praeterita*, Vol. I, Chap. IV.)

reliable manservant to look after them at Kreuznach was almost as comforting to Mrs Bishop as the thought of Effie's companionship.

On the 19th John and Effie went to stay with the Maxwells at Pollok House six miles from Glasgow. Lady Matilda had made arrangements for John to see the Duke of Hamilton's missals and manuscripts at Hamilton Palace (now demolished) close by. The Duke had asked them to dine on the 22nd and John told his father that if he did not accept the invitation it would seriously offend both the Duke and the Maxwells, so he was afraid it would mean postponing his arrival in London yet one more day. He would have to look at the Duke's collection on the morning after the dinner, the Friday, as it was not likely to be shown by candlelight; therefore the first train by which he could leave Glasgow would be the five o'clock in the afternoon, and this, if he slept at Carlisle, would not bring him home until ten on the evening of Saturday, the 24th. In these circumstances he felt it would be much better to take the express from Glasgow on Saturday morning at ten which would bring him to London at half past eleven on Christmas Eve, and to Denmark Hill 'just in time to wish each other a happy Christmas'. (Although Effie was included in these plans, he never wrote 'we'; it was always 'I' as if he were travelling alone.)

Mr Ruskin, though he had deplored the time wasted at Bowerswell, would have been so gratified by the invitation to Hamilton Palace that it is unlikely he would have minded the delay in such a cause, but he immediately vetoed the Saturday express. Both he and Mrs Ruskin were terrified of railroads, particularly of fast trains, and of travelling in the dark, and although it was impossible in December not to have some hours of travelling in darkness, they must be the minimum.*

With the extraordinary sweetness and docility with which John gave in to his father in all little things (it is not often recognised to what an extent he got his own way in anything that was really important to him), he arranged to go to Durham on Saturday in

---

* An appalling railway accident had occurred in the dark near Dublin on October 5 which had greatly increased the old couple's natural fears. Such horrifying details of it were given in *The Times* that Mrs Ruskin had written on October 10 to her husband while he was in Liverpool on business, 'I would much rather your absence was prolonged a week than that you should risk travelling by railroad in the dark.' (Bembridge.)

daylight and spend two nights there, leave Durham at eight on Monday morning, the 26th, and be in London by half past seven that evening. This was the mail train; the express always went later in the day. There seems to have been no question of his travelling on the 25th; not only was it a Sunday, when the Ruskins never travelled if they could possibly help it, but Mr Ruskin would not have had his old coachman out on Christmas Day, and the idea of John not being met at the station was unthinkable.

John wrote good-naturedly from Hamilton on Thursday evening: 'I cannot manage it better . . . If you have anything particular to say, and this reaches you on Saturday, morning, I daresay I shall be able to get your letter out of the Durham post office on Sunday.'

These details are given not only for the glimpses of travel and postal facilities of the day, but to show in fairness to Mr Ruskin how much the time of their arrival mattered to him and to explain why he was afterwards so furious with Effie for not coming by that particular train after all.

In this same letter of Thursday, John's last from Scotland, he described the visit to Hamilton: 'I have been all the evening looking over the M.SS. with the Duke, and another missal admirer—a Mr Sneed* (Mr S nothing much)—nobody but Duke and duchess and we two bibliomanes at dinner. House much too stately for my mind though perfectly warm and comfortable but five servants waiting on four people are a nuisance. The M.SS are of course magnificent but I would not give my £180 one† for *any* one I have yet seen.'[7]

The reason Effie was not at the dinner is explained in a letter from her to Rawdon Brown of January 19, 1854:

I have not told you anything about our Scotch visit to Pollok and Hamilton Palace but I did not join John in the last from a fit of Tic, but he thought the Missals wonderful, the Duke goodnatured, the Duchess sulky. They asked us a second time but I could not go as the noble pair quarrelled (entre nous) although it is well known. The Duchess is Romanist now and

* This was no doubt the Rev. Walter Sneyd (1809–88). Both he and the Duke were fellows of the Society of Antiquaries.

† An early fourteenth-century Book of Hours from France, now owned by Major J. R. Abbey and known as the Ruskin Hours. (J. S. Dearden: *Catalogue of Ruskin's Illuminated Manuscripts*, No. 34.)

was giving away the family plate to the Priests.* She left the Palace but returned in two days, but not being expected Lord Elgin gave me a hint to stay with his sister Lady Matilda Maxwell at Pollok till John returned.

This letter contains the first mention of Effie's tic—short for *tic douloureux* or facial neuralgia—in Effie's case a more or less violent contraction of the nerves above the eyebrow which, at its worst, was actually visible. It was to plague her for the next few months.

* The Duchess was Princess Marie, youngest daughter of the reigning Grand Duke of Baden. She had married in 1843 the Marquess of Douglas who succeeded as 11th Duke in 1852. Their sons were brought up as Church of England but their daughter as a Catholic. The 'noble pair' did not separate. He died in mysterious circumstances in Paris in 1863, possibly murdered by his wife's cousin, Napoleon III. (*Victorian Sidelights* by A. M. W. Stirling: Benn, 1954.)

# MILLAIS AND MRS GRAY

✸

On the very day that Effie arrived at the Maxwells', Millais, in London, was writing a startling letter to Mrs Gray—all the more startling when it is realised that he had only met her for the first time in Edinburgh when she went there for Ruskin's lectures. The letter is undated but is inscribed by Mrs Gray on the envelope: '19th Dec$^r$/53 1st letter' and postmarked 'Perth—EC 20':

83 Gower St

My dear Mrs Gray

I have no time to answer your letter as fully as I would wish as it is nearly 5 o'clock—the only Post whereby you could receive this, when you will be expecting it. I have been delayed by a friend calling.

Believe me *I will do everything you can desire of me*, so keep your mind perfectly at rest—I should never have written to your daughter had not Ruskin been cognisant to the correspondence, and approving of it, or at least not admitting a care in the matter—If he is such a plotting and scheming fellow, as to take notes secretly to bring against his wife,* such a quiet scoundrel ought to be ducked in a mill pond. His conduct is so provokingly gentle that it is folly to kick against such a man. From this time, I will never write again to his wife, as it will *be better*, and will exclude the possibility of his further complaining, although sufficient has past to enable him to do so, at any time he may think fit. One is never safe against such a brooding selfish lot as those Ruskins. His absence in the Highlands seemed purposely to give me an opportunity of being in his

---

* We know that Ruskin did on one occasion at least note down Effie's conversation (see p. 232). Millais refers again to these 'notes' in his next letter and Effie herself mentions them on p. 142. Bell Scott also mentions that Ruskin made notes of Effie's defects. See Source Note 1, p. 276, *To The Highlands*.

wife's society—His wickedness must be without parallel if he kept himself away to the end that has come about, as I am sometimes inclined to think. Altogether his conduct is incomprehensible—he is either crazed, or anything but a desirable acquaintance.

The *worst of all is the wretchedness* of her position. Whenever they go to visit she will be left to herself in the company of any stranger present, for Ruskin appears to delight in selfish solitude. Why he ever had the audacity of marrying with no better intentions is a mystery to me. I must confess that it appears to me that he cares for nothing beyond his Mother and Father, which makes the insolence of his finding fault with his wife (to whom he has acted from the beginning most disgustingly) more apparent. I shall never dine at Denmark Hill again, and will not call at Herne Hill to see either, but will leave a card which will suffice. I shall be out of England next year so that there can be no more interference from me. If I have meddled more than my place would justify it was from the flagrant nature of the affair—I am only anxious to do the best for your daughter. I consider Ruskin's treatment of her so sickening that for quietness' sake she should as much as possible prevent his travelling, or staying a summer in company with a friend, *who cannot but observe* his hopeless apathy in *everything regarding her happiness.* I cannot conceal the truth from you, that she has more to put up with than any living woman. Again I must promise you that I will never more give occasion for the Ruskins to further aggravate her on my account. *Everything on my part will be as you wish*—I have scarcely time to sign to save [*sic*] post

Ever yours sincerely

J. E. Millais

I will write tomorrow more intelligibly

I think the Ruskins must not perceive too great a desire on your part to keep quiet, and submit to anything, as they will imagine it to be fear. She has all the right on her side and believe me the Father would see that also if he knew all.[1]

This last line shows that Millais himself, unlike the Grays and the old Ruskins, already 'knew all'. Effie must have confided in him during their walks alone together at Glenfinlas while John was trying to change the course of a very different stream. The next day Millais wrote again:

Tuesday afternoon [December 20]

I am afraid my answer to your kind and judicious letter was dreadfully incoherent, but now I will endeavour to reply more satisfactorily.

Although you know John Ruskin's odd propensity for roaming away by himself from all human creatures and their habitations, yet you cannot be aware of the abstracted way in which he neglects his wife. It is utterly impossible for a friend to sojourn with them for any length of time without absolutely being compelled in common courtesy to attend to her. I assure you that Ruskin only expressed approval and delight at perceiving that your daughter and myself agreed so well together, and when *I spoke to him about his extraordinary indifference to her attractions* (which could not be but excessively unpleasing, and conducive to her unhappiness) he only apathetically laughed and said he thought all women ought to depend upon themselves for engrossing employment, and such like cold inhuman absurdities. There was something so revolting to me about this sickly treatment of her just cause of complaint and discontent, that I never again ventured to speak on the subject, as I could not depend upon keeping my temper. When she and my brother visited Bowerswell, he was all for my accompanying them, and returning with her, which I refused to do, although I knew he would have been quite as happy without my society. In fact he appeared *purposely to connive at the result*—seemingly callous, and methodically writing all that he himself brought about, to his parents, like a boy of ten years of age.* He is an undeniable giant as an author, but a poor weak creature in everything else, bland, and heartless, and unworthy—with his great talents—of *any* woman possessing affection, and sensibility.

Do not imagine that I am induced through circumstances to speak thus depreciatingly of him, or that this is a hasty conclusion of his character. An open enemy is preferable to a cool

* This was unjust: every mention of Effie in Ruskin's daily letters during the six months of their stay in Scotland has been quoted in the preceding pages.

friend, and Ruskin is one of the latter order and therefore odious
in my sight—I think his Inquisitorial practice of noting down
everything which could forward an excuse for complaining
against his own wife, is the *most unmanly, and debased proceeding
I ever heard of*, but even that is nothing in comparison with his
aggravating unsociability which she has to put up with. You
were kind enough to be plain spoken with me in your letter,
and I will be the same with you—it is of no use conventionally
disguising my opinion from you, however biased it may be,
and however painful I cannot resist unreservedly avowing it:
you will avert many disagreeable casualties, and greatly increase your daughter's comfort by *permitting always one, or other,
of her sisters to be with her*. It is a sufficient inducement (not to
speak of her appearance) that these cunning London men de-
tect neglect, and unconcern, on Ruskin's part, and her unhappiness, to make them impudent and importunate. With a companion this evil can be greatly frustrated, as she would not be
left by herself to receive strangers, and gallant rakes, who can
always find an excuse for calling, and who look upon Ruskin
as a kind of milksop. I have met many of these fellows even
before I knew Ruskin, and have heard them circulating over
dinner tables the most unwarrantable insinuations, and now I
find myself continually questioned regarding my experience of
their married life.

I believe you will have every reason to be satisfied with me,
as your desire is not more earnest than mine to hasten the
interests of the Countess.* My intention is simply to call and
leave a card at Herne Hill and the same at Denmark Hill after
which I will carefully avoid (if they should invite me) dining
there, by managing to get engaged elsewhere. When the summer comes I shall, I trust, be away on the Continent, after
completing Glenfinlas, which I would leave as it is, had not
Ruskin spoken about it since, to the effect, that he should consider it an insult to his Father, besides himself, if I did not
finish it. Of course I cannot obviate or foresee the chances of

* The name by which Effie was known at Glenfinlas. Millais had written
to Collins on July 20, 'I leave off this for a moment to play battledore with
the Countess. We give ourselves titles here as there are no people to dispute
them. I am a Duke.'

meeting the Countess in society, but as she rarely goes out, and myself as seldom, I don't think such a meeting likely. I have written a letter, (the last I will write) telling her I will *not call and see her*, as proposed, to escape the suspicion of the Father, and Mother, who will naturally enquire whether I have been there or not, and will think it strange after our intimacy. *Should she, and yourself*, consider it more prudent for me to call as though nothing had happened I will do so. I regret very much, (in spite of the wonderful advance my pupil has made in her drawing) that I had not taught her more, as I am convinced she will find it one of her greatest, and most absorbing recreations. I will take care to send her sketches and engravings to copy, which she can return by Crawley—by this means a kind of friendship will be continued which will satisfy the curiosity of most people who will imagine I go there as before. Sometimes I uselessly wish that I never had accompanied Ruskin to the Highlands. It may be beneficial in the end to their position, in regard to each other, as it has disturbed the settled dullness of their existence, *and any change was preferable* to the life they have been living (I should rather say the life that *she has been enduring*), for I believe he is complacent, and happy enough. I have seen nothing but the most placid and patient submission on her part to his will, and yet there is a *stealthy*, bad, dissatisfaction in his nature which is very trying, and disgusting. I sincerely hope that all this is not so new to you, but that you will (from previous knowledge) be prepared to hear what is so distressing for me to recount, and that this unfortunate business may blow over, like all the other calamities and grievances that have gone before us. If I have not answered as you desired pray let me know, as I am only anxious to accede to your wishes. I send this with the two drawings of George [Gray] and the Governess [Delphine].

With many thanks for your kindness, and best remembrances to Mr Gray and your family believe me

Ever yours most sincerely
John Everett Millais

I do not think I shall go to the Bridge of Turk before next Autumn, if I go at all. March is out of the question, as it would

be suicide. Although I do not enjoy life much, yet I cannot believe that I am justified in killing myself.
*I will remember my promise of drawing Sophia for you.*[2]

Admiral Sir William James, Effie's grandson, in *The Order of Release*, in which these two letters are quoted, prefaces them with the remarks: 'Millais occasionally corresponded with Effie, which was perfectly natural between close friends, and Ruskin raised no objection, but as soon as he was again in thrall to his parents a sinister construction was put on this correspondence which came to the ears of Effie's mother.' It could not have been the influence of the old Ruskins which put a stop to the correspondence for they did not even know about it. Effie and John did not arrive home until a week after Millais wrote his first letter to Mrs Gray, and John in his letters home made no mention at all of Millais and Effie writing to each other.

Sir William James continues: 'Millais's two letters to Mrs Gray, written in December, reveal the strong currents that, unknown to Effie, were running under the calm surface of life at Glenfinlas.'

Unknown to Effie? Is it not far more likely that Effie talked over the situation with her mother and that the letter was written with her entire approval if not at her request? Effie left Bowerswell on December 17; Millais received Mrs Gray's letter on the 19th (a Monday). It may well have been written before Effie left; she and her mother may even have drafted it together. It is anyway highly unlikely that Effie was unaware of it. If Mrs Gray had written without her knowledge how could it have been explained to her why Millais suddenly stopped writing? It is possible, though, that the idea of appealing to Millais came from Mrs Gray. She must have known by this time that Effie and Millais were in love, or at any rate that Millais was dangerously in love with Effie, and as she was not as yet aware of the unnatural terms on which John and Effie were living together, she was still doing all in her power to try to hold the marriage together.

Something must have happened during those four days while Ruskin was at Bowerswell to make Mrs Gray think it necessary to put a stop to the correspondence between Effie and Millais. What could it have been? Had Ruskin's suspicions been aroused in some way? Could Effie have received a letter from Millais while he was there, or written one to him, which she tried to hide from John? (It transpires later that Effie wrote to Millais asking him to destroy all her letters. Would she have done this if there had been nothing in them that the whole world could not see?) Or did Ruskin produce notes of Effie's conversation and behaviour in the Highlands which made it plain that he knew more of what was going on than she had realised? All we know for certain from these two letters of Millais's to Mrs Gray is that Ruskin had complained in some way of Effie's conduct and that Millais's name had been brought into it. It is quite possible, however, that Ruskin's complaints were not nearly as serious as Millais's letters lead one to imagine.

It is not surprising that Millais spent a thoroughly miserable Christmas. In a letter of the 26th to Mr Combe he expressed the wish that they had all spent a more cheerful Christmas than he had; he had eaten no dinner and was strolling about London between church services.[3] Nor could Effie and John in Durham have been much happier. The presence of Sophie must have been a help to them. One can imagine the three of them at the Christmas service in the cathedral. John at any rate would have been able to forget himself in his interest in the building (he had written in his letter of the 22nd that seeing Durham Cathedral had long been an object with him), merely retaining perhaps an underlying sense of all's being wrong.

The day after they got back to Herne Hill he wrote his final letter to his mother-in-law:

My dear Mrs Gray—

I had your kind note with the green pebble, which is excessively pretty and I am very much obliged to you for sending me this clear piece.

I will write you word of Effie's health; but I fear I shall have little cheering information to give you. She passes her days in sullen melancholy, and nothing can help her but an entire change of heart. With sincere regards to Mr Gray and George believe me

affectionately Yours
J Ruskin[4]

# UNHAPPY NEW YEAR

❋

Effie began the new year with a letter to her mother which shows how rapidly the marriage was disintegrating. It was written exactly a week after their Christmas day in Durham, and though evidently not the first she had written since getting home is the first to have been preserved:

Sunday, 1st January, 54

About my own concerns I shall now tell you that after expressing my opinion to John about the last letter he wrote to Millais he changed its tone somewhat next day and did not urge him to come out, so that we have heard nothing of him since and shall not until he writes to ask John to sit for his likeness when I shall certainly hear what his future intentions are— Mr Ruskin was abusing him last night for not having finished the Picture in time for this next [Academy] Exhibition. I dined there last night and am to do so again today. Mr Ruskin told me that he could not let me have Frank [his old coachman] once a week to take me into town this year, that he could not bear cold and that I was to order a fly at his expense when I wanted to go out at night. I said that I was much obliged but that I am so little able to visit out and so anxious not to increase their expenses that Frank once a week would be enough if they could spare him. I thought it necessary to say this although the other plan will render me so far more independent. However they seemed anxious to let me be quite separate and I told them any arrangement they liked would be quite agreeable to me. They have sent me their usual New Year's present and Sophie 5/–.* She is always to take tea in the little room upstairs whilst I am there at dinner and come down afterwards. All their conversation was about themselves and John's early signs of

* There is an entry in Mr Ruskin's account book under Charities and Gifts—'Jan 2 1854 Effie Sophia 25/–.' (Bembridge.)

greatness which they related and he listened to with great com-
placency. His Father spouted John's Poetry at twelve and
demanded John's admiration of the beauty of the metre which
John objected to giving. I thought the lines pretty.

We talked of the German plan and John peevishly looking up
told me not to begin talking of what had been settled six months
ago. I said I had only heard two days ago from Mrs Bishop as
he had seen by her letter* and that I thought it better to speak
to his Father and we settled the whole thing in five minutes,
agreeably I suppose to all parties and most so to themselves—
so that I will either come down with Sophie to see you before
I go on the 9th of May or immediately on my return. Mr
Ruskin thought it was much better than returning to Perth
whilst they were in Switzerland. I offered, of course, any plan
they liked but Mrs Ruskin said, 'Oh! John has promised to
come with us and you can't travel with us, Mr Ruskin won't be
put out of his way in the least thing and never has been, and
we travel days and days from 9 in the morning till 7 at night
and I never get tired.' She was not the least cross and merely
spoke the truth. Mr Ruskin then said that he could not be
away later than July as all the French Countesses† were coming
over, and that John would take us to Kreuznach, see us fixed
there and come back to bring me home. John began making
some trifling objection about Mrs Bishop perhaps not keeping
her time. His Mother told him to be quiet and not raise
objections.

When we came home I told John I wished to have a conversation with him as I did not wish to begin another year in this
uncomfortable state and that I merely wished him to know that
one of his objections to my conduct was not helping him in his
work and that he must understand that I was quite ready to
do anything he might desire and help him in his work—I took
all the hard things he said to me and which it is useless repeat-
ing. You may be quite sure I will try my best with them and
everything I do will be well weighed one day, but it is a hard

* This is the letter mentioned on p. 116. It had been written from Naples
on December 12, 1853.

† The five daughters of Pedro Domecq, Mr Ruskin's late partner. Four
of them had married Counts, and the other a Baron.

trial to know that I am all day long considered by them all as a maniac in the house, and everything I say or do considered and viewed in that light. They are such peculiar people that I will not judge them, although I must repeat that I think that their superior gifts make them even more responsible in the use of their intellects. John proceeded to say that his marriage with me was the greatest crime he had ever committed in acting in opposition to his parents than [? then].* John's pity and polite behaviour to [me] is simply put on, he says, because he considers it his duty to be kind to anybody so unhappily diseased,† and far more he said, but I cannot distress you, but his calm philosophy I was glad to put an end to and it makes me quite ill this morning to think of it. I do not think you will hear any more about my affairs from me. I have now nothing more to tell and you cannot expect that I can ever be happy. Unfortunately perhaps I have what my Father calls "the lots of heart" that belong to my name, and although I must make up a sort of blind to make these people not uncomfortable on my account I know too well what I have lost in this world to care for the happiness that other women have in trifles when they have lost the substance. Sophie is very happy and was quite delighted with the letter she had from Delphine . . .

Miss Ainsworth‡ comes the end of this week—I think it will do me good and I will just do the best I can. I hear Sophie all her lessons regularly and find it very good for me.

Ever yrs

E

* This shows that John did not consider it was his parents who had persuaded him into marrying Effie as has been stated in many of his biographies. The truth is that they had consented to his marriage only because they feared an occurrence of the illness which his disappointment over Adèle Domecq had brought on. (See Note 1 to this chapter, p. 280.)

† John had long maintained that Effie was suffering from 'a nervous disease affecting the brain' and had written to Mr Gray to this effect in July, 1849. (*Effie in Venice*, p. 35.)

‡ The Misses Mary and Harriet Ainsworth ran the school, Avonbank, at Stratford-on-Avon, which Effie had attended for a year in 1841. We learn from Mr Ruskin's diary that Miss Ainsworth dined twice at Denmark Hill during her visit, on the 15th and 18th of January, but we are not told which sister it was—though probably Miss Mary as she was the one who corresponded with Effie.

Sophie was at this time ten years and two months old, having been born on October 28, 1843. As most of John's alleged cruelty to Effie during the next three months was relayed through her, one must bear her age in mind. She was from all accounts an extremely bright child and a very good mimic. She must have known that there was some drama going on. Children love drama and it would have been her normal instinct to create more of it rather than tone it down. On the other hand there is no reason to think that she was not scrupulously truthful, and Effie's accounts of her conversation certainly ring true. The reader will have to judge for himself how much to rely on the evidence of this child.

It is known from John's published diary that he took Sophie for a walk on this same January 1, and thereafter for the next few weeks there are several mentions in his diary of walking with her or drawing for her.

Meanwhile Millais and Effie were keeping in touch through her mother, and from Millais's next letter to Mrs Gray we get a lively impression of Sophie:

83 Gower St. Tuesday evening
[January 17—postmarked January 18]

I intended answering your letter before this but desired to make the sketch of Sophia first so that I might tell you the result which I think is satisfactory—Ruskin sat to me this morning and expressed himself immensely delighted with her likeness. Having done these drawings for you I thought it would look unkind of me not to make a sketch of him for his loving parents who would naturally conceive it to be strange that I had never made them a present of a portrait in the same manner. I am going likewise to draw old Mr Ruskin for his son who seems to be highly pleased at the notion of possessing a good likeness of his Father*—In his sitting he has scarcely alluded to Socialism but amuses me with all sorts of strange suggestions as to what I should do. He is very bland and affable towards me, at times absolutely tender; I cannot understand him, for some little time back he wrote me a most extraordinary letter of which

* If Millais did do a drawing of Mr Ruskin it has not come to light. His sketch of John is reproduced on p. 163, and of Sophie on p. 162.

you may have heard, quite in *another strain.*\* We never speak about what has passed and nothing is said about the Countess (by the bye I don't know whether you are aware that his wife always went by that title in the Highlands)—Occasionally he says that she is much pleased with her drawing or something of that kind.

What a delightful little shrewd damsel Sophia is. She was so patient and anxious to sit her best, never relaxing until her poor little head wavered about in sheer inability to hold it steady any longer. *I do not praise her to please you*, but I think her *extremely beautiful*, and that she will even improve, as yet she does not seem to have the slightest idea of it herself which makes her prettier—I am afraid that ignorance cannot last long. Since I have been here I cannot say that circumstances have been propitious in advancing my happiness. The oldest and best friend I ever had left me on Friday on his way to Syria, where he will remain 3 or 4 years. Therefore now I am almost entirely left to my own resources. All my family leave me alone in the house for a fortnight tomorrow. I have refused to accompany them as I have every other invitation.

As soon as I finish Ruskin's portrait I shall join my friend at Cairo and begin a new life, or rather try and end this one.

This gives the exact date of Holman Hunt's departure from London, Friday, January 13, which he does not mention himself. In his memoirs he writes, without giving any date, 'I took a cab and made a round of calls on all my friends to say good-bye. The dear old Millais was astonished when I said I was going that night by the mail train. John [Millais] came back with me and helped me to pack. Some bachelor friends rallied me, saying they should go and dine leisurely and come on to my lodgings later. When they arrived I had gone, and Millais had accompanied me to the station. I had not had time to dine, and Millais rushed to the buffet and seized any likely food he could, tossing it after me into the moving carriage. What a leave-taking it was with him in my heart when the train started! Did other men have such a sacred friendship as that we had formed?'[2]

\* This is no doubt the letter to which Effie referred in hers of January 1, p. 127.

Ruskin recorded in his diary that he sat to Millais on January 12 and again on the 19th. There is no entry at all for the 17th when we know from Millais's letter that he also sat. These sittings took place in Millais's studio[3] at 83 Gower Street (now No. 7), a few doors from Bedford Square. Sophie had also sat several times to Millais before Millais reported that his sketch of her was finished. Effie's brother, Sir Albert Gray, states that he was told by William Millais that 'Mrs Ruskin used to bring the girls in her carriage to the studio in Gower Street and call for them after the sitting. He remembers one occasion when the bell rang that Millais threw himself on the sofa and begged him to go and receive the girls—he could not go out and receive Mrs Ruskin. He had in fact determined not to see her again.'[4]

Albert was only three when these events took place so it must have been many years afterwards that he was told of them by William. Nevertheless, because he made a mistake in saying 'the girls' it does not necessarily mean that his other recollection was mistaken. Effie may quite possibly on one occasion have taken Sophie for a sitting; it is more likely, though, that she went with Ruskin himself or with Crawley.

None of Effie's letters home between January 1 and February 27 has survived, but as she had written, 'I do not think you will hear any more about my affairs from me', they were presumably of little interest. The gap is partly filled by two letters to Rawdon Brown. The first, of January 19, is mostly to do with Brown's own concerns and Venice friends. About his book she wrote: 'I have been busy transcribing for John all notes concerning its publication from your own letters and also recopying some of the letters of the manuscript.' John was working on Brown's book as well as getting on very slowly with *Modern Painters* and in January there are three entries in his diary about Brown.[5]

Effie's second letter to Brown of February 4 tells of her daily life:

As to myself I get on the best way I can, like many others I suppose. I suffer a good deal but I think we all deserve that, don't we? Lady Eastlake shakes her head at me sometimes for looking weary and then kisses me. In fact to tell you the truth I could speak to you about myself for a week but that would be a sad bore for you and not kind I think even to tell you the facts. I am in truth often with colour in my cheeks a very poor

creature. I am very subject to *Tic* above the left eye which is
the form my weakness takes when I am weary or excited by
any distress. Alas! this year has been so awful! Seeing so much
distress that cannot be relieved I have even been in so morbid a
state as to fancy everybody was unhappy. I am better when I
drive into London or work at the Museum which I do twice a
week* but I pay for it by having to go to bed and have *Tic*
for half the night. Don't fancy I sit still or mope—I am as busy
all day as can be and never sit still or lie down unless I can't
work which I am most thankful to say is only when these at-
tacks come on—but as all my days are like the rest: here is one
—I rise at eight, have prayers and breakfast at nine—I hear
Sophie practise an hour, then her spelling, Dictation, arith-
metic, English reading which brings me to twelve o'clock. I
draw for an hour or see about mending anything in the house
or sewing for myself. Dinner half past one—at three go out for
a walk—come in and dress for tea; from five to six I draw again;
6 tea—after tea I play for a little to Sophie and John if at home;
then I write letters, vide [*sic*] Diaries and read a little and go
to bed after seeing Sophie's hair in curl papers and tucked up
about 9½ . . . I have been giving dinner parties and intend
going on doing so as I think it my duty and it is a pleasure and
the only way I can ever see anybody as they won't call on me,
I am so far away and I have no carriage to see them in the
forenoon. Mama told me I should try, and I had a nice party
on Thursday [the 2nd]—the Milmans, Murrays, Lord Glenelg,
Lady Eastlake, pretty Mrs Boyle and Mr Halliday.†

* John, too, often went to the British Museum at this time. A diary entry
of his for January 6 reads: 'To British Museum with Millais all day.' Did
Effie hope to run into Millais accidentally at the Museum so close to
Gower Street?

† Mike Halliday, having been at Glenfinlas, was a link between Effie
and Millais. After Halliday had been to Herne Hill, Millais would go to
his gloomy chambers at 3 Robert Street, Adelphi, to hear all about Effie
and the people dining with her. On the day of this particular dinner-party,
February 2, Walter Deverell died and Millais, who had been in the house
at the time, went round afterwards to Halliday to hear about Effie and
to find sympathy. Of Effie's other guests, Mrs Boyle was the talented artist
known as 'E.V.B.' Born Eleanor Vere Gordon, she was the wife of Richard
Cavendish Boyle, son of the Earl of Cork and Rector of Marston Bigot,
Somerset. She was a life-long friend of Lady Eastlake's and wrote Effie a

These dinner-parties of Effie's were criticised by Mr Ruskin in a letter to Mr Gray. In it he aired all his other grievances against Effie too and as we are to hear so much of the grievances on the other side it seems only fair to let him have his full say:

*Private & Confidential*                                   London 16 Febry 1854

My dear Sir

Your letter of 30 Dmr I received in course and I paid Effie £2 for the meal which you took the trouble to send—It was very good—at that time John and Effie were coming South—I took the carriage and went myself at 8 evening to Gr North Railway—I found John only. Effie could not get up to leave Durham at 8 or 9 morning—John having named hour to arrive, not to alarm us was forced to come on—Effie always indifferent about coming to Herne Hill or about our being uneasy—came by Express late in the day and arrived at 12 night—and 3 people by Express costing £2 extra*—The night was severe and Crawley could scarcely find Cabs. Her arrival must have been unpleasant but I did all I could to make it otherwise—She had told her servants to expect her at 7. Since she returned she complains of ill health and the place not agreeing with her—but I see no look of ill health nor is she ever unable to go to parties or Theatres—She had our carriage every Wednesday to town but she wished to vary the day—I then said—Take a carriage when you want it and I will pay—she sent me a Letter saying she could not be half an hour in a carriage without severe headache—but in place of them she would ask me

---

very sympathetic letter after she left John. The Murrays were John Murray, the publisher, and his wife, whom the Ruskins had first met in 1848. He was the son of Byron's publisher and the originator of Murray's Hand-Books. Lord Glenelg the Ruskins had also known for six years. As Charles Grant he had held several minor government posts. It was the Milmans, it may be remembered, who had asked Effie to the Duke of Wellington's funeral. They never liked John, perhaps because he abused St Paul's to Dean Milman.

* Higher fares were charged on express trains by some railway companies at that time. The single first class fare from Durham to London was 51/3 and the Express 68/9. Sophie would have travelled half price but the full express rate must have been paid for Crawley so Mr Ruskin's calculation of £2 was if anything a little under the total extra cost.

to *increase John's means* for other things as he had lately *complained* of *want* of *means*—I confess I was a little astonished at this announcement seeing that in the few years since their marriage they have had from me £15,500 and spent all except a short Lease of House\* and value of furniture—John says he only told her he was determined to live within his income and never made any such complaint. I deem it proper to name all this to you that in case of my Death you may better understand their position. Mrs Ruskin says poverty will do them good but I do not wish my Son to become dependent—and people are quite mistaken as to my property—People fancy because I do not see much Company that I hoard money—my heirs will find the Contrary†—You and Effie first said that £1074 was very liberal—and I have since added a free House to this— but they have spent nearer £2000 a year, but Effie tho' remarkably clever—has as yet few rational ideas of Income and Expenditure—She is young and her folly is the natural fruit of your folly and mine—If she had when young got the Household tastes of her Mother and her domestic turn—her character would have been different but you sent her about visiting and thinking of Dress till she became unsettled and restless, and then to these Boarding Schools‡ where mistresses pilfer parents and teach Daughters the most approved mode of ruining Husbands—then came my folly putting them in Park Street to get into good Society and they paid the cost but made too much racket for the best Society—but they have some clever acquaintances. They now give Dinners in the Windsor stile with only Desert on the Table and pine apples but I believe though many will laugh and think another stile would better have suited the rank of both our families that Effie does it cleverly and as cheap as anybody could—but unluckily for me I dislike their ways of saving as much as their extravagence. The buying bad things—employing bad workmen,§ taking the skin off

---

\* The lease of the Herne Hill house did not expire until 1886.

† When he died ten years later he left to his widow £37,000 and the Denmark Hill house, and to John £120,000, various leases and freehold properties and pictures valued at £10,000.

‡ Effie went to only one boarding school, Avonbank at Stratford-on-Avon.

§ It may be remembered that Effie and John had complained of the shoddy work and dishonesty of Mr Ruskin's employee, Mr Snell.

Tradesmen and Servants to make a dash is neither management
nor economy in my mind—but it is good so far as showing
some wish to save at all—Effie seemed determined always to
get John away from us—I therefore care less about Dinners
and even £150 a year going to hired Carriages (for in spite of
the Carriage Headache I am paying £3 a week for drives to
Town)*—if she proves content—She showed her dislike to Mrs
Ruskin and me and this place to the surprise of our friends,
directly she was married—but I observe Mrs R and she are
more comfortable latterly—Her Temper is quick but not bad—
I keep out of its way and her voice is very sweet. The nature of
my Son's pursuits takes up his Time and thoughts and Effie
never cared for him enough to make her Husband's fame a
greater object than making a figure herself in Society. She will
never be domestic but he is justly proud of her in Company—
Her danger is to herself first in giving even this early Life to a
continual pursuit of pleasure—In Venice her constant companion was a mere devotee of pleasure Lady S who has I believe become deranged†—but Effie works very well when she
likes—though I am not sure it be domestic work—I care little
about Flash Dinner Dresses—If ordinary dress both of Husband
and Wife Linen &c. be not as scrupulously attended to—but I
am very fastidious. My son seems happy enough—I never saw
him in better spirits—and my main object is to live in agreement with him.

By your carrying to Effie what I wrote to you in confidence—
you have made a Breach between her and me that will never
be closed.‡ If you do so again you will only make disturbance
and quarrel and it is not for the interest of either of them to

* In his account book he noted under Sundries for 1854, 'For Crozier for
carriage Effie £46-3.' (Bembridge.) As Effie left in April this does work
out at £3 a week. George Crozier kept a livery stable at Grove Lane,
Camberwell.

† Lady Sorell. She was French and the widow of Sir Thomas Sorell who
had been Consul-General in Venice from 1834 to 1846, when he died. She
knew everyone in Venice and had been very kind to Effie. She went
temporarily out of her mind with grief at the death of a daughter, and was
at this time in a home in Milan. She died as the result of burns in the
summer of 1865.

‡ Mr Gray had often passed on Mr Ruskin's criticism to Effie so he may
not have been thinking of any one particular breach of confidence.

quarrel with me—you can do no good by noticing anything from me—for it is only enough for Effie to suspect John takes any suggestion from us to make her do the contrary—If she drove to Town 3 days a week and had Company the other 3 —she would tell you she neither went out nor saw Company— and she really persuades herself that she leads a quiet Life— You can do no good but might do much harm. Let us see what they spend at the end of the year—If you and Mrs Gray after a time, see anything you think you could mend—you may try— but as my Son is now happy at his book—you will, I repeat, only mar everything by Reports now—I tell you of pecuniary matters for as she does not seem to think she gets money enough you should hear both sides—Kindest regards to Mrs Gray, I am my dear Sir yrs very truly JJ. Ruskin.

This is the last letter written by Mr Ruskin to any of the Grays.

# SOPHIE AS GO-BETWEEN

❋

To the old Ruskins, unaware of the true circumstances, Effie must have been a terrible trial. How could they have understood her sullenness and discontent when, according to their lights, she had everything in the world to make her happy with their incomparable son? In reading her next few letters one must ask oneself how far she exaggerated John's cruelty to her. We hear only the case for the prosecution. A woman in love, separated for ever, as she then thought, from the man she loved, and unwanted by her husband and his parents, she had every reason to feel despair,* yet would not her very hopelessness have magnified and distorted her wrongs? She believed that the Ruskins were trying to drive her mad as well as to get her into a compromising situation with Millais, and it is possible that she did become temporarily a little deranged as she continued with growing hysteria to pour out to her mother accusations of inhuman behaviour against John and his parents:

Saturday [25 February]—Monday/27 Feb/54

I have a great deal to write to you about and cannot therefore send off my letter today, not only on account of its length as that I have been sick two days and not out and have already written some letters . . . By the way, my Missal is lost somewhere by John and he does not recollect where. He remembers having it at Perth—was it left behind with you and could you kindly look and see if it was by chance left behind in your cabinet? He has bought two yesterday, one of the time of St Louis and very fine—he paid 100 Guineas for them.† No wonder he

* 'Hope seemed impossible, interest in Life gone' she wrote in her diary two years later when recollecting her feelings at this time.

† John noted in his diary on the 26th: 'On Friday the 24th I got the greatest treasure in all my life: St Louis' Psalter'. This illuminated manuscript is now one of the greatest treasures of the Fitzwilliam Museum, Cambridge. It is now known to be the Psalter and Book of Hours of Queen

*138*

doesn't pay my debts but that is only inconvenient and does no harm beyond inconvenience. He has taken them to Denmarkhill to keep with the rest and I suppose he has bought another today as Sophie met him at D.H. Gate coming in with a book in his hand and he said he was to remain there this evening to shew it to them.

The end of Sophie's being so much at D.H. and their toadying her so absurdly has had the effect that you might imagine on the mind of a child observing as she is. She has now had an opportunity, as I have never hindered her going, of getting thoroughly bored, first with their way of going on, and the things they have told her about her family and myself have made her examine for herself both the truth of their statements and judge how far they practise the Christian Doctrines they preach. Her eyes were fully opened yesterday—I was awoke by John saying he was going to D.H. to breakfast and would take Sophie with him. I made no objections; she went and did not return till twelve o'clock. I asked her why she had been so long of coming to her lessons; she said they had kept her, and she then recounted to me the scene—which *she* considered so wrong. John was in his study and his Mother fondling him and going on in her usual style when Lucy* came to say that Mr Palgrave was down stairs having come by appointment to see the Turners. He asked for John—John sent the first time to say he was engaged. The visitor was not satisfied—he sent up again—when John said, "What a bore, Mother, what shall I say?"—His Mother said, "Oh! say he is in town with me."— "Oh! but," hesitated Lucy, "that will not be quite true."— "Lucy," said Mrs R, "hold your tongue and don't interfere. Won't that do, darling?" to John—"Yes, Mother," returned he, "quite well for we are going into town by and bye you

---

Isabelle, St Louis's sister. Before Ruskin it was owned by John Boykett Jarman, and was sold after Ruskin's death to Henry Yates Thompson. In 1919 a body of subscribers connected with Cambridge University bought it for £4,000 at the first sale of Thompson's books and presented it to the Fitzwilliam.

* Lucy Tovey, the parlour-maid at Denmark Hill from 1829 to 1874. Ruskin then installed her and her sister as managers of his model tea-shop at 29 Paddington Street.

know!'' They then shook Sophie who was making a little noise and told her to creep out of the house so that he might not hear that anybody was in the house—and that she was to tell me that if Mr Palgrave came up to visit me I was to say John was in town, and if he stayed I was to give him his tea and send down to let John know so that he might remain at D.H. and not come up, but if Mr P went away he would return to his tea. All this Sophie pondered over not to their advantage as the whole talk at breakfast had been about truth and our duty to our neighbours—which extremely disgusted her. When she told me what I was to do with Mr Palgrave I said I would do no such thing as keep him or any other young man like him to spend the evening here and John out of the House. On his appearing it turned out to be the one George was at the Charterhouse with so he paid me but a short visit and went.*

Upon his departure Sophie still had their conduct on her mind and began telling me all John had told her since she had been here etc as he has treated her quite as his confidant, and also Mr and Mrs R the same. I leave it to you and Papa to imagine my astonishment at their disclosures to so young a girl, although indeed nothing should surprize me that they do. The baseness of their line of action is something to me perfectly astonishing, Mr and Mrs R openly telling her everything that could lower her opinion of her parents and flatter herself, Mrs R kissing her and saying she wished she could have the charge of her—for her mother was a weak ignorant woman, and I, a poor, silly creature simply raised into respectability by my husband's talents—that I thought myself very clever and that people made much of me but it was all John's great abilities and that I was merely a Scotch girl with bad manners and that I had

---

* Both the Palgrave brothers, Francis (1824–97) of *The Golden Treasury* fame, and Gifford (1826–88), had been at Charterhouse; Francis as a day boy from 1838 to 1843 and Gifford as a boarder from 1838 to 1844. George Gray, born in 1829, had been at Charterhouse 1841–4. It is more probable that the brother who came to call was Gifford who had returned from the East (where he was a Jesuit missionary) in 1853. He was less likely to have seen the Turners for he was not yet a friend of Ruskin's, whereas Ruskin already knew Francis well and had asked him the year before to come any afternoon to Denmark Hill and walk with him. (Letter of March 14, 1853, *Works*, Vol. 10, p. xliii.)

even taught John some very bad habits such as making that noise with his nose—and that Papa and Mama had spoiled me so that I had grown up a spoiled silly creature that I was— that she had had such experience in bringing up children. Upon this she makes Sophie eat a great hard Pear so that her stomach has ached ever since and some sponge cake all against her will. She said so much that it would be nonsense recounting it all but Sophie acts them to perfection and likes to do so, so that she will give you some specimens.

John's revelations are much more serious and I think it perfectly disgusting his trying to corrupt Sophie's mind by such disclosures and I am sure My Father and you will be filled with indignation at such unmanly conduct. He told her so much that it would keep you reading and me writing, a whole week, but fancy him telling that *child* everything against us that he possibly could. She said to me, 'I am telling you, deary, to warn you because he says he is going to begin his harsh treatment whenever you come back from Germany, that there is not time for it to have effect before you go away, but that when you return, as you won't go to Perth and remain there, he is to try what harshness will do to break your spirit. He is hardly ever going to speak to you and is going to spend nearly all his time at D.H. He says, you are so wicked that he was warned by all his friends not to have anything to do with you, but that you were so bold and impudent and made such advances to him that you just threw your snares over him in the same way that you had done over Millais, and that you were all the cause of Millais' present unhappiness (Fancy!!), and that I was so in love with Millais that I thought of nothing but him, and he really thought I was, with the exception of *you*, the most intriguing woman he had ever known and that he would write a book—so big (making a motion with his hands)—about my conduct and get a divorce from me tomorrow.' Fancy putting such ideas into her head—indeed it would disquiet anybody. Upon my word they would almost make a Saint a Sinner. I am sure Papa will never permit Alice to go through this ordeal, and John boasts that he is to try everything he can to have her next, as Mrs R said to Sophie that "she may be talked to and not allowed to grow up and be blinded," and he told Sophie if he comes back from Switzerland he is to take me to Perth and bring Alice back to see how they agree.

He next read Sophie some of my conversations in the Highlands, "the Notes", and commented thereon, and also one of my letters to him before marriage—commenting on my duplicity. He said he could not endure me and did not mind whether I was ill or well—but, with an Emphasis, that he would do his duty to me, which Sophie naturally thought a curious contradiction to his expressions and daily conduct. He is a perfect villain to make such a systematic plan of deception as I must tell you much more, and although I must put up for the present, and I do wish Millais was gone as John is loading him with flattery and trying to get me into some fresh scrape that may be a means of recovering Millais' friendship and lowering me in his estimation. He must be trying something of this kind since he says he is the noblest fellow he knows, and when Sophie asked him why he said to Millais that a sketch of her was the finest thing he had done or something like that and he was improving every day, and told me it was a vile thing and a daub, he said, Oh he would not hurt his feelings for the world, and* Millais likes flattery! I have no doubt he gives him so much that he is disgusted but still it would be well he knew, I think, that John is very different there to what he is here. He sits to him on Thursday [March 2].

I must next speak about Crawley who will be the next sacrifice if he is not very prudent, and I want your advice thereon. I had not an idea but that he got on quite well with them at Denmarkhill, but on Saturday it appears that there was some misunderstanding about John's shirts and Crawley's pride had been hurt by finding that they make remarks on the way his Master is dressed, that Old Anne† and Mrs R do anything with him they like and change Crawley's ways of doing things. This has arisen for long without my knowing anything about it. In the evening when Sophie was giving him his French lesson she repeated some of Mrs R's remarks upon him, which caused

* Here begins page 5, headed 'Monday', but the letter runs straight on.
† Anne Strachan, John's old nurse, who had first entered the service of John's paternal grandfather when she was fifteen. John was devoted to her. She died in 1871.

an explosion of all the rest of his opinions on things in general since he came here. He said, "Well, Miss Sophie, the whole truth is this that they just hate me at D.H. because I won't gossip with them about my Master and Missus. It's perfectly disgusting to me to see servants talking about their Masters' affairs and I never have joined, and there Miss Sophie I'll just tell you what they do down there of an evening—they listen to all they hear, first in the diningroom, and then at night Old Anne gets out wine and fruit cake and they sit and gossip until they get half sleepy and tipsy—Lucy is the only one who is quiet—but they tell the most dreadful lies about my missus and I cannot stay there and see how they go on. It is perfectly shameful to see the way they treat Missus, and I am often dreadfully sorry for Missus. I am very glad I am going with her to Germany. I think my Master a very silly man, but I will work (you may tell my Missus) day and night for him so that he may not observe that I am attentive to my Missus's wants, for I *have observed* since I came back, especially this year, that just because I have been a little more attached to her he has hardly ever spoken to me. It is perfectly shameful the way they treat her, and I can tell you Miss Sophie if my Missus was not here I would give up my place tomorrow. And what I am so afraid of is these servants gossiping and their speaking of my Master and Missus all over Camberwell—just think how dreadful that would be Miss Sophie!! And that's the whole truth Miss Sophie. It makes me so ill I can't have my French tonight, Miss."

Just imagine all this and think over it. I do hope Crawley will be prudent, as really he is quite a comfort to me. I have nobody else who cares a pin here whether I am dead or alive; in fact, however humiliating, it is a satisfaction to have someone in the house who observes and who could, if necessary, tell the truth. I, of course, have never taken the least notice of their behaviour to Sophie. As Mrs R kindly informed her, "You had better not tell Effie these things, dear, for she would hate you and then you would be sent home."

I am to all appearance on perfectly good terms with them. Only with John I am quiet. He has told Sophie that he watches everything I do or say, therefore it is impossible I can talk about anything that comes uppermost. I do not know what on earth they are such fools for, especially John as were it not for the pain of exposure I have him most completely in my power. I must tell you all these things just to show you how impossible any behaviour is to help things straight for all our sakes when their object is to get rid of me, to have John altogether with them again. At any price they are resolved to do this, but they seem to wish if possible to disgust me to such a degree as to force me—or else get me—into some scrape. John has been trying again to get me by taunts to write to Millais. He accepted that St Agnes drawing* etc, it now hangs before me, and then he said, didn't I still write to him and where was the harm if he gave me drawings? I said the drawing was his as much as mine and to send it back if he liked. Then he was excessively angry at my telling him, after some words in which he called the Fords "Liars" the other night, to find that I was writing a letter to Clare to discontinue my correspondence with him. He was extremely displeased and said, "Well—you must let Clare distinctly understand that it is quite against my wish, and moreover that I think you are doing so simply because you are tired corresponding with him." (There is nothing I do to which a bad motive is not instantly attached.) My letter to him will go next Mail; it is not yet finished but I have put John's words as he desires.†

I suppose by the autumn something will be done by the R's— do not think any manifestation will come from me. It is impossible for me to tell you all until I am obliged to seek my Father's advice—but I feel better in my health and as it is impossible by any means of mine to stop their folly I will just go on as I am doing. Jane Boswell‡ will soon be here and then

* This is a pen and ink drawing, washed with colour, illustrating Tennyson's poem *St Agnes' Eve*. It is signed with Millais's monogram and dated 1854. It is reproduced in James, p. 216.

† Clare was still in Naples as an attaché. He remained a life-long friend of Effie's. In 1857 he married Bene, daughter of Marchese Garofalo of Naples, and died in 1899.

‡ Jane Douglas Boswell was a very old friend of the Grays. She was the second of the five daughters of Hamilton Boswell who had married Jane Douglas, heiress of Garrallan, Old Cumnock, Ayrshire. She was coming to Herne Hill for a visit of three weeks.

we go for some days to Oxford and then abroad so that I trust this summer will come and go without anything. It troubles me excessively to write to you about all these things but my position now admits of no other plan and I leave it to your judgement whether or not to give Millais any hints. You must write to him as his picture of Sophie I sent on Saturday. I wish that picture of John was done.

I have just received your letter and will make Sophie write. I am busy today as Mary is leaving.* I keep a most particular account of all my expenses in my day Book but it is impossible to know what John spends since he gets hundreds unknown to me from his Father every now and then . . . We dine tomorrow with Lady James for a wonder.

Ever Yrs Effie[1]

Tuesday [February 28]

I told you yesterday that we were to dine with Lady James today. What does John do but go to her without even telling me yesterday and say that he wishes to beg off to dine with his Father and Mother who have the Pritchards† today, but that on her asking me, I would dine there with pleasure. This he tells me on coming home. I told him I really would not go, and this morning I am going into London to explain to her that I cannot dine out at any large party by myself.‡ This made him very angry, my refusal to go. He told Sophie privately that he was sure I would go and only said no last night to make a fuss—but on finding that I am in earnest, he told me I was to write to Naples to tell Mrs Bishop that I was not to be allowed to join her in Germany and that I was either to stay here all the summer alone or go to Perth. He is perfectly enraged that I do not lose my temper or appear annoyed. He said last night that it was no merit my not getting into a passion

---

* Mary had been with Effie since the summer of 1851. She left because she found life at Herne Hill too dull. (*Effie in Venice*, p. 327.)

† John Pritchard was a rich landowner in Shropshire and M.P. for Bridgnorth. His wife was a sister of Rev. Osborne Gordon who had been Ruskin's private tutor at Oxford.

‡ Effie had met Sir Walter and Lady James soon after her marriage. They lived at 11 Whitehall Place.

as I had no temper to lose. Sophie is perfectly astonished at him and says now she thinks you and Papa much more religious people than the Ruskins. What am I to do with her? All this is dreadfully bad for her. And what will you write to Millais, for really he must know and be told something of all this or else he will commit some indiscretion from John's false manner to him, and if I let Sophie go and see him she will tell him everything and then he will be put in a passion. I cannot shut my eyes to the Ruskins' wish to draw me into scrapes, therefor it is quite impossible for either you or my Father to advise a submission which might end in their success since they are perfectly blinded by their selfishness.

Don't trouble about me but advise me. I cannot do wrong that good may come. I hope and think I am doing right and I feel better for it.[2]

She left this letter unsigned and added on a small scrap of paper: 'I have just left my letter open to say that I have had a long visit from Lady E [Eastlake], kind and true as ever. Nothing new however. Just hearing the different *on dits*. I will tell you when I get home.'

Her next letter seems to show for the first time that she really was in love:

Thursday [March 2]

Your letter has come to hand. Do not fear their opening your letters. John is away all day and yours generally come at 2½. I think you see the thing quite plainly even without my telling you more. Mrs R was here today, the first time since she has been home, and took Sophie down to Denmarkhill and there walked in the garden and gave her a lecture on the impropriety of my not going to Lady James's. She said, "There, Sophie, was an instance of your sister's character. She *might* have obliged her husband and gone to please him. A wife should obey her husband in everything but what is against God's commands." Sophie just laughs at them all and is much fonder of me, but I cannot think such goings on at all fit for so young a girl. It will teach her, I fear, both to exaggerate a little and to act a part as Mrs R always asks her if she doesn't see the thing

*Cruel Treatment of a Master to his Pupil*. Drawing by Millais showing Ruskin on the left, while Millais teases Effie with a piece of fern.

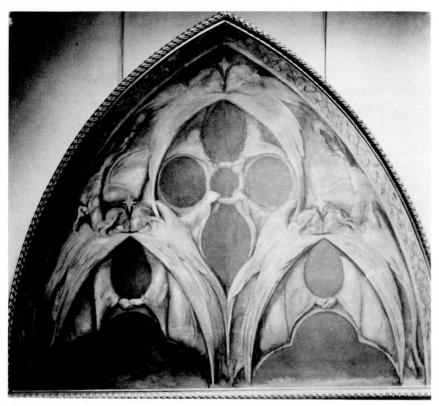

Design for a Gothic Window painted by Millais at Glenfinlas.
(*See pp. 81–2.*)

as she does, and as Sophie doesn't at all, but quite the contrary, she either remains silent or has to invent an evasive reply.

I must now speak principally of Everett, and you can either send him this to read or write the substance of it. I think you see John's plan clearly in regard to him. If I cannot go on with the Ruskins I will do so at least till I see you in autumn or before it—but about Millais there is no doubt that he (John) is acting in a most decided manner to get me into a scrape. About this drawing of St Agnes he most completely, as far as I can learn from Sophie, encouraged him to send it, telling him that it was the finest thing he had done and that I would not know how to thank him etc. Well, Millais I have no doubt takes this for permission, knowing how much pleasure the drawing would give me. He sends it and writes John a most kind note telling me to accept it. John asks me what I thought of it and wasn't it the finest thing I had seen, such an ornament to my room &c. It was hung up and he expressed himself highly pleased with the position. Well! last night I just thought, as I am now so accustomed to his ways, that notwithstanding all his approval that he might lead me into a mess, and Everett too, and I said, "Now you are going to Millais tomorrow, what are you going to say to him from me? Do you really quite approve of my having this drawing and are you to tell him so?" "No," said he, "I do *not* think you should take it—but you and Millais must settle that between yourselves." I said that was quite impossible as I did not hold any intercourse with him. He looked incredulous and I said, "I will send the drawing back in the morning," quite cooly. He said nothing, but I suppose had not expected that I could part with so lovely a possession. This morning he came in and said that he was going to say to Millais that I was to keep it, and then turning to me said, "You know it is not what either you or I feel or think but what will save Millais' feelings. No wonder Cupid is represented with an emaciated Body and Claws sometimes when Love makes such a fool of a man like that. I shall tell him that the sooner he gets over it the better." Now he told Sophie that he knew that when he treated me harshly next winter it would, he thought, force me to write and complain to Everett, and what did he care?

It is quite horrible to be obliged to think such things of one's fellow creatures but it is quite impossible not to see the R's settled wish and idée fixe is to impute something to me which will give them power, and as they have nothing, their malice is next to insane, and if I do not act on the defensive I have no preservative to my honor, for to please them is to destroy myself. John sees all the worth of securing Everett's good opinion, and Everett knows my position so well that he is most anxious to promote my happiness in the only way he properly can, by encouraging me to draw. I draw perpetually and after tomorrow when I am going to send Sophie for her cloak and to bid him goodbye, as I cannot properly send her again now that John has talked to her in such a manner about us, I am never going to mention his name even if John wishes it. Don't you think I am right after the manner he has spoken to me, and now he constantly praises Everett. Whether he praises or blames him is not of the slightest consequence to me—as my opinion [of] him as a man is quite independent of his genius— whilst John only cares for that and considers him accordingly. If Everett never painted another stroke John would talk sentimentally about the fine things he had done and abuse his personal weakness in giving in. As long as he does fine things John will never let him alone but will attach him to himself. As he said the other day, all his hopes for the Fine Arts are fixed on the P.R.B. School in England and that people would say how true *his* writings were.

I am for my own sake most thankful he has so arranged that St Agnes still hangs before me. It is the most touching thing you ever beheld. The Saint's face looking out on the snow with the mouth opened and dying-looking is exactly like Millais'— which however, fortunately, has not struck John who said the only part of the picture he didn't like was the face which was ugly but that Millais had touched it and it was better, but it strikes me very much. I think I see Millais reading the poem to me and talking about it with me. I wish he was gone—I cannot bear to think of what he must endure painting John. When I think of all his [John's] double dealing I wonder how I can speak to him at all, and his conduct to Sophie is too detestable. Do not fear for her affection! I have some hopes of still going to Germany since Mrs R told Sophie it would look too odd my being left here alone—but none of them have mentioned it to me.

*Friday* [the 3rd] I asked John this morning what he had said to Millais about the drawing, he said, "I am not going to say anything to him"—So you see—it is quite impossible to get John to say clearly what he thinks for two days together. Millais, I know, will still be good enough to send me things to copy whilst he remains in this country and all this will annoy and bother him excessively. I suppose I must speak of him sometimes too. Things must just take their course, and you must write to Millais most fully about me, at the same time be sure and do so exactly as you would speak and I tell you. I am excessively anxious not to blame the Ruskins more than I can help, nor impute any motives to them which their conduct would not justify, but it is impossible to blind myself to their doings without losing all perceptions of right and wrong, and Millais is very much concerned in this as well as me and I would rather do anything than that his name should be dragged before the public, and I agree with you that towards winter, after he has gone and no intercourse between us, that if they do not behave better I must then do something without any disadvantage to either of us. For however much he wishes from his regard for me to help me it would be an irreparable misery to himself, although he would try not to feel it. [It] would hurt his independence, and his character stands so deservedly high that as the founder of a new school, and in a great position in this Country, it would be a lasting sorrow to have that reputation tarnished in the slightest degree. It is a very very important thing for him to keep clear of us altogether and you may tell him not to think it selfish but imperatively necessary and his first duty to go as soon as possible. Things may change but he must not hesitate now. I have been so worried that I quite forgot the Milmans' dinner yesterday. Only think! Yrs Ever[3]

Again she forgot to sign her letter. She was evidently quite distraught. Mrs Gray must already have written to. Millais after receiving Effie's letter of February 27, for he was replying to it on the very day Effie was writing the last part of the one above:

83 Gower Street
Friday morning 3d March/54.

I am very much obliged for your letter as I shall now be more careful than ever. It is only right that I should know of Ruskin's deceit, that I may act accordingly. *Something must be done by you* if she continues to be martyred, as it is *grossly sinful* to permit matters to stand as they do. *Nothing more shall be sent by me.* I should never have sent drawings at all had it not been for Ruskin Himself permitting me to do so. I enclose a letter from him received lately which will tell you everything. If I had only myself to consult, I should write immediately and refuse to go on further with the portrait, which is the most hateful task I ever had to perform, but I am so anxious that Effie should not suffer further for any act of mine that I will put up with anything rather than increase her suffering.

Surely such a quiet scoundrel as this man never existed, he comes here sitting as blandly as ever, talking the whole time in apparently a most interested way.* Do you think I can get off finishing his portrait without doing harm to the Countess? If so I could leave almost immediately, in May, or 1st of June. My family are going to leave this house then, and are perfectly reconciled to my going abroad.†

I have not painted anything since, nor do I think it likely until I get away from hearing about this. It incenses and disgusts me to hear of this matter, and yet naturally I desire to know all. He was sitting here yesterday and mentioned about sending a little girl's head I have painted,‡ to Herne Hill for the Countess to see. *It is my opinion that some steps should be speedily taken* to protect her from this incessant harassing be-

---

* According to Sir William Rothenstein in *Men and Memories* (Vol. I, p. 141), Henry Acland told him: 'Ruskin later insisted that Millais should finish the portrait; it was a duty to Art. Millais came, Ruskin stood, and the work was completed, without a word having passed between them.' So much for hearsay.

† His parents had taken South Cottage at Kingston-on-Thames where they were very happy and lived for the rest of their lives.

‡ Probably the head of Annie Miller, the model Hunt had discovered and was in love with. Millais wrote to Hunt on April 10: 'Annie Miller has been sitting to me and I have been painting a little head from her. She is a good little girl, and behaves herself very properly.'

haviour of the Rs. If they are bent upon obtaining a separation you will be obliged (in pity for her sake) to consent, for human nature can never stand such treatment.

I am not sufficiently acquainted with Law to know whether something more than a separation could be obtained, but I think you should enquire into the matter. Sophie has come in with Crawley to bid me goodbye.[4]

The following note from John was enclosed in Millais's letter:

Sunday evening February 26
My dear Millais

I shall be with you on Thursday [March 2] at eleven—as you desire in your last note.

The St Agnes is placed in the principal place in the drawing-room—Effie says "I only praise you to try and make you like me again". I shall therefore never praise you any more, except in writing and speaking of you—when of course I shall say exactly what I should have said if I had had no acquaintance with you.

Believe me faithfully Yours
J Ruskin.

Effie herself, writing a second time to her mother on Friday, March 3, described Sophie's last visit to Millais:

I wrote you a long letter this morning. Since sending it Sophie has been to Millais' and he had got your letter. He understands perfectly and will be off as soon as possible. He is in a perfect rage with the Ruskins and said that they were a lot of Babies, and at first told Sophie not to tell him anything it would make him so angry, but she told him all, and that if it was not for fear of hurting me he would not paint another stroke to John's picture and is to write to you about that. I hope he will finish it as soon as possible. He farther told Sophie that it was quite wrong my putting up with them and that I should get divorced from John directly and that if I did not write to you and my Father what John's conduct to me had been that he would, as I ought to have Papa's advice, but that he would not like to take a step and would rather I did it, but that if I did not he would not hesitate as he thought it quite wrong my being treated in this way, and wicked to continue. He said anything more monstrous than talking to Sophie he never heard and that she was to warn me not to be tempted in any sort of way to write him a single word.

I will think over all this for a few days and when my mind is made up I will write to my Father, reserving always to myself the wish that whatever you may feel on the subject you will not allow your feelings to communicate in any way with the R's without my consent.

This you have always been wise enough to do. Many thanks for all your Love—I hope I may never give you concern. These trials have been for seven years nearly [in fact for nearly six]; they might have gone on 27, only it is better that they should have an end before either these people kill me or lead me into a scrape. Ever Yr E.

I shall not write for some days. Don't write what I said this morning to Millais, it is useless and he knows as well as us what to do.

The next few days of waiting must have been almost unbearably anxious ones for the Grays, and they must have been very worried about Sophie too who was being used by everyone as a go-between. No one seems to have said anything to her without an ulterior motive. John and his parents told her things which they evidently intended her to pass on to Effie; Effie and Millais exchanged messages through her, and even Crawley made her confidences which he must have known she would not keep to herself; moreover, inadvertently at least, she would have revealed to the Ruskins much of what Effie did and said. All these adults undoubtedly heard from her just what they wanted to hear, for it would have been most unnatural for a child of ten not to have coloured her revelations to suit the eager ears of her listeners and heighten the drama. How important she must have felt and how dull life at Bowerswell must have seemed when eventually she returned home.

The effect of all this on her bright little mind can only be guessed at. She grew into a lovely girl as can be seen from Millais's two pictures, *Autumn Leaves* and *Apple Blossoms*, for both of which she sat as a model. Nevertheless it is known (from a letter from Millais to Holman Hunt) that in 1868, when she was twenty-four, she had a breakdown and was away from home for almost two years with what was called 'hysteria'. This may not, of course, have had anything to do with her experiences at Herne Hill; indeed it rather seems to bear out a story in the Millais family that she and Millais became too fond of each other and that Effie sent her away. There is no doubt that Millais was devotedly attached to her and that there was some tragic mystery in her life.

In spite of Sophie's beauty she did not marry until 1873 when she was thirty. Her husband was James Caird of a Dundee shipping family with whom she was very unhappy.\* She died in 1882 leaving one daughter, Beatrice. Millais painted a sad and lovely portrait of Sophie two years before her death.† Perhaps he, more than anyone, knew the secrets of her short life, and in her hauntingly sad expression portrayed an old sadness of his own.

\* Mr Caird had in fact appeared on the scene as early as 1865 when Effie wrote to her mother that if Mr Caird was 'intelligent and well informed he would just suit Sophie'.

† Now owned by Sir Ralph Millais, who also possesses a portrait of Beatrice Caird painted by Millais in 1879 and reproduced in Millais, Vol. II, p. 211.

# THE TRUTH AT LAST

✿

Three days later Effie at last told her parents the truth about her married life:

Herne Hill 7th March*

My dearest Father—I have received my Mother's and George's kind letters this morning and feel very thankful that I have your and their approval in the course of conduct I have been endeavouring to pursue for some time—and in fact unless matters had become so sad for me as to threaten my Life I should not have on any account, but feeling that the necessity for acting in concert with you might by being longer delayed cause you and others connected with my Life greater sorrow in the end. I therefore, as I feel now so ill and in perpetual nervous distress, and feel that perhaps I may be adding to yours by a silence which I have kept on John Ruskin's conduct to me ever since I left your care, although I have lately and on my last visit home shown you how very unhappy I was.

You are aware that since 1848 to this last year I have never made any formal complaint to you. There were many reasons for my silence, the principal being of course my great love for you and my dear Mother—fearing to trouble you when you were in great difficulties [financial ones] yourselves, when I tried to look on my unfortunate position as one where, whatever I internally suffered, at least removed me from being a burthen on you—and I resolved that no annoyance which I suffered should give you any. I pass over all other discussions and reasons at present till I see you as I could fill Volumes. To come to the present moment, when even now I was unwilling

* Effie put the wrong date on this letter. It was post-marked March 6, and Perth March 7.

to tell you all, fearing your anger against John Ruskin who has so illtreated and abused me, and his Parents who have so seconded him, although so far they are innocent, not knowing the gravity of the offence with which I charge him and from which proceeds all the rest. But they have been most guilty in the education they have given him and ought not to have treated me as they have done. I wish neither to be uncharitable nor to take advantage of any of them but I am so ruined and nervous in both mind and body that as they are so anxious to get rid of me, and I have not the satisfaction of feeling that any one is the least the better for my forbearance and suffering, I have duly considered the step I am about to take in telling you all. Feeling very ill last week and in the greatest perplexity about my duty to you—I went and consulted Lady Eastlake and also partly Lord Glenelg, the two persons in London for whom I have most respect. I did not open my mind to the latter as I did to the former but as I could perfectly rely on their prudence and wisdom I took the advice of Lady E to permit her to make the necessary enquiries of How English Law would treat such a case as mine.* You may perhaps at first wonder that I should apply to anyone in preference to yourself—but I was still unwilling to ask you to act for me until I saw I could not avoid giving you trouble and that of a most serious nature. I enclose Lady E's most kind and noble letter, it will best show you what she is, as well as perhaps help you, although cases of this description may have come under your own knowledge in the course of your Life. I have therefor simply to tell you that I do not think I am John Ruskin's Wife at all—and I entreat you to assist me to get released from the unnatural position in which I stand to Him. To go back to the day of my marriage the 10th of April 1848. I went as you know away to the Highlands.† I had never been told the duties of married persons to each other and knew little or nothing about their relations in the closest union on earth. For days John talked about this relation to me but avowed no intention of making me his Wife.

* This may have been the first occasion on which Effie fully confided in Lady Eastlake. It is more likely, though, that Lady Eastlake had known the truth for a long time and had been urging Effie to tell her parents.

† They had spent their wedding night at Blair Atholl.

He alleged various reasons, Hatred to children, religious motives, a desire to preserve my beauty, and finally this last year told me his true reason (and this to me is as villainous as all the rest), that he had imagined women were quite different to what he saw I was, and that the reason he did not make me his Wife was because he was disgusted with my person the first evening 10th April.* After I began to see things better I argued with him and took the Bible but he soon silenced me and I was not sufficiently awake to what position I was in. Then he said after 6 years he would marry me, when I was 25. This last year we spoke about it. I did say what I thought in May.† He then said, as I professed quite a dislike to him, that it would be *sinful* to enter into such a connexion, as if I was not very *wicked* I was at least insane and the responsibility that I might have children was too great, as I was quite unfit to bring them up. These are some of the facts. You may imagine what I have gone through— and besides all this the temptations his neglect threw me in the way of. If he had only been kind, I might have lived and died in my maiden state, but in addition to this brutality his leaving me on every occasion—his threats for the future of a wish to break my spirit—and only last night when he wished to put his arm round me (for I believe he was cold) I bade him leave me, he said he had a good mind to beat me and that he had never admired Romanism so much, as if he had a Confessor for me he would soon bring me to my senses. I don't think, poor creature, he knows anything about human creatures—but he is so gifted otherwise and so cold at the same time that he never thinks of people's feelings and yet with his eloquence will always command admiration. I cannot bear his presence and something you will feel is imperative. Once this year I did threaten him with Law, but I really did not know myself about it, as it was in Edinburgh and he said, "Well, and if I was to take

---

* It was suggested in *Effie in Venice* (p. 21) that Ruskin suffered a traumatic shock on his wedding night when he discovered that Effie had pubic hair. Nothing had prepared him for this. He had never been to an art school and none of the pictures and statues on public exhibition at that time depicted female nudes with hair anywhere on their bodies. Ruskin's later love for little girls may well have stemmed from his disgust with this aspect of puberty.

† Her twenty-fifth birthday on May 7, 1853.

all the blame?" I think he might not oppose my protest—In point of fact, could He?

I should not think of entering your House excepting as free as I was before I left it. All this you must consider over and find out what you can do. Thank God for all his goodness to me which has enabled me to Live up to this time in his fear and in I trust a virtuous Life—the glory is all his and under him I have been kept from sin by the remembrance of the example you and my dear Mother have ever shown me. If I have not written you clearly enough you must put it down to illness and agitation, for you will hardly wonder this keeping up of appearances makes me often sick.

Yr affectionate Daughter    Effie Gray[1]

The signature was no doubt intentional. On the inside flap of the envelope she had written: 'Return me Lady E's letter. I have sent a box to Mama today which she will be so good as to put in her storeroom for me. It contains my Dairies [*sic*] and things she thought I had better send.'

Mrs Gray must have written to Millais within a few days, and his reply, postmarked March 15, shows beyond all doubt that Effie had fully confided in him while they were at Glenfinlas:

I confess in spite of the distress it must occasion that I am glad that you know all. You will better understand now how all the Highland affair came about, and how little right Ruskin has to complain of her conduct. I think the most generous way of looking upon his behaviour is to believe him partially out of his mind. It is needless for me to say how deeply I sympathise with you in this miserable affair and how I pity her in her present position which I trust will be changed. I shall hope to hear from you again shortly.[2]

Some immediate action was evidently expected of Mr Gray—but what? He was in a difficult predicament. After some slight pushing from Mrs Gray he decided to come down to see Mr Ruskin.

In the meantime Delphine, the nursery governess at Bowerswell, had been dismissed after nearly three years and was to leave before Sophie's return. The reason for this is not given. We only hear of it

from Effie's next letter to her mother of March 20: 'I quite agree
with you about Sophie and Delphine not meeting. Sophie is constantly asking now when she is to go back and the whole reason is
that she may be with Delphine. She was begging me the other day
to let her tell Delphine everything when she went home, and I
simply told her that Delphine was not one of the family and I would
not permit her to tell her anything, at which she stared and said,
"Why not?" '

It seems hard on Sophie that having been encouraged to gossip
with Crawley she was not allowed to tell her beloved governess
anything of what was going on.

Effie ended her letter of the 20th: 'Old Mr R is going from home
tomorrow for ten days.* They were all here yesterday for a wonder
and admired Millais's St Agnes. When you write to him [Millais]
again say that I am sorry I cannot send Sophie to him again, as he
begged me through her to let her go back. I fear John questioning
her. I have just got Papa's note. His letter never came and I cannot
think where it can be. It would be no use coming till Mr R's return.'

Three days later she was writing again:

No word of the missing letter yet—and I do not think it can
have fallen into Ruskin hands at any rate, for I told John last
night about not going to Germany, a project which I think
greatly relieved his mind as now he fancies he will go off to
Switzerland without the bore of going to the German Spas and
without the expence. He was however angry that I simply told
him my plans without enlightening his mind on any of my ideas
and I went to sleep whilst he continued declaring that my
insolence was unpardonable and that the only thing for me was
a good beating with a *common* stick. What I put my not going
on was his own saying that I was not to go &c . . . I think Papa
should come up after your Preachings as you say. Mr R is
expected to be from home ten days at least and it should be
about that time . . . I also told Crawley about my not going
and hinted that he had better be making up his mind whether
to go with his Master or not. I quite approve of what you said
about his not going to Everett and I don't suppose he would
think of it without Everett asked him which he would not

* He went to Wrexham, Worcester and Liverpool on business.

think of doing. I had William [Millais] dining here two days ago. He sang beautifully and spoke of being in Perth this summer as usual. He had not seen Everett for four days but Mr Halliday who was also here said that he was hunting constantly* and it was putting new life in him and he was working very hard at some heads. I am not able to draw at all just now, my mind is in such a state of constant thinking—although I do not think any one would believe it from my manner but it is mere manner as my head is incapable of giving the least attention to any thing requiring . . .

Jane Boswell makes me laugh in spite of myself.† She wrote home the other day that John R was more to be admired at a distance than near and would have driven her mad years ago, that *Piety* was the Ruskin Fine Art—he showed it by quitting the House often before breakfast and not returning till night to read *prayers* at 9½. She thinks the Old people quite an "invention of the Enemy" and thinks the way Mrs R speaks to Sophie of me and you all the height of wickedness. She says she is to put great faith in her instincts for the future since she took the greatest dislike to them all the first year of my marriage, but John made himself so agreeable in Edinburgh that she changed her opinion.‡ However now she returns to the belief that all Geniuses are *Mad, John* forming no exception to the rule. She would have broken his head years ago—had he offered to beat her—she thinks.

He is quite as much occupied with his "poor Mother" as usual in his Father's absence and we hardly ever see him . . . *Friday.* I saw Lady E [Eastlake] last night; she is much grieved at Lord G's [Glenelg] not coming to me. She thinks he will still come. She once thought of going to him herself but that would not do.§ All that Papa says is excellent . . . I shall approve of

---

* He hunted with the Hitchin Harriers. It was a new sport to him.

† Although Effie had told her mother that Jane Boswell was coming to stay, this is the first mention of her being in the house.

‡ John had written to his father about Jane Boswell from Edinburgh: 'A great friend of Effie's—A Middleaged maiden lady. Very clever and witty. Not troublesome but needs some attention for Effie's sake who stayed long in her house.' (November 27, 1853.)

§ Lord Glenelg, a bachelor of seventy-five, was of a very shy and timid disposition. He did nothing to help Effie but after she had left Ruskin he

whatever he thinks proper to be done. Lady E thinks it quite
right his going to Old Mr R. When Papa comes to town you
ask where I could meet him. I can go anywhere to see him
wherever that may be. If he is staying in an Inn I could go
there but if with a friend I could arrange somewhere else quite
easily.

In her next letter of March 26, after describing some people who
came to tea the day before, she went on:

John fled to Denmark Hill on a hint from me to his intense
relief. He is taking tea with Mrs R. His father is at Wrexham
today and I have not heard when he returns. I have not heard
anything from Lord G and do not in the least expect it. I quite
puzzle John who cannot, he said to Sophie, make me out at
present and wanted to know if she had any idea what was the
reason of my change of conduct. He cannot make me out. I
hardly ever address him but in company and then nobody
would ever guess that we were not as usual. Jane [Boswell]
is of opinion he is quite mad but he makes himself most agreeable to her. I am still taking Quinine, I do not find it does me
either good or harm. I do not think any medicine could make
me better at present. Sometimes I think my mind will never get
composed again for any length of time. Music soothes or rather
excites me out of myself, but even that requires to be the very
best to make me forget for a little and feel less ill. Don't be
alarmed about me. J.R. says I am the most collected of my sex.

On Friday I took them to Exeter Hall to hear the Hymn of
Praise and Requiem. The Queen, Prince and Princess Royal
came which I was glad of for Sophie and Jane Boswell's sake
as they thought it quite a sight. The music was superb.* I
made Crawley go and he said it made him quite melancholy
the whole of the next day. I do not know what the worthy

---

wrote to her on July 10 apologising for his neglect. He told Lady Eastlake
'of the sad alteration he had remarked' in Effie and quite believed she
would not have lived if she had remained with Ruskin. (Letter from Lady
Eastlake to Effie, June 25, 1854.)

* The Requiem was Mozart's and the choir and orchestra those of the
Sacred Harmonic Society. Exeter Hall was in the Strand. It was pulled
down in 1907, and the Strand Palace Hotel now occupies the site.

Crawley is meditating at present. I told him that I was not going to Germany and that my plans were very unsettled. He declared his willingness to follow me to a village, if I was to be left by the R's, but as I said I was to go to Perth and would be with you and Papa, he may make up his mind to go with John for the sake of seeing foreign parts—He is an excellent good fellow and I should be very sorry if he became an inmate of D.H. He is far too good for them. Jane thinks Mrs R a dreadful old humbug. I wonder what she will say [when she hears the truth about the marriage]? I am quite determined to have no conversation with any of them on the subject!—unless I am obliged. What I chiefly dislike in all of them is their terrible want of honest truth and candour and never saying what they really think. I would not argue or talk with them on such a subject for the world. I hope I will be spared this. I would answer any question put to me properly by a third party. But I do not think the R's use their faculties but for the purpose of twisting others to their own views and I feel quite convinced that I do much better at present in trying to suppose John anybody or nobody.

Effie's next letter is written, like most of her others, on folded sheets of white paper, so that each sheet has the normal four pages. The first sheet of this one, however, has been torn in half so that pages three and four are missing. Clare Stuart Wortley believed that this was the work of her mother (Effie's daughter, Lady Stuart of Wortley) who had begun the sorting and arranging of Effie's letters. Lady Stuart of Wortley once told Clare that she had torn up part of one of Effie's letters because it was too intimate. Judging from the context it seems that the missing page of the following letter must be the one she destroyed:

My dearest Mother, 30th March

I had yours last evening and feel quite thankful to hear that Papa has fixed a day to come . . . I am glad he proposes Wednesday fortnight as Mr Ruskin will be back next week and Jane Boswell's three weeks visit will be over. She is not however to leave the neighbourhood as she wishes to be near me—to see what becomes of me—but it is quite time that things were settled. Everybody who has to do with me, until something is done, becomes concerned in these domestic affairs and it is very difficult indeed, the position I am in being so sad, to make any body happy or comfortable, and Jane has written home giving some hints and particulars of John's conduct as she thought it her duty to let her Mother know. She asked my leave to do this and after some thought I felt she was quite justified in doing so, they are quite safe. These two or three mornings I have come down quite exhausted for John has found out a new method [here comes the break where the page has been neatly torn off] what did he mean by this? I tell you this to show you that Papa must be very decided and quite prepared for all sorts of eloquence of this kind to screen his own conduct, and as he fears nothing, says the public are fools and that he daresays I have gained their good opinion by my pretty face, and also that I am too cunning to lose my character and not have some steady friends, he will perhaps do some unheard of thing since he seems to think himself quite perfect and really to believe it and me quite mad. It is quite fearful to go on this way. He is naturally quite loathsome to me but of course I did not abuse him for not having married me as just at present he might worry me more than he does. Is he not perfectly awful? It is astonishing however that during most part of the day when he is gone Jane and I get on so nicely, although the subject is never out of our heads, and I am so much the better of her. We went yesterday to Tottenham to show Jane Mr Windus's pictures. They are so lovely and I saw there Millais' "Isabella",* very large and wonderful, done when he was 19, also some interesting drawings of the P.R.B. school and me sitting sewing on the Rocks at Glenfinlas, the small oil picture† . . . I have

---

* *Lorenzo and Isabella*, a subject taken from Keats's poem, was painted in 1848 and exhibited at the Royal Academy in 1849. It was the first of Millais's pictures to be signed PRB. It is now in the Walker Art Gallery, Liverpool. Benjamin Godfrey Windus, a retired coach-builder, was one of the first to buy Pre-Raphaelite pictures. He also had a wonderful collection of Turners at his house on the Green at Tottenham. Ruskin, who had the run of his house, says in *Praeterita*, that without this access to Windus's pictures he would never have been able to write *Modern Painters*.

† This is the little picture described on p. 68 and reproduced on p. 83. Called *The Waterfall* it is now at the Delaware Art Center, Wilmington, U.S.A.

Sophie Gray. Water-colour painted by Millais at Gower Street in 1854.
(*See p. 130.*)

John Ruskin. Water-colour painted by Millais on January 17, 1854.
(*See p. 130.*)

also pruned all my wall trees and nailed them all tidy. And the girls' dresses are done. I shall send Alice's home. As to myself I am in very bad order. John won't pay me what he owes and I feel so unsettled and not knowing what is to become of me that I have only got myself a black silk and made myself a spring bonnet to be clean as I think a woman under no circumstances should be dirty, but all my things would require looking over and renewing . . . Jane's kindest love—she says she has got into a D's nest but luckily we know who can overcome them.

Ever yrs Effie

I feel so irritated at John now that I should like to pitch my wedding ring at him on the 10th [of April] but I suppose I must refrain from this however.[3]

It is not surprising that Effie did not 'abuse' John at this stage for 'not marrying' her. Indeed she probably made herself as odious and unattractive to him as possible for fear of any last minute attempt on his part to consummate the marriage, for this would have ruined all her plans.

# PLANS FOR ESCAPE

✸

Meanwhile Mrs Gray at Bowerswell was evidently almost as demented as Effie herself, for on April 1 Effie was writing to her:

I am very sorry to hear you are making yourself ill and worried with my affairs. Do try and be comforted and composed. Nothing ought to give you uneasiness and I see more and more every day that it is quite imperative that things should come to a height and not go on. Here has a letter come last night from Mrs Bishop to John imploring him to let me go and stating the serious inconvenience to her his not letting me. John writes her a nonsense letter condoling and putting my conduct in the worst light and saying he never approved of the plan, and yet this morning said to me he would give me a last chance to go and if I still liked would not send the letter. I said as he said he did not approve of the plan even yet, that that, if I had not made different arrangements, would have prevented me under any circumstances going. Every thing he does is twisted uneven, and so unsteady and incorrect that I told him he must not expect me to consult or talk with him about anything. He sent in Sophie last night to say that instead of his being in my debt that I was in his £15. I went to him and told him we had better settle our accounts once for all. So we made a separate statement and he said to Sophie, after I had made my statement good, that he was sorry to find that he was £60 in my debt instead. I was thankful I had my accounts arranged as I have different little bills in town which his not paying me this money has prevented me discharging . . .

I cannot think he has got Papa's letter [the lost letter to Effie]—and they have fixed to go away the 9th of May* . . . Although I say nothing ought to give you uneasiness, I mean

* This was the original date as mentioned in Mr Ruskin's letter of December 15, p. 116.

simply as regards my conduct. The more Jane sees and hears of John the more she says it would be impossible to go on with him. His extremely bland manners, and his actions so opposite, render him most dangerous. To estimate the annoyance it must necessarily give Papa and you is impossible, but who could have foreseen all these things, and trials come that must be met and I hope we shall see a way to escape. Papa and I will talk everything over and not do anything rashly—you may be sure he won't, and as for me I will be guided by his prudence and counsel, but I do not see what more I have to say as if I talked it would only be to tell more unkindness and abuse.

Try and keep easy and not get worried—in ten days now I will hope for Papa. Mr R comes on Monday. Mrs R still goes on questioning Sophie. Jane Boswell says she feels as if she had lived months instead of weeks here and feels John's personal rudeness to her. With all his bland speeches he never has offered to show her a thing and she says the commonest Farmer would be more polite to his guest.

On Monday, April 3, she wrote her last letter to her father:

I did not write anything about my affairs in George's letter last night as John was sitting in the room and might have asked to read my letter as I never can be sure. You need not write to me again till you do so to tell me where to find you as I should like to see you and hear your opinion before you meet Mr R. He comes today. We all dine at D.H. on Wednesday.

Do not fear my having any scene either with John or the old people. My composure is of far too great consequence to me at present to lose it. I am almost too weak and ill for anything and my health is so critical that it requires the strongest exertion to keep myself going at all, and as to losing my temper, things are far too serious. I have a difficulty I confess to go on with such deceitful people, it makes me sick—and at times impatient inwardly, but not angry. Their system of lying is however so rooted that Sophie on Saturday told me that John and his Mother talk such lies and nonsense that she was obliged twice to tell them that what John said was untrue. He told his Mother that I had gone into such a passion with Sophie for taking the

Kettle off the fire, upon which Mrs R condoled and said poor little Sophie. She replied that I had certainly reproved her but had not been at all angry. The child is perfectly disgusted with them. She makes a little noise with her mouth in eating and Mrs R told her not to do that as it was a proof of being *imbecile*. She then gave John and Sophie such an account of how she washed her Body in the morning, using such terms that although it was no laughing matter to hear Sophie describe them, still it was worth any of Molière. They next abused George [Gray] and said he was a great fool, and finally John is trying to get Sophie into an impatient state to be home and told her privately this morning that he was quite sure Mama and I were determined not to let Delphine and she meet* and that he would not wonder if I did not take her home after the term. He next came to me and said it was disgraceful behaving in such a way and breaking my promises to that poor little girl and that Sophie had been abusing Mama and me downstairs (she tells me she is quite willing to do anything you like and that John tells lies), and that he must know my plans now to tell his Father. I said that he knew I would go before they left for Switzerland. I hope this will quiet him and that he will ask no more . . .

Till you are on the spot, *I never mention my affairs to anyone.* Any letter of mine will but faintly give my Mother and you ideas on the matter. Much of course will depend on the Ruskins and how they take it. If they are anxious for my departure never to see me again, I should think they would not throw difficulties in the way, but if Old Mr R thinks they will lose caste you must prepare yourself for every sort of iniquity. As I fear no sort of examination however painful, my sense of right is so strong that you will find me quite determined and I cannot throw off the responsibility of my Conscience. Where is the use however of writing?

Good bye my dear Father, I trust you will be brought safely here and that we may both be guided towards the right way.

Her next letter to her mother is undated but it transpires that it

* This was true.

was written on April 6. It tells of the development of her plans for escape:

I have a line from Papa and will let him know in time about meeting him. It appears to me still that it would be *very* premature to go to Mr R the very afternoon of his arrival. My affairs unhappily cannot be disposed of so quickly and will require mature deliberation. I say unhappily because if my interests are to be consulted, and Papa warns me constantly not to be rash, this I think would be about as rash a measure as could be proposed since it appears to me highly necessary to know before having personal communication with the R's—to know how much or how little they will be obliged to accede to our wishes whatever these may be determined on to be, after due consultation. I may be quite wrong and Papa may take an entirely different view of the case but at any rate it is quite necessary he should be master of all the facts of the case before going and plunging into such a matter to the Rs, and two or three half-hours won't do this.

I will be most happy if I am well enough to go to the Wharf* and take him to his Hotel but I entreat of him not to dream of seeing Mr Ruskin till afterwards. This is the most important event of my life upon which all my future depends. Everything now is but a choice of evils but the thing must be done. If I am left and the Rs work farther on my understanding I fear the result would end in their triumph. My Father and you would never be happy if I had any illness which left me in the state they would not (and I think I am not uncharitable) be very sorry to see me in. I am to have a meeting at Lady E's tomorrow upon this subject and will give you the particulars.

Jane and Sophie with me dined yesterday at D.H. Mr Dale,† his son [Lawford], and the Pritchards were there. Jane and Sophie were in town all day. I was on the sofa in the most

* This shows that Mr Gray was coming by the steamer which left Dundee on Wednesday, April 12, and was due to arrive on the 14th.
† The Rev. Thomas Dale, Vicar of St Pancras. Ruskin as a boy had been his pupil when he was incumbent of St Matthew's Chapel, Denmark Hill. From Mr Ruskin's diary we know that this dinner-party was on April 5. (Bembridge.)

nervous state all day and in such pain all over my body proceeding from I do not know what that I thought I could not go
and yet it was so necessary that I went. Jane is perfectly rabid
on the subject of the R's, especially Mrs R. She was so disgusted
with her conversation last night that she thinks she must have
been quite drunk* . . . She never imagined such wicked people
and thinks London must be the centre of attraction for such
monsters . . .

Today I had a meeting at Lady Eastlake's. Mr Brown of
Venice was of our debate. It is quite necessary to speak to
some man who knows about these things and about *me* and my
life and I felt it quite a blessing his arrival in London two days
ago. Lady E and I agreed that nobody could have been found
better. He and she agreed to this and with me that nothing
could be more rash or premature than seeing Mr R before
more is arranged since things cannot be retarded and I cannot
suffer longer. The question was decided that Papa must first
hear all I have to say (they seemed to imagine You would
likely come also, I wish indeed you could) and then consult
with Twiss or Lushington†—state to him the case—name nobody—and ask his advice as a Lawyer and then personally and
what he would advise were the case his Daughter's, and then
act accordingly. Papa will see the force of this. He must not
think because I have consulted these *two* friends here and they
agree with me that the right thing must be done and very
deliberately, that I either undervalue his talents, ability, desire
to relieve me, or forget the expence and anxiety it will cause
him—but what can I do?—and as Mr Brown also disapproved
of me going to the Wharf I would rather go to the Hotel at
three and see if he has arrived, or return later. I must excite
no suspicions. Could Crawley go and help him to land and have
a fly waiting?

* Jane Boswell wrote to Effie after she left Ruskin: 'So others as well as
me think old Madam gets *drunk* . . . If old Madam was not drunk that night
I dined at D.H. I can only say the imitation was excellent.' (June 1, 1854.
Morgan.)

† Travers Twiss, D.C.L., was Vicar-General of the Archbishop of Canterbury and acted as advocate in the Consistory, or Ecclesiastical, Courts.
Stephen Lushington was a Judge of the Consistory Courts. Cases of divorce
and annulment were tried in the Ecclesiastical Courts up till 1857.

Mr Brown has seen some of his friends already. In asking about us as, of course, apart from anything remarkable, he finds *I* stand high in London and John is supposed to behave infamously to me—in short some say he is mad. This is Important to know.

I have this moment received your valuable letter; it is everything it should be and I am very glad Papa did not, and does not, intend seeing Mr R.* I am a very bad letter writer especially just now, but nothing can be wiser than all you say. If you could persuade Papa to bring you it would be much more proper, and indeed it is almost unavoidable—you will probably have to be sent for after, and it would be much better to come together. Lady E and Mr B talked of you and Papa equally and seemed to look on it as a matter of course. Papa is most kind, and nobody is more clear headed, but he must remember that these are matters quite beyond the common run of Life and must be treated by people accustomed to extreme cases and who have had the same passing under their eyes before, and two or three days at most will settle all our talks.

I have thought of what would be done with John after things are so far advanced as that old Mr R must be told—John must go to D.H., it will only be *sleeping* where he *lives*. After a Lawyer knows the case I will not sleep with him, and You, if not Papa, also should come to be with me here. All this will be easily arranged when you come. Papa must really allow you every freedom in this affair and nothing could be more judicious than all the advice you have given me. I don't think the R's have a suspicion.

John has just put my debt into my hands without uttering a word. After asking him for it twice I told him he must ask his Father, for to take the Housemoney to pay my accounts (what he proposed) was what I would not do. He said nothing but came to me with some haver in the afternoon about being anxious to keep this bad point of my character from his Father. I said, "What! asking you to pay up debts? I'll bear that blame." I don't know what he may have said to his Father but here is

---

* This means that Mr Gray did not intend to see Mr Ruskin before consulting with Effie and the lawyers. It was still his intention, though, to confront Mr Ruskin personally while he was in London.

the money, which is the great point . . . I cannot write more.[1]

Rawdon Brown's sudden arrival in England seems to have been unexpected by Effie. He already knew Lady Eastlake through the Murrays. Brown had been at Charterhouse with John Murray, and Lady Eastlake was not only a great friend of the Murrays but connected to them by marriage, her youngest sister, Matilda, having married Mrs Murray's brother, James Smith.

Brown had come to London to try to hurry his book through the press, and it is through Effie's letters to him that we know the details of her escape. According to Mr Ruskin's diary he called at Denmark Hill on April 6, the very day of this meeting between himself, Effie and Lady Eastlake.

# EFFIE'S FLIGHT

❀

On Monday, April 10, Effie's sixth wedding anniversary, she wrote off a desperate little note to her mother:

You really must come here. I think when Jane goes and things begin to be arranged it would be most improper for me to be here alone as I am quite afraid of John and you do not know what he might not do. Brown thinks him quite mad, although he says he may have a method in his madness and suggests that the Grandfather's suicide has still its effects in John's conduct.* I am very ill and so nervous that I cannot meet these coming events without your advice and presence as well as Papa's. Crawley has been in bed three days—Ever Yrs Effie.

This day six years ago we anticipated very different results. God will defend the right. I am quite decided that to live on any terms with this man is to continue in sin.[1]

On this same day Effie got John to sign a most extraordinary document. It is on an ordinary four-page sheet of cream paper. The first three pages are filled with her questions; the fourth contains John's reply which is in his own writing:

In reference to certain drawings made for me (Effie Ruskin)

* John's grandfather, John Thomas Ruskin, had committed suicide at Bowerswell in 1817, shortly after the death of his wife. (It was ten years later that Mr Gray bought the house.) John's mother, then Margaret Cox, was John Thomas's niece and lived at Bowerswell with him. The story was told by Sir Albert Gray, Effie's brother, who had heard it from an old aunt at Perth, that the old man had appeared one day in her room with a fearful gash in his throat and that she had held the wound together until the doctor came, but in vain. She married her cousin, John James Ruskin, the following year but she retained such a horror of Bowerswell that she refused ever to enter the house again.

and given or sent to me by J. Everett Millais Esqr A.R.A. *by* and *with* the express approval of John Ruskin Esq I wish the latter (in consequence of my having wished to return various drawings given to me by Mr Millais, and having been forbidden to do so by John Ruskin Esqr who expressed a fear of wounding Mr Millais' feelings by such a course) to make me (Effie Ruskin) distinctly understand if I am to keep said gifts. To prevent Mr J Ruskin's declaring at any future time, that I kept any Gift which he did not most entirely approve from that Gentleman of anything now in my possession—I request a signature in Mr J. Ruskin's handwriting to this effect.

2ndly The same in regard to a desire I have that Mr J. Ruskin should state whether I have any other thing whatever in my possession, that Mr J. Ruskin wishes me to return from whosoever received, which I have heretofore accepted and retained in the belief that I had Mr J. Ruskin's express approval in so doing.

I, (Effie Ruskin) have devised and written this letter to prevent future misunderstandings on this point.

John replied most reasonably:

Mr Ruskin confirms the statement of this letter: thinking it better to accept the drawings than to wound Mr Millais' feelings: and, not having knowledge of his wife's feelings in any respect, cannot take upon him to say that it is either wrong or right in her to accept any present from any person. But as far as his knowledge of her feelings extends—that he has no objection to her retaining any presents she has hitherto received.*

J. Ruskin

10th April 1854

Millais himself was writing miserably to Hunt from Gower Street on this very day, April 10: 'I never see the Ruskins now except Ruskin himself, who is to sit to me again next Thursday [the 13th]. I have been out very little into Society this Winter, deriving

* Effie evidently took the St Agnes drawing with her when she left, for in Millais's *Life* it is listed as belonging to George Gray. It is now in the possession of Effie's grandson, Admiral Sir William James.

scarcely any pleasure from anything. The desire for work gets less every day of my life. I shall die a pauper if I do not alter soon. I try hard sometimes to think of subjects but nothing ever seems worth painting . . . London is dreadfully miserable and I think you were wise to get away from it. I daresay you know now that war is declared against Russia, and every day we expect to hear of some frightful battle* . . . I see a great deal of Leech† now. Yesterday we took a walk in the park together, and nearly every woman we saw was lovely.'

It was spring and he was in love.

Effie also wrote on this busy day, April 10, to Rawdon Brown who was staying with his great friends the Cheneys at 4 Audley Square. As he was now fully in her confidence she could write to him openly:

Taking advantage of the extremely rare occurence of John's dining here yesterday, I talked to him for about 20 minutes about your book and what ought to be done to meet your wishes respecting its appearance in public. The result of this conversation was the note he wrote in the evening which I requested to read when finished . . . I told him that he must go himself [to the publishers, Smith, Elder] and do everything he could, that he knew perfectly it was no more than two or three evenings work his looking over the sheets, being so accustomed to this kind of work and it could all be done before he left, and whilst you were perhaps still here . . . I would like to see you as

---

* England had declared war on Russia on March 27. Effie was too preoccupied to notice it—at any rate she makes no mention of it in her letters.

† John Leech (1817–64), principally a humorous artist and as good a draughtsman as Millais. He contributed to *Punch* from its foundation in 1841 until his death. He was chiefly known for his sporting drawings, particularly the 1854 hunting series of 'Tom Noddy' (Mike Halliday in fact) though he perpetrated many of the 'collapse of stout party' variety as well. All his drawings are signed JL. It was he who had introduced Millais to hunting this year and a delightful drawing by him (reproduced in Millais, Vol. I, p. 266) shows Millais out hunting in his first season. The next year Millais introduced Leech to salmon-fishing and stalking. Their adventures together as Mr Briggs and his friend appeared in *Punch* in 1857 and 1861. His sketch of Millais fishing near Perth in 1855 is now in the National Portrait Gallery.

I am most distressed that any of my affairs should retard anything to your advantage or make things less easier for you. And I can hardly write what I exactly want to say as I am so nervous and weak. But this brings me to another point of the note, viz, the invitation part. I pointed out to John the visible impropriety of asking you to come here and work in his study and live in his House—which I never quit and he hardly ever enters but to sleep. I merely notice this to you to show you one instance of the positions he places me in. These occur so perpetually, and as I generally never hear of them at all till they are all arranged, I have not the power of remonstrance. I told him that you would think him very extraordinary to make such a proposal. He said he was extraordinary and that if you did not know it before you were as well to know it now. He certainly, he said, should not alter his note, that I was a fool and to that he had long made up his mind. Improper indeed! It was just like my notions. As if I did not know perfectly that it was absolutely necessary for him to work at D. Hill. I said I really could see no necessity but his own will. He was then silent. You see it is a perpetual struggle. When can I see you?—This day Monday April 10th six years ago I was preparing for my marriage— and my Mother was dressing me for the Ceremony! I thought to be very happy—I do not know if I shall get over all this. Yrs Truly Effie.

I have no more dependence on J.R. than a piece of slippery ice. Delay is no longer possible. But he may be of the greatest use to you I still think. I am to be in town tomorrow and Thursday but till two on Wednesday I will be in.

Ruskin sent his letter to Rawdon Brown in spite of Effie's protests. A dull letter on the surface, it is lit up by the story behind it:

Herne Hill, Sunday Evening [April 9]

Dear Mr Brown,—I have been thinking over what you said to me as you were going away last night, and am going into town to see Mr Smith about it to-morrow . . . I think they would be glad if I would write them a short preface . . . I fear I shall hardly be able to read the proofs with the care I had hoped, just in the course of preparations for leaving town . . . Now

Effie's friend, Miss Boswell, leaves us on Friday [the 14th]. On Saturday next, a comfortable room here would be ready for you—and my study, a large and light room, at your service all day long, as I have another at Denmark Hill. We should leave you on the 9th of May, master of the house—with two servants, not together perhaps equal to Joan,* but enough to boil your kettle and warm your soup. Mr Rich would see the sheets through all the *mess* and confusion of the first proofs, and the last clean proofs would be sent out to you daily, so that you might see them clear of mistakes. If you could spare five or six weeks and bear the dulness of the place, this would be the safest way. I would write the preface immediately,† and the publishers would let you and me together pretty nearly do what we liked.

I trust you will believe my very great assurance that you will give me heartfelt pleasure if you will adopt this plan, and with Effie's best regards, both to yourself and to your kind friends, with whom you are staying, believe me affectionately yours, J. Ruskin.[2]

Effie had made no such fuss about having a man to stay in the house when she had heard in Venice that John's Oxford friend, Charles Newton, a bachelor whose romantic looks were very attractive to her, was coming to visit them at the Casa Wezlar,‡ but now, such was her distrust of the Ruskins that she looked with suspicion on everything they did or proposed to do. She and John had reached the stage where neither of them could do right in the eyes of the other.

Effie wrote to Brown again on the 11th about his book and ended her letter: 'I told you I was to be at home till two tomorrow but I don't want you to come here unless you quite like [to] yourself as I think you may not like to in the present state of things . . . Kindest regards to your friends and *mine* [the Cheneys]. They were always

---

* Rawdon Brown's housekeeper, a Venetian in spite of her name.

† In the end Ruskin did not write a preface for the book.

‡ 'Who do you think we are going to have for a visitor to occupy our pretty little spare room and French Bed?—Mr Newton who is coming out immediately on his way to Mytilene in Lesbos to which place he has been appointed Consul.' (Effie to her mother, January 16, 1852. *Effie in Venice*, p. 247.)

very kind to me. As for John, he is as hypocritical about the *Cheneys* as in other things. He says they are intensely worldly, know nothing about Art etc, but as he thinks everybody who do not flatter him mad or bad—this is not singular.'

The betrayal of marital confidences and the embroiling of mutual friends in marital disputes is one of the most embarrassing aspects of a ruptured marriage. There is something very distasteful in the deceitful part played by Rawdon Brown at this time. After all, Ruskin had done so much for him; it is unlikely that Smith, Elder, or any other publisher would have accepted his book if it had not been for Ruskin's strong recommendation; and it was the publication of this book which led to Brown's appointment by Lord Palmerston, in 1862, to calendar Venetian State Papers with English associations—a task which occupied him for the rest of his life and brought in sufficient remuneration to set his mind at rest from all financial worry. Did Ruskin ever know of the treacherous part played by Brown in the break-up of his marriage? It seems unlikely, for their friendship not only survived but became much closer as the years went by. Brown also remained close friends with Effie for the rest of his life.

Lady Eastlake was not quite sure of Brown's trustworthiness as a friend. 'My dearest Effie,' she wrote on April 13, 'my heart is exceedingly occupied with you and I find it difficult to be patient *for* you—so that I can more keenly enter into your exceeding state of suffering . . . I am thankful your mother comes as well, for you will need her softer comfort and she need to give it too . . . I have not seen Mr Brown since—he could not dine with us yesterday. I am sure of his kindness but I think he would sacrifice himself too much to mercenary interests—especially that *openness* which you ought to *court* when this [case] comes on. I know your mother feels as I do in this which is a great comfort to me. God bless you my dearest child and lead you through this thorny way. Your truly affectionate Eliz Eastlake.'

From this letter it is known that Mrs Gray had decided to come to London with her husband. At six o'clock the following evening, Friday, April 14 (Good Friday as it happened), Effie was writing a note to Rawdon Brown from the lodgings at 28 Bury Street, St James's, which her father had taken. The Dundee boat was late, she told him, and she had been waiting three hours for her parents to arrive. In the end she was obliged to return to Herne Hill without seeing them for fear of arousing suspicion by her prolonged absence. Crawley's illness had prevented his going to the docks to meet them. Effie must have trusted Crawley implicitly to think of sending him to the docks. One wonders whether Crawley ever told Ruskin how these secret plans had been carried out.

The Grays arrived later on that evening and apparently Effie saw them in London next day. (How did she manage to get up to London so often without arousing suspicion?) By the Monday, Mr Gray, after taking legal advice, had abandoned the idea of seeing Mr Ruskin, and it was planned that Effie, when she left, should pretend she was going home for an ordinary visit and should not let the Ruskins know that she never intended to return until she was safely on her way. This we gather from a hurried little letter to Rawdon Brown written from Herne Hill on Easter Monday:

I have not time for more than a word. All seems going well. I hope it is the same with you. Lady E will tell you more than I can. Papa is quite hopeful about my case, having found a similar one decided last year. The parties married the same spring as myself—where the simple *fact* against the Husband procured a verdict in favor of the wife. Papa thinks nothing more can be done and I am off to Scotland on Wednesday. Tell the Cheneys and bid them not to speak about me till I am gone. The Ruskins have not a suspicion. What a state of astonishment they will be in on Wednesday night! My father and Mother are at [torn] 8 Bury St, St James. I would like you just to see them, and they you, but don't know if you will be passing there—or if you would.*

Dear friend if I never see you again God bless and prosper all your undertakings. Return thanks to him for me that I can go through these things

Yrs Effie

* Rawdon Brown had never met Mr or Mrs Gray. He evidently did call on them in Bury Street, for Mrs Gray was surprised to find him so young looking. (See p. 205.)

The next day, Millais, unaware of the change of plan and still thinking that Mr Gray intended to confront the Ruskins when he came to London, was writing to Mrs Gray:

83 Gower St
Tuesday the 18th April/54

I hesitated immediately answering your letter, conceiving it just possible that you were coming to Town on Good Friday, as it seemed you intended coming the Friday following, when my letter would have crossed you on your way, but from J.R.'s manner and conversation I imagine you must have meant this week, as he is just as calm as ever and I can scarcely believe but that he will be somewhat disturbed by your appearance and purport in London, which I should not fail to perceive. I am now finishing his portrait; the face is painted and I have a very little more to do from him, two days more will suffice. He comes Wednesday and I will try and get him to come again on Friday as it will be as well to get all the sitting over at once. I have been a long time about it, but I am surprised to find it achieved at all. Next week I hope to be in Wales where I shall find something enough like Glenfinlas to finish the waterfall from and then it will be all over.

I can perfectly understand the dreadful state of mind of the poor Countess, but you *must impress* upon her the weakness of overmuch distress in the matter. She can have *nothing to blame herself for,* and *with that knowledge should go bravely through it.*

It is only the wretchedness of Society that makes us attach so much importance to disclosures of the kind, making thousands endure a slow inward martyrdom for years rather than suffer a temporary exposure of facts. She must also remember that under the circumstances there was no chance of her condition improving with time—I believe he would grow every day more selfish and intolerant, but she knows best what she would have had to contend with, and cannot but feel that an entire change is both now her duty, and the only way of insuring a chance of some enjoyable quiet in her life. I cannot tell you how thankful I am to you for writing to me on this subject. It is much better that Sophie should not come and see me.

And then on the advice of the lawyers their departure was postponed for a week. Effie wrote to Rawdon Brown to tell him this on the same day that Millais was writing to Mrs Gray, Tuesday the 18th. She added, 'Be so good as to caution your friends the Cheneys if you have told them as it is of the greatest consequence that the R's should not know for a week. We shall probably go next Wednesday week.'

It was a wonder that the news did not get out, for Lady Eastlake, who was going into the country to stay with her mother, had written to Mrs Gray on this same day, 'Sir Charles [Eastlake] will probably see Mr Murray in my absence and make him acquainted with the subject, for his shop [50 Albemarle Street] is the great rendezvous of report and rumours, and I would like him prepared with the *truth*, and by her wish.' (Sir Charles himself had only just heard the truth.) 'I told my dear husband before I saw your parents,' Lady Eastlake wrote to Effie (also on the 18th). 'I felt that the time had come—and his manly indignation has only added strength to my own feelings.' Through her husband, the President of the Royal Academy, and through her own wide circle of friends, Lady Eastlake was able to do Ruskin a great deal of harm. Apart from her affection for Effie she seems to have had an intense personal dislike of Ruskin. When Eastlake was Keeper (as it was then called) of the National Gallery, Ruskin had written a very long letter to *The Times* in January, 1847, attacking him for buying bad pictures and for destroying good ones by cleaning them. This may have accounted for some of Lady Eastlake's antipathy.

Apparently Effie sent off her luggage in advance, for George Gray in Perth, who must have heard by now that Effie was to leave secretly, wrote to his mother in London on April 22, 'I am glad to see that J.R. had not suspected any movement when he saw the luggage leaving'. It does seem almost incredible that John was entirely unaware of what was going on—unaware even that the Grays were in London, and unsuspicious of the amount of luggage Effie was taking. Was it possible that Mr Gray's lost letter had fallen into his hands and that he was aware all the time of Effie's intentions?

Millais evidently saw the Grays while they were in London though he did not see Effie. Now he knew that Effie was so soon to escape he could write to Mrs Gray in a much more cheerful vein:

Sunday evening [April 23]

I felt much inclined to pay you another visit, but think it perhaps better to see no more of you at present. I must however repeat the delight it gives me to think that the Countess is likely soon to have a substantial "Order of release" for herself, which I trust will occasion as much satisfaction as the reverse incident gives her in the picture. Altogether this business is quite incomplete without the stage accompanyments of muslin fairies and blue lights. When you get back to Perth the poor illused Countess (who has been imprisoned so many years) must return to her former happy life, playing, dancing, and *drawing*, and never for a moment permit her thoughts to rest upon the tragic farce in which she has so patiently played a suffering part. I assure you the knowledge that she is going home has a most beneficial influence upon me, as I now begin to feel unloosened from a dreadful thought which had taken up all my attention since I was in the Highlands, to the destruction of all painting—I don't think any number of years would have restored in me a sensation of quiet if it had always remained as it was.[3]

Their departure, planned for Wednesday the 26th, was put forward to the Tuesday. George was charged by his mother with the arrangements for their arrival in Perth. 'I have great pleasure in informing you,' she wrote to him on the 24th, 'that Dr Lee's opinion is in the highest degree satisfactory. He was perfectly thunderstruck with the case and had read John's Books and thought him a Jesuit— but now he thinks him mad—and shudders at what she must have gone through and said to her to take her course by the Law—that it was the most proper for her to do and the only one a father and mother could approve of. He has not the least doubt but he will be at once backed by Dr Locock at the proper time.* We leave tomorrow morning at 8 and will come straight to Perth arriving at ½ past 12 at night so you will order our beds to be ready and have a

---

* These two doctors were appointed by the Court to act in Effie's suit. Robert Lee (1793–1877), obstetric physician, was a lecturer on midwifery and diseases of women at St George's Hospital. Charles Locock (1799–1875) was first physician accoucheur to Queen Victoria and attended the birth of all her children. He was created a baronet in 1857.

cab waiting us at the station, tomorrow evening ½ past twelve. All is beautifully arranged. J.R. has been made under providence to play into our hands to the last Moment in a most wonderful manner.'

It might have been more seemly if Mrs Gray had shown some sorrow at the break-up of her daughter's marriage, yet the tone of jubilation in this letter to George was very natural. There was the release of tension after months of anxious doubt, the joy of so soon having Effie, and Sophie, home again, and the satisfaction of knowing that the case would almost certainly be settled in Effie's favour without too much delay; above all there was the happy realisation, having seen Millais again, that Effie's eventual future with him was secure. In this Mrs Gray herself had played a considerable part, keeping him on ice, so to speak, by her frequent letters until Ruskin could be conveniently disposed of. She had never really liked Ruskin, had always been a little in awe of him, whereas she and Millais thoroughly understood and approved of each other. But what exactly she had in mind when she wrote that Ruskin had played into their hands to the last moment in a wonderful way is never made clear. Her words seem to imply some positive action on his part, whereas perhaps she really meant that he had played into their hands by refraining from any action at all. If, for instance, he had had some suspicion of the charge that was so soon to be brought against him and had made a last minute attempt to exercise his conjugal rights in order to refute it, all their plans would have been ruined.

Effie was also writing off excitedly to Rawdon Brown on this same day, April 24: 'When you get this I shall be far on my way to Scotland as arranged. Everything is nicely ordered and I feel I can go on with the case with the greatest confidence.'

The day after she got home she sent Brown a full account of her escape:

Bowerswell 27th April

We arrived safely at home yesterday morning at two o'clock and I lose no time in sending you a line to tell you this as I think you will be anxious to know that all went well with me.

J.R. went to the Station at 9 o'clock with me.\* There, as he
was parading up and down, not uttering a word or saying that
he would expect to hear from me when I reached Perth, Mr
Stirling of Keir came and spoke to both of us as he was going
North. I was glad of this as John might wish it to be thought
by and bye that he did not know of my going—and as he stood
talking for some minutes with Mr S I thought it a fortunate
circumstance. 20 miles out of London my Father and Mother
were waiting. Sophie jumped out to her Father, and Mama
came in beside me.† I gave Papa a parcel directed to Mrs
Ruskin containing my Accounts and all my Keys—these were
to be delivered by the Lawyer and another Gentleman at six
at Denmarkhill when John and his Father were each to be
called out and a Paper delivered to each of them. I hope Papa
would hear from the lawyers what happened before leaving
yesterday morning by the Steamer. I trust to see them safely
here tomorrow. Mama and I continued our journey, arriving at
Edinburgh at nine, and finding a train for Perth we thought
better to go on. We arrived at the station and found George
my brother waiting who had thought we might perhaps appear,
and was overjoyed to receive me and did not say much about
the Ruskins excepting one or two sentences of so violent a
nature that I am glad to think we are 400 miles north of
D. Hill.‡

The reason why the journey was put forward to the 25th was no

\* And with Sophie, who left with Effie, so that as far as John knew this
was just an ordinary departure for a visit to Bowerswell. Mr and Mrs Gray
must have gone by an earlier train to Hitchin where they met Effie's train.
Mrs Gray had told George that they were leaving at 8. It seems that they
had managed to keep their visit to London a complete secret from the
Ruskins.

† Effie must have made a mistake about the distance. Her train left
King's Cross at 9.30 and the first stop was Hitchin about thirty miles
from London where it was due at 10.10. It stopped there only two minutes
so Sophie would certainly have had to jump out to give Mrs Gray time to
get in. Mr Gray and Sophie returned to London and took the boat next day
to Dundee.

‡ George Gray went to Australia to sheep farm in 1856 but he was not
very successful and returned after ten years. He never married and died at
Bowerswell in 1924, aged ninety-five.

doubt to enable Mr Gray to deliver Effie's parcel to the lawyer and still catch the Wednesday steamer. One thing Effie did not mention in her letter was that Crawley went with her to Bowerswell. He remained there a few days before returning to John. He was almost certainly in the plot. It is unlikely, though, that Sophie was in it; Effie would have been too frightened of the Ruskins questioning her, and she probably did not even know that her parents were in London. After the train started, however, Effie must have told her the truth so that she could be ready to change places quickly with her mother.

Many people may agree with Andrew Jameson when he wrote to his sister Mrs Gray: 'I almost wish Mr Gray had taken his first plan and seen his [Ruskin's] father before resorting to the last remedy.' Effie's secret flight laid her open to a charge of deceitfulness.

# RUSKIN'S DEFENCE

Ruskin was to stay at Denmark Hill while Effie was away. Assuming that he had no suspicion of the charge which was soon to be brought against him, it must have been with a tremendous sense of freedom and relief that he saw her off from King's Cross Station on the morning of Tuesday, April 25, believing that he was not to be bothered with her again for several months. In exactly a fortnight's time he would be setting out with his parents on one of those tours of Switzerland he loved so much. The Monday night had been the coldest April night within living memory. The thermometer had fallen to 15° (17° below freezing) and all the blossom in the Surrey orchards had turned to rust overnight.[1] Mr Ruskin, who was very proud of his pear trees, would have fussed dreadfully over this, not knowing how much more there would be to worry him before the day was out.

Frederick Furnivall, a young disciple of John's, was coming to Denmark Hill in the afternoon with some of his friends,[2] but as he had not been asked to dinner it is unlikely that he would still have been there at six when John and his father were called out. A citation to Court in Effie's suit of nullity was served on John and a packet containing Effie's wedding ring, keys, account book and a letter for Mrs Ruskin was delivered to his father.*

There is a copy of Effie's letter to Mrs Ruskin in the Bowerswell Papers:

Herne Hill
April 25—1854

My [crossed out] dear Mrs Ruskin

You have doubtless been wondering why I did not, as was usual with me, pay you a visit at Denmark Hill to bid you

---

* Mr Ruskin's diary entry for that day was laconic: 'Effie went to Scotland—John at six got citation.' (Bembridge.)

goodbye before going to Scotland, but I felt that owing to the circumstances which induce my addressing you this letter that rendered it not only impossible for me to see you now or indeed ever again—but also required that I should state to you the reasons of my sending you my Keys, House Book wherein will be found a statement of this year's account—together with an explanation of the money received and spent by me, and also you will find enclosed my marriage ring which I return by this means to your son, with whom I can never hold farther intercourse or communication.

You are aware that I was married by the Scottish form in my father's house on the 10th of April 1848.

From that day to this, your son has never made me his wife, or wished to do so, as he at first overcame my judgment, which was ignorant on such points, by a variety of arguments which even showing him the words of Scripture did not refute or cause him to change his opinions in the least about. Whilst we were at Salisbury, when you caused me to be put in another room on account of an illness, which he told me his Father supposed to arise from his recent connexion with me, he used to laugh and say his Father was imagining things very different to what they were.* His conduct and manner went from bad to worse until I felt I could no longer submit to his threats of personal cruelty and desires to get rid of me in any manner consistent with *his own* safety and comparative freedom. I always resisted the idea of a *separation* and would take no steps in such a matter, and threatened him with the course I have now pursued if he did not treat me in a becoming manner. He said, "Well what if I do take all the blame, you would make a great piece of work for your Father and go home and lose your position."

I have gone through this winter and thought at last that I must either die or consult my parents to take proper steps to ascertain what relief could be got, since your son almost daily heaps one insult upon another, more especially accusing me of *Insanity*. My Father and Mother came instantly they knew what

---

* They had stayed at the White Hart Inn at Salisbury in July, 1848, together with the old couple. It was there, while John was ill and his parents fussing over him, that Effie had her first quarrel with Mrs Ruskin. (*Effie in Venice*, p. 24.)

I suffered to Town and are only sorry I have lived in such an unnatural position so long. I believe you have been all along in total ignorance of this behaviour of your son's. The Law will let you know what I have demanded, and I put it to you and Mr Ruskin to consider what a very great temporal loss, in every point of view, your son's conduct has entailed upon me for these best six years of my life.* Your son first said he would marry me when *I* was 25—then on arriving at that age last year†—I enquired on what terms we were to live, he said I was quite *mad*, quite unfit to bring up children, and beside did not love or respect him sufficiently. I said *that* was quite *impossible* after his perpetual *neglect*—but that I never would refuse to gratify his wishes. He then put it off again and said he should try and break my spirit to enduce me to leave him and return to Perth as I bored him. I think *he* will be glad I have taken this step. I hear that our affairs are perfectly known in London society; and nothing more will be said, since the fact of our marriage not having been consummated was known to *many* and your son's personal neglect of me *notoriously condemned*— this has likewise been the case in Perth.‡ My parents have entirely approved of the steps I have taken and my Mother accompanies me to Scotland. All accounts besides the House Books will be found filed in the store-room and any things at Herne Hill amongst the glass, furniture &c that your son considers my property you will, I feel assured, be good enough [to] send after me.

I remain yours truly
Euphemia C. Gray[3]

Although none of the Ruskins would have been sorry to see the last of Effie, her accusations must have come as a terrible blow to the old couple. Mrs Ruskin would not have grasped the worldly consequences so quickly, and besides she had no false pride, whereas Mr Ruskin,

---

* This seems to show that the question of damages had already been discussed with the lawyers.

† On May 7. She was born in 1828.

‡ Effie's niece, Eliza Jameson, reported to Charles Stuart Wortley, (Effie's son-in-law) that Effie was known in Perth from the first year of her marriage as 'the virgin wife'. (Stuart Wortley.)

acutely sensitive as he was to the slightest slur on his son's honour and to the good opinion of the world, must have been deeply wounded by this insult to his son, especially as it would be so difficult to keep all the circumstances secret.

It is known from his diary that the next day he called on Mr Rutter, his solicitor, and on Mr Pott, a proctor—i.e. a solicitor in the Ecclesiastical Courts. John Champley Rutter, of the firm of Rutter and Trotter, was his friend as well as his solicitor and one of the trustees of John's marriage settlement. Five letters from Mr Rutter to Mr Ruskin, written in the course of the next four months, have been preserved[4] and make it clear that he and Mr Ruskin managed the case between them while John merely abided passively by their advice. Mr Ruskin, in his efforts to put all the blame on Effie, made her out to be so objectionable that Mr Rutter congratulated them on their 'Release from such a Woman'. It was Mr Ruskin's desire that the case should go through as quickly, cheaply and privately as possible—so privately indeed that Mr Rutter was given the almost impossible task of keeping all knowledge of it from his partners and even from his clerks, which meant that he had to write every letter connected with it in his own hand. In order to expedite the proceedings John was advised not to put in a defence. Nevertheless, on April 27, two days after receiving the citation, he wrote a statement giving his side of the marriage story. This statement was never used, and together with another document signed by him three months later, was lodged in a drawer of the solicitor's desk where it remained for the next seventy years.

John Champley Rutter was succeeded by his son Henry (Ruskin's solicitor), who in his turn was succeeded by Harry Morgan Veitch. Mr Veitch died in April, 1924, and in June of that year it was brought to the notice of Effie's brother, Sir Albert Gray, K.C., that Mr Veitch's widow was in possession of two documents written by Ruskin in reference to his marriage. Although Mrs Veitch was very badly off and had been told that the documents would be worth a great deal of money in America, she was anxious that they should be returned to the family most concerned with them. Albert Gray saw them and agreed to buy them for £40 with the intention of destroying the one of April 27 which he believed to be inimical to his sister's reputation.

Albert Gray was not aware when he bought these documents that not only was their existence known to Alexander Wedderburn, K.C., Ruskin's only surviving literary executor, but that Wedderburn had already put in a claim for them. As soon as Wedderburn discovered that Sir Albert had bought them he renewed his claim, and after a great deal of correspondence Sir Albert reluctantly relinquished them, much to the indignation of two of Effie's daughters who had contributed part of the purchase money. Sir Albert copied the documents before sending them to Wedderburn, and at the death of Sir Albert's widow in 1938 (Sir Albert himself died in 1928) these copies were given to the Bodleian Library at Oxford with the proviso that they were not to be published for thirty years.[5]

In 1950 the original documents were published for the first time in Howard Whitehouse's *Vindication of Ruskin*, Whitehouse having been authorised to release them by Wedderburn's son. The first of these documents, which is entirely in Ruskin's own writing and which is the one Sir Albert wished to destroy, is given below in its chronological place in this story, April 27, 1854:

## General Facts

I was married—in her father's house—to Euphemia Chalmers Gray, on the 10th April 1848. She entered her 21st year on the 7th May in that year. Immediately after our marriage, we agreed that we would not consummate it, at all events for some little time; in order that my wife's state of health might not interfere with a proposed journey on the Continent.

Soon afterwards we agreed that the marriage should not be consummated until my wife was five and twenty.

Before that period had arrived, I had become aware of points in her character which caused me to regard with excessive pain the idea of having children by her, and therefore, neither before nor after that period, either pressed or forced consummation, but I offered it again and again, and whenever I offered it, it was refused by her.

Her feelings of affection towards me appeared gradually to become extinguished; and were at last replaced by a hatred so great that she told me, about the end of September or beginning of October, 1853, we being then in Scotland, that if she ever were to suffer the pains of eternal torment, they could not be worse to her than going home to live at Herne Hill with me.

I took her home, nevertheless. We arrived in London on the day after Christmas Day 1853. From that time to this she has remained in resolute anger—venting itself in unexplained insults; and rejecting every attempt of mine to caress her as if I had been a wild beast.

She informed me some days ago—about the 14th or 15th of April, that she intended to go down to Scotland on Tuesday the 25th, to which proposal I assented; understanding that she was to stay with her parents for three months, while I went to Switzerland with my father and mother. I saw her depart by the railway at ½ past 9 on Tuesday morning, and was surprised to receive the citation to court the same afternoon.

### Details relating to the above statement

1st   Reasons for our agreement not to consummate marriage.

I offered marriage by letter, to Miss Gray, in the autumn of 1847, and was accepted. Letters passed between us almost daily from that time until I went to Scotland in March 1848, to marry her. I met her at her uncle, Mr Sheriff [Andrew] Jameson's at Edinburgh; there some fortnight before our proposed marriage Miss Gray informed me that her father "had lost immense sums by railroads", and Mr Gray, coming over himself, told me he was entirely ruined, and must leave his house immediately. His distress appeared very great; and the fortnight or ten days preceding our marriage were passed in great suffering both by Miss Gray and myself—in consequence of revelations of ruin—concealed till that time, at least from *me*.*

---

* He had known before this that Mr Gray had suffered some loss, though not the extent of it. His mother had written to him in September, 1847, '. . . he [Mr Gray] has I believe at present been overpersuaded by friends and brought himself into some difficulties with Railroads.' (Stuart Wortley.) Mr Ruskin, when he came to draw up a marriage settlement in March, 1848, was surprised and angered at discovering how near bankruptcy Mr Gray was. (*Effie in Venice*, p. 17.) There is no doubt that the first months of Ruskin's marriage were clouded by Effie's intense anxiety over her father's finances.

The whole family rested on me for support and encouragement—Mr Gray declaring I was their "sheet anchor"—But no
effort whatever was made to involve me in their embarrass-
ments—nor did I give the slightest hope of my being able to
assist Mr Gray, who I believed, must assuredly have become
bankrupt. But I expressed no surprise or indignation at the
concealment of his affairs from me, although it had entirely
destroyed the immediate happiness of my marriage.

Miss Gray appeared in a most weak and nervous state in
consequence of this distress—and I was at first afraid of subject-
ing her system to any new trials—My own passion was also
much subdued by anxiety; and I had no difficulty in refraining
from consummation on the first night. On speaking to her on
the subject the second night we agreed that it would be better
to defer consummation for a little time. For my own part I
married in order to have a companion—not for passions sake;*
and I was particularly anxious that my wife should be well and
strong in order that she might be able to climb Swiss hills with
me that year. I had seen much grief arise from the double
excitement of possession and marriage travelling and was delighted to find that my wife seemed quite relieved at the suggestion. We tried thus living separate for some little time, and
then agreed that we would continue to do so till my wife should
be five and twenty, as we wished to travel a great deal—and
thought that in five years we should be settled for good. The
letters written to Miss Gray before our marriage are all in my
possession and will show that I had no intention of this kind
previously. My wife asked me to give her these letters some days
ago—I fortunately refused, thinking she would mislay them, as
she did not now care about them, but she doubtless intended
to destroy them.

2 Reasons for the aversion felt by my wife towards me.

This aversion had nothing to do with our mode of living
together. It arose first from my steady resistance to the en-
deavours of my wife to withdraw me from the influence of my
parents, and to get me into close alliance with her own family.
She tried to get me to persuade my Father to put her brother

* Ruskin's love letters to Effie, written during their engagement and
quoted in James (pp. 47-93), refute this.

into his countinghouse: and was much offended at my refusal
to do so:* she then lost no opportunity of speaking against both
of my parents; and, every day, was more bitterly mortified at
her failure in influencing me. On one occasion, she having been
rude to my mother, I rebuked her firmly, and she never forgave
either my mother or me.†

I married her, thinking her so young and affectionate that I
might influence her as I chose, and make of her just such a wife
as I wanted. It appeared that *she* married *me* thinking she could
make of me just the *husband she* wanted. I was grieved and disappointed at finding I could not change her; and she was
humiliated and irritated at finding she could not change
me.

I have no doubt she felt at first considerable regard for me,
but never a devoted or unselfish one. She had been indulged
in all her wishes from her youth; and now felt all restraint an
insult. She sometimes expressed doubts of its being *right* to live
as we were living; but always continuing to express her wish to
live so. I gravely charged her to tell me, if she thought she
would be happier in consummating marriage: or healthier, I
being willing at any time to consummate it: but I answered to
her doubts of its being right, that many of the best characters
in church history had preserved virginity in marriage, and that
it could not be wrong to do for a time what they had done
through life.

It may be thought strange that I *could* abstain from a woman
who to most people was so attractive. But though her face was
beautiful, her person was not formed to excite passion. On
the contrary, there were certain circumstances in her person
which completely checked it.‡ I did not think either, that there
could be anything in my own person particularly attractive to

---

* This is true. (*Effie in Venice*, p. 26.)

† This happened while the four of them were staying in Salisbury in
June, 1848. (*Effie in Venice*, p. 24.)

‡ There is no evidence that Effie was in any way malformed. She was
almost certainly the only naked woman Ruskin ever saw so these unattractive 'circumstances', which he thought to be personal to her, he might
have found in any mature woman. He may, though, have had in mind
something quite different such as a personal smell which is an important
factor.

*her*: but believed that she loved me, as I loved her, with little mingling of desire.

Had she treated me as a kind and devoted wife would have done, I should soon have longed to possess her, body and heart. But every day that we lived together, there was less sympathy between us, and I soon began to observe characteristics which gave me so much grief and anxiety that I wrote to her father saying they could be accounted for in no other way than by supposing that there was slight nervous affection of the brain.* It is of no use to trace the progress of alienation. Perhaps the principal cause of it—next to her resolute effort to detach me from my parents, was her always thinking that I ought to attend *her*, instead of *herself* attending me. When I had drawing or writing to do—instead of sitting with me as I drew or wrote, she went about on her own quests: and then complained that "I left her alone."

For the last half year, she seems to have had no other end in life than the expression of her anger against me or my parents: and having destroyed her own happiness, she has sought wildly for some method of recovering it, without humbling her pride. This it seems, she thinks she can effect by a separation from me, grounded on an accusation of impotence. Probably she now supposes this accusation a just one—and thinks I deceived her in offering consummation. This can of course be ascertained by medical examination, but after what has now passed, I cannot take her to be my wife or to bear me children. This is the point of difficulty with me. I can prove my virility at once, but I do not wish to receive back into my house this woman who has made such a charge against me.

27 April
1854

John Ruskin[6]

Ruskin seemed to think that proof of virility would have been a complete defence. This was not so, nor is it so today, for the com-

---

* We are never told what symptoms in Effie led the Ruskins to believe, or at any rate to state, that she was suffering from an affection of the brain. Mr Ruskin evidently suggested her mental condition to Mr Rutter as a possible line of defence, for Rutter wrote to him on May 23: 'What you state about the Woman's Brain I have been thinking might cut both ways . . . might not the irritant arise from want of consummation?' (R–CT.)

plaint in a nullity suit is that a *particular* relationship is not a true marriage. As Mr Lushington laid down in another case at about this time, it would obviously be impossible for a wife to prove that her husband was impotent with all women, and the law does not impose any such obligation on her. Nevertheless, in those days a nullity suit could not be instituted on the grounds of non-consummation until the couple had lived together for three years. If Ruskin had been married before, and sired a dozen children, potency with his first wife would have been no defence to Effie's suit. On the other hand his enemies were equally mistaken in saying that because of his impotence with Effie he was incapable of making a real marriage with any other woman.

His only possible line of defence would have been his claim that intercourse had been repeatedly offered by him and refused by Effie, the inference then being that neither of them had really put their capacity as marriage partners to the test. He would have had to satisfy the judge, however, that his offers had been more than verbal ones and that Effie's resistance had been as strong at the beginning as it certainly would have been had he made any such attempt in the last six months of their married life.

Whether Ruskin would have been capable of carrying out his offer is another matter. Many years later he wrote to Mrs Cowper Temple, his great confidante at the time of his love for Rose la Touche, 'Have I not often told you that I was another Rousseau?'[7] He was referring to the habit of masturbation of which Rousseau in his *Confessions* says he was never able to break himself. And this no doubt was the basis of his assertion that his virility could be proved at once.

One is brought to the conclusion that Ruskin was not impotent, though he might have proved to be so with Effie had he tried to consummate the marriage after five years of living with her in chastity, and that his statement, though it withheld much truth, told no untruth, with the exception of his claim to have married for companionship rather than passion.

# LADY EASTLAKE RAMPANT

✺

Meanwhile Effie at Bowerswell was writing to Rawdon Brown. After describing her journey home, which has already been quoted, she continued:

I am already better, the quiet of this lovely place and seeing all the children so happy and gay, and feeling that I am really away from those wicked people fills me with such thankfulness that already a quiet happiness has settled on my spirits and I feel I have everything to be grateful for in having been preserved through such years of misery. I am convinced that new troubles were just preparing for me for we find from Crawley that after John had seen his Parents on their way home in Autumn he intends to retrace his steps and go to *Rome*. I never heard a hint of this and think he must also in this be deceiving his Parents. Since he nearly died there once, they always vowed he never should go, and when I asked him to take me, he used to say he hated Rome and besides had given a promise never to go. I think him the most complete Jesuit ever was born and I doubt not that they will get him—perhaps he will not declare himself till his people are dead. Crawley told my brother this and says he is to take the first opportunity to leave them. If John had not Parents I am convinced that at this moment he is so mad, and besides has always had such an idea of becoming a Monk, that he would fly really to Rome and become one in earnest. We shall see.*

* John had first gone to Rome in 1840 and did not return there until 1872 after the death of both his parents; he then hated it as much as ever. He went there again in May, 1874, and wrote to Joan Severn, 'I verily believe that, were I a Christian at all, Rome would make a Romanist of me in a fortnight.' (*Works*, Vol. 23, p. xx.)

On this same day, Thursday, April 27, Lady Eastlake was writing
to Effie from Fitzroy Square:

I have been longing to write to you and longing to tell you
how some of your friends have received this intelligence—received in some cases first from me—Much as you were loved
and respected you were never so much so as now—not by me
only but by all whom this sad tale has reached and who know
not only what you have suffered, but *how* you have borne it.
Your dear mother will tell you how late and long I was with
her on Monday evening (so long ago it seems now!) we both
felt that the worst was indeed past, and that we could dwell now
more exclusively on the comfort of your coming liberation and
unsullied name. But still Tuesday morning woke me early to
thoughts of what was actually going on and imagination was
too busy with you to submit to any *quiet*. I was almost as restless
as you have so long been—My dear husband was a great relief
and comfort to me and *is*—he calls you "a heroine of the best
kind" and occasionally he *gratifies* me by sentiments of a somewhat opposite kind regarding one who I wish could be struck
out of your memory as utterly as he will be and already is out
of the respect of all good people.

On Tuesday evening I saw dear Mrs Murray.* She begged
me to come upstairs [at 50 Albemarle Street]—and only her
gentle sister was with her. I asked the sister whether Menie
could bear to hear what would *terribly* interest her—and she
assured me there was no fear for her health now†—and then
by that time your sorrows were so forcibly before me that I
could not conceal my emotion and the story was out in its sad
outline before I well knew what I said. Never shall I forget the
tender womanly *anguish* with which dear Mrs Murray caught at
it—hiding her face on the sofa to conceal her sobs—all sympathy and pity—too much even for *indignation* to be uttered—
and midst all, the sorrow for the *loss* of you.—"Oh! that I could

* Marion (Menie) Murray was a daughter of Alexander Smith, a banker
of Edinburgh. She had married John Murray in 1847 and it was her brother
who had married Lady Eastlake's sister.

† She was recovering from the birth on April 1 of her third child and
second son, Hallam.

have seen her sweet face once more—and she has been so often
at this door to ask for me"—Ah, dear child—those are true
sweet friends who will ever give you the hand of comfort.[1]

Thus did Lady Eastlake go the round of her friends stirring them
up with obvious relish against Ruskin. For the most part the ladies'
reactions were like Mrs Murray's and the gentlemen's like Sir
Charles's. Only old Lady Charlemont, a lady-in-waiting to Queen
Victoria, who had presented Effie at Court in 1850, was unable to
comprehend the nature of Ruskin's villainy. '. . . the good lady with
all her kind heart', Lady Eastlake told Effie, 'seems to have a confused *head*, and perhaps from her misfortunes [her husband was
frequently unfaithful] has formed such a very low estimate of the
male sex that she heaped upon J.R. every possible and impossible
wickedness of motive and aim that has characterised the *roué* part of
the novels of the last half century—none of them being *his* particular
wickedness which was too new for her apparently to comprehend . . .
I asked her if the Queen were to hear the story at all whether she
could take care that H.M. heard it *rightly*, but she seemed to have
too great a fear of the little woman even for that, and told me
frankly that she could not.'[*2]

On this same day, April 27, Millais was writing to Mrs Gray:

As I expected Ruskin did not come this morning. He wrote a
letter last night saying that he could not come today but would
sit again next week. I have written a reply asking him to come
next Monday . . . I went to the R.A. last Monday [the 24th]
and saw the exhibition. Sir Charles Eastlake was there and

* Lady Charlemont, *née* Anne Bermingham, had married the 2nd Earl
of Charlemont in 1802. Her four children had all died young and she had
treated Effie like a daughter. Whether the Queen ever heard the story
rightly or not is unknown, but she refused to receive Effie at Court after
her marriage to Millais although Effie had twice been to a Drawing-Room
at Buckingham Palace as Mrs John Ruskin. This must have caused Effie
great unhappiness, for when Millais lay in his last illness and the Queen
sent Princess Louise to ask whether there was anything she could do for him,
he replied, 'Yes, let her receive my wife.' The Queen consented, and
Princess Louise, then Marchioness of Lorne, offered to present her privately
at Windsor. If Effie had not been almost blind by that time she would have
had the gratification of seeing her name twice in the Court Circular, on
July 2 and July 4, 1896. Six weeks later Millais was dead.

expressed much mysterious regret that I had not finished Ruskin's portrait in time. Lady E's likeness is there, painted by Boxall,* very good, but not very like.

In about ten days time I will have completed Ruskin altogether, in the picture, and shall set off immediately for Wales. I don't think they can be otherwise than satisfied, for Ruskin himself brought Hunt, the watercolour painter,† to criticise the face and figure, according to my wish, Hunt being a man in whom J R has entire confidence—the result was more than agreeable to me, and evidently gave Ruskin great pleasure, more particularly regarding the portrait itself.

*Friday*—I have just come from the private view where I met Lady Eastlake who spoke a few words upon the subject. I was glad to hear that she had received good news about the Countess since your return. *Everybody glory [sic] in the step she has taken* and only wonder at her delaying so long. I intend calling on Lady E on Monday or Tuesday—I can scarcely as yet perfectly realise the altered state of things. "Awey-ye-goo"‡ should now be the Countess's motto after leaving J R for ever. I did not hear what most people said at the R.A. as I generally escaped when the subject was mentioned—As you say it will be but a nine days wonder and it will be all over. One great battle with the Russians will swamp the little talk there will be for the present. In the mean time she is out of it all, and when she sees her friends again it will be an old story. I should like to hear that she is as happy again as she was before she left Bowerswell for the first time . . .

I am sure the Countess would be happy if she knew all her friends say about her—

* William Boxall, A.R.A. (1808–79). He was a great friend of Lady Eastlake's and, according to her, warmly espoused Effie's cause. He became an R.A. in 1863, was Director of the National Gallery from 1865 to 1874, and was knighted in 1867. He often dined at Denmark Hill, and had been dining there with John and Effie two days before Effie left. (Mr Ruskin's Diary, Bembridge.)

† William Henry Hunt (1790–1864), an old friend of Ruskin's. He was primarily a still-life painter, but of the four pictures of his which hung at Denmark Hill, two, especially painted for Ruskin, were of heads of a Negro boy and a country girl.

‡ The title of Millais's sketch at Glenfinlas reproduced on p. 211.

I will let you know what passes between myself and J R directly afterwards.

There was no more talk of joining Holman Hunt abroad. Millais wrote off joyfully to Hunt on May 4: 'Now I have plenty of news for you. First (which I know will interest you as you are aware of the circumstances) Mrs Ruskin, that was, has been taken away by her parents who have been in London arranging everything for her release, which she will most likely have in about four months time from now. The Exhibition is open and your picture [*The Light of the World*] the only picture considered by thinking men.'

Lady Eastlake described to Mrs Gray this meeting with Millais at the Private View, which was exceptionally early that year, Friday, April 28:

I was most thankful for your letter, for I had been much longing much [*sic*] for tidings of my dear *child* who is ever in my thoughts. Especially had I longed to know how her last hour in company with that J. R. had passed, and your account tallies much with my anticipations. I am convinced that you have only *forestalled* him in the act of separation and that if Mr Gray had not acted with such excellent promptitude and prudence now, he might have had a far more difficult task to perform a year hence. Thus I feel more and more comforted that the decision is already *over*.

I continue to hear the same buzz of pity for her and indignation at him, and I continue to tell the tale whenever and wherever I think the *truth* can do good. Yesterday was the Private View at the Royal Academy (she was with me last year there!)* and the story was circulating busily through the rooms . . . I had not been long there when I saw Millais, so I went to him with a cordial heart, and asked a few commonplaces. We found ourselves suddenly in the *subject*,—my cheek white, his *crimson*. I asked him if he had heard anything from the other side, and he told me that he had had a note from J.R. on the *Wednesday*, merely saying in usual terms that he should delay a sitting till next week. Millais said that he did not know how he should bear to see him—truly I think it useless his finishing a picture

* When *The Order of Release* was exhibited.

which *nobody* will *look* at. He had known nothing of the *truth* and asked me with painful blushes if I had.* Our conversation was very short from the numbers of acquaintances that beset me, and from knowledge of matters it was constrained, but I think he felt that I had a great respect for him.

At last came news that the Ruskins had been seen. Rawdon Brown hastened to inform Effie in a letter of May 1 but the same news is told in a more lively way by Lady Eastlake two days later:

Now dearest for the tidings I have picked up of the R's. Would you believe that father and son were boldly at the Water Colour Exhibition on Saturday [April 29] in the middle of the day! Good Roberts† fell in with them, and with his *honesty* he said "I could not *blink* the matter" so he went to them and said he could not pretend to be ignorant of what all the world was speaking of, and which had given him a sorer heartache than he had known for some time—and asked them if it were true. The young man treated it *lightly* and said that Mrs Ruskin was gone to Scotland—and hummed and ha'ed—but the old man interposed that his son had been *entrapped* into the marriage!— that he had been attached to a French Countess and was an easy prey!—but they had overlooked that, and your father's absence of wealth! etc, etc, and as the place was not the best in the world for discussing such a matter he took his precious son by the arm, and said "Come along John—we shall have to *pay* for it—but never mind we have you to ourselves now"—These words are exactly what Roberts heard and repeated to me—he repeated them to Sir Charles afterwards. Your father will understand no better perhaps than we do the allusion to *paying*. I would fain hope it means something more than the *costs*. I am convinced the son *never* meant to *return*, and that you are right

* This shows that although Lady Eastlake was aware of Effie's and Millais's interest in each other, she did not know that Effie had fully confided in Millais, nor did Millais seem to know that Lady Eastlake had been, for some weeks at least, fully in Effie's confidence.

† David Roberts (1796–1864), landscape painter. Most of his work was of scenes abroad. Ruskin was to write about him on June 5 from Geneva: 'Roberts is a contemptible mannerist and paints worse every day.' Letter to Dr H. A. Oldfield (Bembridge).

in foreseeing his ending in Rome (if he be not there already) only that it is too good a place even for him . . . Your servants* came here on Monday . . . my tears started at the sight of them. What two nice girls . . . The old Mrs R and the old man too had been very harsh and rude to them and would fain have turned them out on Saturday [the 29th], but they had protested against leaving until *today* [May 3] . . . J.R. had not returned to the house till Monday except on Sunday for a moment.

In a later letter Lady Eastlake wrote very humanly: 'I did not hear from your servants the account of the Ruskin *surprise*. I was rather too scrupulous of asking and regretted afterwards that I had not been bolder. I trust the old man's fury fell at first partially on his son.'

Rawdon Brown's account of Roberts's speaking to the Ruskins at the Water Colour Exhibition was almost identical, the only addition being that 'the father, when Roberts said what all your friends think of you, rejoined by vituperating your *temper*!, and *extravagance*. He also said something about Mr Gray and railroad shares.'

To this Effie replied by return, 'Their conduct is so much what I expected that it just tallies with all the rest. The son is too great a coward to say much, but the wicked old man I know would be too angry not to say some ridiculous things which only serve to show his own dreadful nature and bad heart. The idea of the *French Countess* made me smile. The lady was only plain Miss Domecq but her fortune procured her a French Baron for a Husband of very questionable character† . . . Mama is going to send Lady E some letters which will show you if *you* care to read them that the marriage was all made up on their side. My father thinks this necessary as they have thought proper to add this falsehood to the rest. He bids me tell you what you knew before, that in 1847 he lost a good deal of

---

* Robina, the Scotch cook, who had come just before they went to Glenfinlas, and Jane, Effie's new maid. Lady Eastlake was trying to find situations for them.

† Adèle Clotilde Domecq was the second of the five daughters of Mr Ruskin's late partner. Although John had been very much in love with her she had never cared for him. She married Baron Duquesne in 1839. John had had the chance, though, of marrying one of her younger sisters, Caroline, who became Countess Béthune. (*Effie in Venice*, p. 159.)

money by the Railroad shares alluded to. Old Mr R did *not think proper* to tell Mr Roberts that he had done the same.'\*[3]

Old Mr Ruskin showed none of the vituperation described by Rawdon Brown when he wrote on May 3 to his old friend William Harrison: 'We are soon moving on a long projected Slow Tour—the first since 1849 about France and Switzerland—that is Mrs R myself and Son—Mrs John Ruskin has returned to her parents who I hope will succeed in making her good as beautiful. To us she returns no more. On our return you shall know further particulars—All I can say at present is that she did not suit my son nor my son her and that she has, acting under the best advise, gone pleasantly away Via the Great Northern.'[4]

This tone of levity, which came to Lady Eastlake's ears, enraged her: 'It is a marvel how people in the 19th century can conduct themselves in a trying and peculiar position like this as those old people are doing,' she told Effie indignantly on May 17. 'Nothing can be more *indecent* and *vulgar* than the affected *glee* at a catastrophe so disgraceful to their wretched son—"that Pre-Raphaelite fellow" as I hear him called.'

It was a pity that Mr Ruskin could not keep up this light tone which was far more dignified than the tirades of abuse he was later to pour out upon Effie. John himself was never either facetious or undignified, and the letter below, written just a week after Effie's departure, shows characteristic restraint:

Monday evening [May 1]

Dear Furnivall,†—Many and sincere thanks for your kind note. You can be of no use to me at present, except by not distrusting

---

\* Mr Ruskin had taken 25 shares in Boulogne Railways whereas Mr Gray had taken 200 as well as speculating in other railway stock. Mr Gray was very nearly ruined whereas Mr Ruskin's loss was a flea bite to him. (*Effie in Venice*, p. 17.)

† Frederick Furnivall (1825–1910) was the young man who had come with some friends to Denmark Hill on the day of Effie's departure. He was Ruskin's chief champion at this time. He was a barrister with chambers in Lincoln's Inn, a member of the Philological Society from 1847 and its secretary from 1862 until his death. It was Effie who had first introduced him to Ruskin in 1849, and his friendship with Ruskin was for many years the chief joy of his life. He was a rich young man, having inherited a fortune from his father, a doctor who had kept a private lunatic asylum, but he lost his money in a bank crash in 1867.

me, nor thinking hardly of me yourself. You cannot contradict reports; the world must for the present have its full swing. Do not vex yourself about it, as far as you are sorry, lest such powers as I may have should be shortened. Be assured that I shall neither be subdued, nor materially changed, by this matter. The worst of it for *me* had long been passed. If you should hear me spoken ill of, ask people to wait a little. If they will not wait, comfort yourself by thinking that time and tide will not wait either.[5]

Millais, in his next letter to Mrs Gray, of May 3, refers to this letter from Ruskin to Furnivall:

I have only time to say that Ruskin did not come Monday, he wrote to me saying that he would sit for his hands upon his return from Switzerland whither he has gone . . . He has written to Furnivall expressing a hope that his friends will not condemn him too hastily, until they hear what he has to say in defence of himself. Of course the story is in the mouth of everybody—some few seem desirous of making the best of it for his sake, conceiving him to be a very different man . . . I met Thackeray who was speaking on the subject last night. Most people look upon J.R. as partly mad.

Two days later Millais wrote again:

I have just received your letter. I made a mistake in saying that J Ruskin was going, or had gone to Switzerland last Tuesday, it was Furnivall's letter that told me this. There is a letter about the picture of a friend of mine in this morning's "Times" which you will doubtless read which proves he cannot have gone yet. My Father saw him standing before the picture he speaks of in the [Royal Academy] Exhibition. He seems to be going about rather more than usual. His excuse for not sitting to me was that he was leaving London instantly and was pressed with excess of business the little time he remained. I should think that he would not dispute the separation as I think he will be much better and happier without her—He says in his last note to me—"I am sadly afraid you will have to

leave the hands *till I come back*—I must be back long before
you will want to leave for the East—if you hold in that mind".
This is nearly all his letter to me, only a remark about the
increase of business which has come upon him. When I spoke
to him about painting the hands from somebody else he very
truthfully said that his hands are unlike other peoples, and that
it would be absurd attaching other folks fingers to his figure,
which I could not deny. I suppose by his note that he will very
shortly return, to say something for himself, which seems assuredly to be his intention, from his letter to Furnivall, who
wrote a sympathising letter to J R upon hearing of the circumstances . . .

The end of next week I hope to be in Wales. A young friend
will accompany me who strange to say saw the Countess when
she was either coming from or going to Bowerswell when with
William (my brother). He was then a lieutenant in the Army
stationed at Glasgow, and having a great desire to see Ruskin,
and myself painting him at Glenfinlas, he made a journey to the
place with some fellow officers. Soon after he sold out and has
since taken to painting—and has become a very agreeable companion.* Ruskin was very anxious that his Father should see
the portrait before he left but I have heard nothing more about
it from him. I wish as eagerly as yourself that he would sit to
me once more and have done with it but I suppose he dislikes
seeing me just now . . . Wish the Countess many *happier* returns
on the day Sunday.†

The letter from Ruskin in *The Times* of May 5 was in praise of
Holman Hunt's *Light of the World* which was then on exhibition at
the Academy together with his *Awakened Conscience*. It is a very long
letter and in it Ruskin writes that he stood in front of the picture for
upwards of an hour to watch the effect it produced upon the passer-
by. He then gives an explanation of its symbolism and pronounces it

---

* This was John Luard (1830–60). Although he took up painting so late,
he exhibited at the Royal Academy from 1855 until his early death. After
Millais's parents moved to Kingston, Gower Street was given up and Luard
and Millais shared a studio at Langham Chambers, Langham Place, for a
few years.

† Her twenty-sixth birthday on May 7.

in his opinion 'one of the very noblest works of sacred art ever produced in this or any other age'.

This letter in *The Times* made the Eastlakes intensely angry. 'Sir Charles was disgusted with it,' reported Millais on May 6; and Lady Eastlake herself wrote about it three days later when telling Effie how Louisa Stewart Mackenzie had reacted to the news of Ruskin's 'villainy'—'She was very *earnest* in manner and her eyes overflowed with tears. On her saying to me at first "do you really think him so utterly devoid of feeling", I said "I think that you can need no further proof than that letter in the Times this morning" (it was on Friday she called). "What man of the slightest heart, losing even a bad wife, could have written such a disgusting farrago not ten days after"—I conclude that you and your people have seen that letter— on Hunt's odious picture—it has condemned him with many—even without knowing any further.' And one of Mrs Gray's old friends wrote that she had read 'the letter in The Times on Friday little thinking what a "Wolf in Sheep's clothing" had written it'.

At least Hunt himself was grateful enough to quote the letter in full in his *Pre-Raphaelitism*.[6]

Ruskin's purpose at this time was evidently to appear as much as possible in public, to carry on as usual and to show that his private life had nothing to do with his public work, and he must have been glad of this opportunity to praise, publicly, a picture by Millais's best friend. When he went abroad he was not running away because he was afraid to face people, as many of his enemies maintained; he went because he had long planned to go, and he went on the very day his father had always intended to go—May 9. Nevertheless, what he suffered at that time, and the amount of harm that was done to him, can be gauged from passages in his letters to Mrs Cowper Temple written fourteen years later. At one moment, when he was afraid there might be some fatal bar in Rose La Touche to prevent the possibility of their marriage, he wrote, '*If a second* time an evil report goes forth about my marriage—my power of doing good by any teaching may be lost—and lost for ever ... the question is a fearful one whether I might not thus finally confirm the calumnies before arising out of my former history.'[7] And three months later, when he believed that all hope of marrying Rose was gone: 'I know now that this thing, whatever it is, has been openly against me from the year 1854 till now.'[8]

# RUSKIN GOES ABROAD

❊

Rawdon Brown was still in London staying with the Cheneys, going
every day from ten till three to read over his *Giustinian* with Mr Rich,
dining out and passing on to Effie every scrap of gossip that came his
way. He had now met 'Milley', as he spelt it, at the Monckton
Milnes's and had been asked to his studio. 'He talked to me about
Giustinian,' he told Effie in a letter of May 6, 'and said that he had
amused him more than anyone since Robinson Crusoe!* A greater
compliment could certainly not have been paid our hero.'

Millais himself described to Mrs Gray this meeting with Brown at
the Monckton Milnes's:

After dinner the conversation turned upon the Countess and
Ruskin, who meets with general condemnation. Like yourself
I was astonished to find Mr Brown such a youthful gentleman—
I had conceived in my mind (I don't know why) that he was
slightly infirm in appearance, and paternal in character, but
I think Mr B will have a young wife yet.† He is very nervous
and quaint [he also had a pronounced lisp], and was very silent
when they were talking of Ruskin's case, whilst Mr Cheney
was eloquently defending the Countess and denouncing J R—
he [Cheney] seems to have suspected the truth many years
ago. Some few are inclined to look upon Ruskin in the kindest
light, and make allowances for his peculiar mind, believing
him to be partly mad. After this dinner I had to go to another
house where I met Sir Charles and Lady Eastlake . . . Lady
Eastlake thinks much worse of him than any other person I
have met . . . I have received a letter this morning [May 6]
from Dr Acland of Oxford . . . By his note I don't fancy that

* It may be remembered that Effie had read some of *Giustinian* aloud at
Glenfinlas. See p. 96.
† Brown never married. He died in Venice in 1883, aged eighty, and is
buried in the Protestant cemetery on the island of San Michele.

he knows anything about what has taken place . . . I am sure
that Dr Acland will have but one opinion, for I remember his
speaking to me [at Glenfinlas] of Ruskin's dreadful indifference
to his wife, and groaning over the unfortunate life the Countess
was doomed to lead . . . numbers of people are beginning to
discover something dreadful about J R's look. I am sure it
would make the Countess laugh if she could hear what is said—
One lady said to Monckton Milnes, "Only think of such a
religious letter coming from such a wicked man."

Lady Eastlake told Effie three days later about this meeting with
Millais: 'He interested me much by his upright simplicity. He
owned to me that he had remonstrated with J.R. on exposing you so
much in the Highlands, but that he laughed and said that he (J.R.)
was much obliged to M for teaching you to draw!'

Effie replied to Rawdon Brown's letter on May 9:

Mr Millais was I am sure very sincere in his admiration about
Giustinian . . . If you go to his studio you will see the famous
picture of J.R. which he [J.R.] does not seem anxious should
be finished but in his own time. Are you not amused at their
keeping to their original day (today 9th) for starting? I am
very much obliged for your hints and continuing to tell me
what is said. I expect to hear from Lady Eastlake that she has
given you the Letters written by the old people to me before
the marriage to read . . . is it not *so* fortunate that Papa has
kept all their Letters in case they should give us any trouble?
I have also journals down to last year which I kept regularly.*
They would serve to put me in mind of many additional details
of my Life if necessary. But I cannot conceive what they can do,
they have nothing in their power. I suppose they will send for
poor quiet Mary and question her but she can tell them nothing

---

* Effie's diaries (which she had sent to Bowerswell for safe keeping on
March 6) have unfortunately disappeared, but the two letters she referred
to, written to her by Mr and Mrs Ruskin while she was engaged, have
survived and are given in the Appendix. Lady Eastlake called them 'the
most extraordinary things' she had ever read. It is difficult to see what she
thought so extraordinary about them.

against me. Supposing the worst and they were to bribe either she or Crawley or both, or George Hobbs,* to say anything they might make up against me, these paid servants, my Father says, always break down under crossexamination. The old Ruskins may be equal to anything, for from what I hear from my Cook to whom he was very harsh, he was in a terrible passion of anger and quite frightened the poor young women who however had the pluck to refuse to leave the house when he ordered them to be turned out. I *don't* think *J.R.* would do this kind of thing even by instigation—although I doubt not that they will try and think over everything to try and say something against me. What can they do that would harm me? —although you may be sure that I quite feel with you that it would be very disagreeable, and I hope *J.R.* will not think of using his eloquent pen for such a bad cause. He can have written to nobody but Mr Furnivall, who is an amiable weak young man, a vegetarian, Christian Socialist and worshipper of men of genius,† as I had a letter from his [John's] greatest admirer and friend, Lady Trevelyan, with whom he maintains a very constant correspondence. She said she had not had a word on the subject from himself or anyone else but me. She was in Northumberland but now in London.

Rawdon Brown replied that it was indeed fortunate that the letters and journals had been preserved. He then added that Ruskin had neither written to him nor called upon him before his departure. 'A meeting would have been very awkward, and I very much rejoice at its being dispensed with, but I rather expected that he would have made some sort of communication to me, did not you?' Could Brown's conscience have been troubling him? It is known from Millais's letter that he had remained very silent when the case was being discussed at the Monckton Milnes's.

* Ruskin's valet for ten years. He had been with them all the time they were in Venice and had left to emigrate to Australia. Effie had never got on with him. His sister, who was for many years Mrs Ruskin's maid, married George Allen, Ruskin's future publisher.

† Furnivall had become a vegetarian while he was an undergraduate at Cambridge, and remained one for twenty-five years. He never touched tobacco or alcohol either. He had become a Christian Socialist in 1849, but later declared himself an agnostic.

Effie had heard by this time, much to her indignation, that
Crawley was to remain in Ruskin's service. This is commented on in
Millais's next letter to Mrs Gray:

Wednesday. [May 10]

I was delighted to receive your long letter this morning. You
must make some allowances for the weakness of human nature
and forgive selfish Crawley for his want of mental stability. He
may consider his master a very great villain, but he must also
consider his worldly interests, and I expect that he will so far
enact the part of a good servant that he will forget all his
former prejudice in favour of his Mistress, and join his Lord and
master, when following in the capacity of dry boot, and sock
bearer, up the Alpine Mountains, in groanings over the in-
sincerity and faithlessness of womankind.* Last night I was at
Sir Robert Inglis's† and met Lady Eastlake who said she thought
you are rather anxious to know whether J R has gone yet. I had
a letter from him dated the 6th of this month, asking some
questions about Hunt's picture, concluding with wishing me
"goodbye" and directing me to address my answer to 7 Billiter
St City,‡ "*to be forwarded*" so that he must have left by this time.
I would send you his letter but imagine you would not care to
see his handwriting again. It is very kind and communicative
and I think I shall receive another shortly. I cannot help believing it would be *much better* for the Countess *not* to hear any
more opinions upon the step she has taken, they will only make
her nervous and excite her. I will tell you of Dr Acland and
[George] Richmond who was there last night, as you perhaps
wish to hear these remarks.

Dr Acland expressed deep sorrow, and doubtless is much of

* Crawley made a wise choice in deciding to stay with Ruskin. They
became very close, and not only did Crawley nurse his master and valet
him but he copied out his manuscripts and took photographs for him as
well. When Ruskin moved to Brantwood he settled Crawley, his wife and
family in a cottage at the gates, and when his wife became insane Ruskin
made Crawley curator of his drawing school at Oxford. Many of Ruskin's
letters to him, in which Ruskin signs himself 'ever' or 'always your affectionate master', are preserved at Bembridge.

† 2nd Baronet. He was a Tory statesman, a Privy Councillor, President
of the Literary Club and Antiquary of the Royal Academy. He lived at
7 Bedford Square.          ‡ Mr Ruskin's office.

the same way of thinking as Lady Trevelyan—one thing he particularly adhered to, was that there is no law (from Religious Authority) which admits of parting persons married by word, excepting upon one plea, referring me to the 5ᵗʰ Chapter of St Matthew.* *He was fully convinced of Ruskin's fault* but thought it might have gone on until the end. I was not surprised at this man's gentle, fearful, way of considering the subject, as he is exceedingly timid. He spoke very kindly, and was quite alive to the misery such a life would have entailed to the Countess. As to Richmond, he pretended to disbelieve what he heard, and asked me whether it was true. He was astonished, and entirely altered his opinion of the Countess who he had always imagined in fault, and frivolous, and unworthy of such a mighty man of intellect. He forgives her for all the thoughtless participation in society and thinks she has behaved altogether *exceedingly well.* He is going to write to JR advising a total silence in the matter. I myself believe that Mr Richmond is rather like Crawley and would carry an extra pair of button boots in behalf of his illused friend. I don't think Mr R[ichmond] would have given out other views in my presence for I perceived an immediate interpretation of my thoughts. It is a pleasant thing to agree in Society—gentlemen retire into corners and talk it over, some expressing grief beyond utterance, placidly imbibing a cream ice, and one man in 20, for the sake of peculiarity, voluntarily acts as counsel for the "Author of Modern Painters" and makes the best of his case.

The Countess must look like another Una and the Lion with a staghound walking by her side. When she goes bathing in the sea at St Andrews mind you make her wear a necklace of corks for there must not be an Ophelia finish to the tragedy† . . .

---

* Verse 33: 'Whosoever shall put away his wife, saving for the cause of fornication, causeth her to commit adultery: and whoever shall marry her who is divorced committeth adultery.' Acland himself was very happily married.

† The Grays were soon going to St Andrews for their usual annual holiday. The 'stag-hound' was Effie's beautiful dog, Roswell. He was really an Irish wolf-hound bred in the Queen's kennels and had only recently been given to Effie. She had him for some years until he became such an awful poacher that he was sent to Australia! Millais painted him with Effie in his picture *Peace Concluded* in 1856. (Millais, Vol. 1, p. 290.)

I have heard that Thomas Carlyle is very boisterous in the question of this *asundering, his judgement is that no woman has any right to complain of any treatment whatsoever,* and should patiently undergo all misery. This is what a number of comfortable, portly, philosophers will say merely in direct opposition of the general public. If the Countess is annoyed at a few odd people, make her draw foreshortened fern. Like all kind friends I tell you the worst news but I think she had better hear the worst at once, if the opposite conclusion of one sage in a thousand is a source of lamentation. I wish she would get as indifferent as the Swiss traveller is. I can easily imagine poor old Mrs R tremblingly going over the habitation of her mistaken boy, it really must have been an affecting scene. Never mind, they have got him now and will keep on either side of him like two policemen, or the two outside horses in the Edinburgh omnibuses, who always suggested the thought that they were taking their companion to the station house—let us hope that this may not be realised in the case of poor J R.

In the new circumstances Millais was light-hearted enough to feel he could go back to the right place to finish the background to his portrait of Ruskin. It is, though, rather surprising that his Pre-Raphaelite conscience had allowed him, even for a moment, to consider finishing the picture in Wales, let alone sticking someone else's hands into Ruskin's cuffs. 'I have made up my mind,' he wrote to Mrs Gray on May 16, 'that far the *shortest way* of finishing Ruskin's portrait will be to return to the old place for a week or so. *I am very anxious to get it off my hands at once,* as I have other things to do. I expect the greater part of the summer I shall be living near Chatsworth (Derbyshire) where I shall be painting. I saw Sir W and Lady Trevelyan coming out of church; they stopped and spoke for a moment. Sir W has had the bad taste to grow a pair of moustaches and looks quite different. The friend I spoke of [John Luard] will accompany me to Glenfinlas and stay there with me. Although it will be dreadfully strange revisiting it, still I feel it a kind of duty to go there again. I don't think the Ruskins, or rather J R, would be satisfied by my painting the rest of the picture otherwise, indeed he said as much when he was sitting.'

Millais also wrote testily to Furnivall on May 16, 'What is the

Lady Eastlake in 1854 painted by William Boxall.
(*See p. 197.*)

*Awey-yegoo.* Drawing by Millais at Glenfinlas, July 31, 1853. From left to right: Ruskin, William Millais, Millais and Effie. (*See p. 197.*)

good of telling me what people have already said about myself, and Mrs R that was? If fashionable gents will quietly settle matters amongst themselves, why let them—it is perfectly immaterial to me—I don't quite see how a report of that kind is to distress or annoy me—I only wish my kind friends would wait until they knew positively that I am married . . . I am going at once to the old place for a week to finish the background.'[1]

But that the rumours passed on by Furnivall did distress and annoy him is shown in a letter written two days later to Mrs Gray:

As I expected I hear now that my name is mixed up in the affair, and by some in a manner that makes it advisable that I do not for the present see anybody connected with you. I say this thinking it just possible that George might come and see me at the old place. Any personal communication with your family just now would certainly forward the scandal, which has reached the extreme limit of invention. There must be a large proportion of vagabonds in the world to set such rumours afloat . . . Some of the most barbarous stories have been in circulation regarding my absence from the R.A. walls, and in connexion with my friend Hunt's works, but next year I hope again to resume my place with a still more conclusive result. All the Summer and Winter I intend working very hard, and this is the chief reason for returning to Glenfinlas where I can sooner complete the portrait which otherwise would be a hindrance to the progress of other more important subjects.

I leave here for the New Trossachs Inn next Tuesday [the 23rd] without stopping at Edinburgh. Ruskin's figure (with the exception of the hands) is *entirely finished* and I trust that the rest will not keep me above a fortnight at most. I will write to you from there and tell you how I get on. Dr Acland promised to write me fully what he thought of the disunity of his two friends, but hitherto he has not fulfilled his promise—I was to have visited him at Oxford but owing to my sudden resolution to depart I have been obliged to put it off to another time. I have called on Lady Eastlake and will call again tomorrow. I hope the Countess grows everyday more callous to the moanings of the few weak, unhealthy people who consider her conduct too hasty, and undignified.

I am sure that nothing will ever make Lady Trevelyan see J R in the wrong, and it will be almost useless trying to explain the wretchedness of her position with him before this change.

I think it probable from what I have heard that J R will make some kind of statement in behalf of himself, very likely in the shape of a pamphlet as he has asked some of his friends to wait awhile and hear what he has to say, before judging harshly of him. His best friends will advise him to be silent.[2]

Lady Trevelyan was one of the few friends who, like Furnivall, remained absolutely staunch to Ruskin, much to Lady Eastlake's disgust. 'I should be glad if Lady Trevelyan came in my way,' she had written to Effie on May 17. 'Mama always calls Sir Walter a "Hamadryad"* which may have confused Lady T's notions of conjugal duty.'

Bell Scott in an unpublished passage from his *Autobiographical Notes* has this to say about Lady Trevelyan's attitude to Effie: 'At the very time of my first visit to Wallington they [the Ruskins] had separated. Every other day Lady Trevelyan laid certain letters aside, these I believe were from Mrs R beseeching sympathy with the painful position of a wife, who, for the first time in her life knew what love was, confessing that John was loathsome to her, and that at any pains and penalties of exposure and shame she must from him be separated. I could not even appear to wish to know the feeling which these letters called up, but it was evident enough that the action of the wife was repudiated, and that Lady Trevelyan would not reply to them or even I think read them.'[3]

There was certainly truth in this and it must have caused Effie great distress for she had been very fond of Lady Trevelyan—perhaps fonder of her than of any other woman friend except Lady Eastlake.†

* A cobra.

† When an opportunity came a few years later for reconciliation Effie rejected it. They met at 34 Onslow Square, the house of Baron Carlo Marochetti, the sculptor, an old friend of Millais's and a great admirer of Effie's. Lady Trevelyan held out her hand and Effie refused to take it. The incident is recounted in a letter from Millais to Mr Gray of December 24, 1857, the day after the meeting took place. 'I was out of the way at the time they met,' he told his father-in-law, 'which I was rather sorry for

Furnivall evidently told Ruskin that Millais was going back to the 'old place' to finish his picture, for Ruskin wrote to Furnivall from Vevay (as he spelt it) on June 9, 'I am very glad of your kind letter—very heartily glad that you liked my lectures*—very supremely glad that Millais has made up his mind to go into Scotland and finish his work properly. What did he say to you—and what do other people say—about his reasons for wishing *not* to go into Scotland? I have no personal reason for asking this—but I wish to know for Millais' own sake poor fellow and you need not fear surprising me by telling me—I know the *facts*—but I want to know the *sayings*! . . . I am very happy among my Alps. I have been drawing a little in a more finished way than usual, and shall have something to show you, I hope, when I come back in August.'[4]

---

as it must have been trying for her [Effie] from the excited state she was in after the affair. Nothing could have been better for Effie than dining there and being made so much of by the Marochettis in the sight of the Ts [Trevelyans] who must have felt ashamed of themselves and occasioned the clumsy attempt at reconciliation.'

Lady Trevelyan died, aged forty-four, in May, 1866, at Neufchâtel while on a tour with Ruskin and her husband. Sir Walter married again the following year when he was seventy.

* The Edinburgh lectures had just been published as a book by Smith, Elder.

# EFFIE'S ORDEAL

In the meantime Effie had become very unwell again. She wrote to Rawdon Brown on May 21 to say that for the last ten days she had been almost entirely in bed or in an armchair incapable of motion or speech. 'The doctor thinks I shall take some time to recover but that nothing is *really* wrong and the great debility I have at times is easily accounted for by past distress.' She told him also that as Ruskin had not appeared in the suit, her lawyer had informed her that the case would probably proceed 'in default'.*

She now had a great ordeal to undergo for which she must find all her strength. On the following Wednesday, May 24, she was going with her father by boat to London to be examined by the Court and by the doctors appointed by the Court. She did not want anyone to know she was in London except Lady Eastlake, Rawdon Brown and the Cheneys.

Her father had written for the same rooms at 28 Bury Street as he had occupied at the time of Effie's flight from John, but when they arrived they found that a lodger was ill in them so they stayed across the road at No. 15.

Millais left London the evening before Effie left Scotland. He travelled by the mail train from Euston Square Station direct to Stirling and from there took the daily coach to Callander, arriving at Brig o' Turk at seven the next evening. He was accompanied by Charles Collins as well as by Luard. 'In spite of the change,' he wrote to Mrs Gray on the day of his departure, 'revisiting the old place will be still a melancholy matter but with two lively companions I will do everything to imagine myself in a different locality. I hope you will write to me at Mrs McIntyre's.† What a dreadful

* Mr Ruskin was being advised by Mr Rutter that the wisest course for his son was to be as passive as possible. Only if there were any danger of John laying himself open to a charge of collusion would he advise putting in an appearance in the suit. (Letter from Rutter of May 23. R–CT.)

† Landlady of the New Trossachs Hotel.

misfortune it is that the Countess will have headaches, surely something can be done to prevent such continued suffering. It is a very
great pity that she has to come up to Town as that will I expect
upset her still more . . . I called upon Lady Eastlake and had a long
talk with her. She thought it quite right that I should escape seeing
any of your family. I expect many will naturally attribute extraordinary reasons for my going again to Scotland but when they hear
their suspicions positively contradicted will have to keep silent. Mr
Furnivall is most curiously busy about all this. He called here
Sunday, I expect to speak again on the subject but I was from home.
I think I told you that Dr Acland wrote to me a long letter, not
containing any definite opinion but all groaning and lamentation.*
Certainly the R's have taken the meanest position in circulating
reports against the poor Countess, which is the very best illustration
of "adding insult to injury". I am so busy packing and getting ready
for my departure that I must finish this.'

The previous day Millais had written to Furnivall:

You will I know have the kindness to contradict any absurd
conjecture about myself and Mrs R ["that was" crossed out]—I
confess that I am *disgusted* with the way in which Society has
been pleased to mix up my name in the affair. I am now going
to the Highlands in the face of all the Scandal not as some
people will *kindly* suppose to see the unfortunate Lady, but
truly to finish the background of Ruskin['s] portrait properly.
I should indeed be sorry to hear that any friend of mine ["th"
crossed out] imagined that I had the *bad taste* to see Mrs R
whilst the ["trial" crossed out] matter is in lawyers hands—I
write this to you as you are often in a position to refute the
writched [*sic*] untruthful rumours which are now afloat and I
beg you will positively state that I shall make a point of avoid-
ing *all persons connected with the business in Scotland*—

For a time I intended to finish the waterfall from Wales but
Ruskin did not seem satisfied with this notion as the rocks are
of quite a different Strata there, so I have made up my mind to
go to the old place and have done with it . . . When people
say I am going to marry Mrs R ["tell" crossed out] ask them

---

* Millais had not told Mrs Gray that Dr Acland had written; he had
told her in his letter of May 18 that the doctor had promised to write.

whether the ceremony has taken place? *or whether they have heard it from me*—At any rate tell them to wait and see—I have been married twice before now by report, everything was settled by the kind public excepting the purchase of the Wedding ring— One report in this matter I heard was current was that I had disappeared with Mrs R *a romantic elopement.* I have not heard anything from the author of modern painters. Certainly he is the author of one modern painter being considerably maligned —I shall wait most calmly to hear his statement in defence of himself. If you hear anything please let me know of it.[1]

On the evening of his arrival at Glenfinlas he wrote to Mrs Gray:

Now that I am here I can scarcely believe that I have ever been away. I have been painting at the old place and have taken my friends to all the familiar spots . . . Most curiously it began raining directly we got to the first Scotch station and has been showery ever since. Returning to the place is so wonderfully strange that all the rest of what has happened appears a dream. Scarcely a leaf is out of place for the new ones have taken nearly the same form and position. In a day or two I will better judge what influence coming here will have upon me . . . I shall not feel happy until that picture is finished. It really is a misery to me and prevents me from thinking of other things. I almost fancy sometimes that it will never be finished but will last all my life. One thing I dread the thought of is Ruskin sitting to me again for the hands. I have been thinking a great deal of him lately and I am sure many allowances should be made for him for he is certainly *mad* or has a slate loose. When I call to mind his ways there seems little doubt but what something was amiss in his head.[2]

While Millais was writing this, Effie was in the steamer on her way to London. Two letters from her to her mother describe what she had to go through after she got there. She must have needed her mother badly during the doctors' examination, but no doubt funds did not run to three return fares and board and lodging for three in Bury Street. Mr Gray had to be there to make a deposition.

The Divorce, Probate and Admiralty Court was not instituted until 1857. Before that date cases to do with matrimonial matters were tried in four Ecclesiastical Courts with their head-quarters at Doctors' Commons at Bennet's Hill, Upper Thames Street—a building comprising a great hall where the cases were heard, chambers for the doctors of law, a dining-room and library.* The Ecclesiastical Courts took evidence by deposition only, and required such depositions to be presented by a proctor on behalf of the deponents. Proctors in these Courts were equivalent to solicitors, and advocates to barristers. It had been necessary, therefore, for Effie to instruct a proctor as well as an ordinary solicitor.

Although Effie and her father both had to go to Doctors' Commons to make a deposition, her case, because she had lived in Camberwell, was heard in yet another Ecclesiastical Court, the Commissary Court of Surrey under the jurisdiction of the Bishop of Winchester. The judges in this Court sat in the Lady Chapel of St Saviour's, Southwark, and it was there that three months later Effie's decree of nullity was granted.

Effie's first letter from London, although undated, was probably written on Sunday, May 28. After describing their arrival, she continued, 'I think I am stronger. Papa brought Mr Webster here this morning.† He was very kind but seems to think that the case may not be over till November—but it may be in July. We are to hear what Mr Glennie‡ says tomorrow. It is simply the length of time required for the forms of court. He says no appearance is made for the Ruskins . . . Mr Webster thinks they mean to brave it out, as another letter has appeared in "The Times" some days ago on Hunt's picture "the Awakened Conscience" in the same strain as the last.§ Dr Locock has been appointed by the court. On being told to wait on me and some details mentioned, he said he knew the case— Lord Lansdowne had been talking to him about it. I shall not require to go into a Court room at all which I am very glad of. I must go first to St Saviour's, Southwark, to swear—and then return here when an Examiner of the Court will come and put some questions to me . . . We think we shall get away Wednesday.'

* This building was finally demolished in 1867.

† John Maule Webster, her solicitor. He had chambers at Lincoln's Inn but lived at the Reform Chambers, 105 Pall Mall, so it would have been easy for him to go round to Bury Street on a Sunday.

‡ John Irving Glennie of 19 Bennet's Hill, Doctors' Commons, her proctor. He was a partner in the firm of Sladen, Glennie, Farquar and Sladen.

§ This was a shorter letter which had appeared on May 25.

Her second letter describes this important day:

Tuesday evening [May 30]
6 o'clock

I have just returned from my long day to find your note. I have left Papa now being examined at Doctors Commons to let us off by the steamer tomorrow at two. Everything has gone on so nicely. I went to St Saviour's Church and took the oath with the Doctors who afterwards came here and then I went to Doctors Commons and was examined by a lawyer in a private room. I have just come back and am tired and ready for dinner. I will reserve further particulars. One thing greatly relieves me and that is that J. R. gets no more citations—they have nothing further to do with him but get the Bills of the Lawyers paid.* We find we have a claim for Damages, but both Father and I have decided we take much higher ground by not asking.† Mr Glennie thinks with us. Thank God we have got over all so well. Till we meet.

The deposition of the doctors who examined her was as follows:

We found that the usual signs of virginity are perfect and that she is naturally and properly formed and there are no

---

* Mr Ruskin recorded in his account book under sundries for 1854: May. John Law Expenses £257–15–10.' (Bembridge.) We know from a letter from Mr Rutter that Effie's costs came to only £139–16–0 of this sum, including 10 guineas each for the two doctors and £44 for journeys and board and lodging in London for 'Mr and Miss Gray'. It is known from the same source that Mr Pott, the proctor, who put in an appearance for John at the final hearing, declined to send in a bill in 'such a peculiar case' (was he too, like Mr Rutter, sworn to secrecy?) but suggested the sum of £50 as 'compensation' for his time and trouble. (R–CT.)

† On July 19, after the final hearing, Mr Rutter was to write to Mr Ruskin that it was 'quite clear' that the Woman was 'not entitled to either Alimony or Damages', so Effie's proud gesture of taking 'higher ground' must have been entirely wasted on the Ruskins. Indeed Mr Ruskin most unfairly wrote about the Grays to his old friend William Alexander, a wine merchant in Edinburgh: 'Their Rage is increased by their having by their own acts deprived themselves of all claim to Alimony.' (December 14, 1854. R–CT.) When the marriage was declared void, the marriage settlement became void also and the whole of the £10,000 which John had settled on Effie was returned to him.

impediments on her part to a proper consummation of the marriage.

Charles Locock M.D.<br>
Robert Lee M.D.<br>
signed at 15 Bury Street St James's<br>
30 May 1854[3]

Effie, in her deposition, listed the places where she and John had lived together, and then continued, 'He used to tell me that he would marry me when I was 25. He had a great dislike to children and he gave that as a reason for abstaining from marrying me . . . I was living with him occupying the same bed for near upon a year after I had attained 25 years of age but it was the same after that as before.'[4]

Mr Gray was merely called upon to swear that the couple had lived together up to the last six weeks.

These sworn depositions were presented by Mr Glennie at the final hearing in July. Effie was not obliged to go to London again or to give any more evidence. She and her father managed to get away from London on the Wednesday, and Lady Eastlake reported to Mrs Gray that she had seen them before they left. 'Effie's coming has been kept perfectly secret,' she wrote on the 31st, 'but now I shall be glad to retort when I hear foolish and malicious people talking about her giving "public evidence before the House of Lords", and "scandal", "exposure" etc. which a few have got hold of—and just assure them that all her evidence is already given and nobody has known the how, where or when.' Ten days later, however, she was regretting that this privacy, so acceptable to Effie, should also be the means of screening the detested 'J.R.'.

Millais's next letter to Mrs Gray was written from the New Trossachs Hotel on the day of Effie's ordeal, May 30:

It occurs to me that a most offensive report may reach you which is common in London and which I fancy originated from a conversation I had with Monkton Milnes who takes Ruskin's part. In endeavouring to make him understand the facts I suppose I must have exhibited more than ordinary interest in the matter, for he at once said he saw as much and came to a

conclusion which has since been circulated, with the addition
that I myself had had the bad taste first to spread it abroad—I
know that you will not believe this but I cannot help speaking
to you about it as it is peculiarly odious.*

*4 O'clock*—I have just been driven home by the rain . . . I
have got on well and I doubt not but what I shall succeed in
getting it finished in the time I hoped. We have not had one
day *entirely* dry since we have been here . . . We sat under Mr
Monteath [the Minister] yesterday and he is coming to dine
with us this afternoon. I called upon him when I arrived here
and he spoke about what has taken place—having been all
along completely deceived in J.R.'s character . . .

I showed Mrs McIntyre the portrait and she said she might
just think it was the man himself. The dreadful swamp that
used to be in front of the Inn is now a part of the upper garden
which the Countess will remember. Mr Stewart [the school-
master] never appears with his telescope now looking out for
visitors. The change of years seems to have happened in a few
months. The Minister has not moved into his new house† yet
but occupies the sitting room [where Ruskin used to sleep].
I often wonder whether J.R. is happy now in his wanderings. I
imagine that in spite of his apparent indifference that he must
feel it at times. I wish that I could write something to amuse
the Countess but this place in the like weather reminds me too
keenly of what happened.

[Later] Mr Monteath has been here and I have seen him
home across what used to be the swamp. He spoke to me on the
subject of the letters he received from the Countess at the time
of her affliction, and upon my assuring him that she would not
object to my seeing them he acceded to my desire and I read

---

* It was on May 5 that Millais had dined with the Monckton Milnes's.
He had doubtless heard of the 'offensive report' from Furnivall, but we
can only guess at its exact nature. Millais's indignation that his name and
Effie's should be coupled together can be charitably attributed to his
desire to shield her rather than to hypocrisy.

† Two years later Millais, with Effie and their baby, took this new manse
at Brig o' Turk for the month of August, and Millais wrote from there to
Mr Gray, 'We have been dining at the Brig of Turk Hotel to day and
visited the old spot where we were parked in company with the Historian of
"Modern Painters".' (August 11, 1856. Morgan.)

them. I hope that he did not wrong in allowing me to look
over them and that *she will not be angry with me for wishing to see
them.* Poor little body, she indeed *suffered.* I had an irresistible
wish to know the contents which are more painful than I could
have anticipated, and I am rewarded for my inquisitiveness
with a sensation of torture to be belabouring the occasion of
so much cruel anguish I don't know which is uppermost, the
above desire or thankfullness that she is out of his power.*

The next letter I write I will try and make her laugh, and
make some drawings . . . Luard is sitting near me and sometimes I look over him and put him right. He is of a desponding
nature and requires similar gentle treatment to another pupil
I once had [meaning Effie] . . . Since I have heard the letters
to Mr Monteath I am more convinced than ever that J.R. is
insane. When I call to mind his manner, and sickly opposition, I wonder with surprise that I did not fall into an open war
with him. I shall refuse to paint his hands as there is just a
chance that mine might refuse to paint and *perhaps* do what I
should afterwards be sorry for. There is *one great satisfaction* with
regard to his picture and that is that I am *confident* that no
living man could do a better. This he cannot justly dispute for I
can challenge the criticism of all those others that he most
admires.

The delight of freedom ought in itself to renew health and
happiness to the Countess . . . As she said in her letter to the
Minister I think it very likely that J.R. will go into the church
of Rome when his parents die . . . but before long I think he will
destroy all doubt in regard to his character by publishing some
absurdity which will at once settle the state of his mind. I disbelieve in the existence of such wickedness in mankind excepting in partial madness. It is so late (12 o'clock) that I must
*awee* to bed. I hope you will not forget me when there is good
news to tell.

Millais complained in his next letter, of June 5, that the weather
justified the construction of another Noah's ark. 'For want of a

---

* It seems almost incredible that the Minister should have shown Effie's
confidential letters to this young man who, on the face of it, had no right
whatsoever to see them.

cunning hairdresser,' he went on, 'I have had to operate upon myself with a pair of nail scissors and I don't think the result quite as happy as it might be . . . Should the Countess find all the world condemn her she can as a last resource obtain a situation in the Burlington Arcade as a hairdresser and cutter.'*

He went on to say that he had read Ruskin's second letter in *The Times* about Hunt's *Awakened Conscience* and could positively state that Ruskin had mistaken the story which he considered so easy to interpret. 'I think he has written it partly to gull the public into believing that he has the feelings of other folk.'

Hunt fully quoted this second letter also in his *Pre-Raphaelitism* and, far from saying that Ruskin had mistaken the symbolism, remarked, 'It could not but gratify and encourage me to read these words of high appreciation.'5

* In those days, H. P. Truefitt, now in Old Bond Street, was at 20 and 21 Burlington Arcade. See p. 71 for description of Effie cutting Millais's hair.

# MILLAIS WAITS

❋

Effie had been terribly seasick on the voyage back to Dundee, but she declared to Rawdon Brown (he had returned to Venice on June 4) that the sickness had been a blessing and had saved her from 'bilious fever'. She really seemed to be altogether better after this journey. 'I am quite a different creature,' she told Brown on June 9. 'In the first place my mind is completely relieved of all anxiety, and I am naturally so happy, that I am able to return to any pursuits that are necessary here with great delight and I look upon myself as much to be envied in getting away instead of dying of misery as many a poor woman who has a worthless wretch to drag on all her days without the possibility of any Release ... I never cared for teaching the children before I was obliged to go away in '48, and now my afflictions have given me, I hope, more patience than I had naturally and I have the charge of three little bodies* here who are a great delight to me. I begged my Father not to engage another Governess for some time as if I was at all able I would like some occupation and there is none so fit for me as that.' She was evidently glad to be able to save her father some expense as well as to find occupation for herself.

On June 10 Lady Eastlake was writing to her excitedly with direct tidings of 'J.R.'. He had borrowed some books from Sir Charles which he had not returned before going away, and Sir Charles had written to old Mr Ruskin, ignoring the fact of his being away, asking for them back. 'And this morning,' wrote Lady Eastlake, 'he received a short letter from J.R. himself—dated June 6th Geneva, in which he apologises for not having returned the books on the score of being so hurried. "I was in much confusion owing to the unexpected necessity of moving all my things from my former house to my father's in the last week before leaving England. (I went

---

* Sophie, Alice and John. Albert and Melville were still in the care of the old nurse, Jeanie.

abroad in order to give my father and mother a happy tour, and his time of departure could not be delayed) so I was not a little hurried." All this speaks for itself—I leave you the easy task of pulling the sophistry to pieces. There was time enough to write that letter about Hunt's picture, which has condemned him in the eyes of the mere world more than anything. He adds that he will return the books "the moment I return—some time in August".'

On June 25 she further reported to Effie that she had heard 'that J.R. *intended* to have written a statement of the truth, but upon second thoughts he felt it would injure you so much that he had made up his mind to refrain! Very convenient forebearance . . . Last Sunday [the 18th] the Bishop of Edinburgh,* Mr Lockhart and Mr Hay (from Rome) were here to dinner and when Miss Farquar and I had left the room (Mr L having started the subject by asking me for you) the gentlemen continued the conversation, and the Bishop, not knowing the real history, was duly informed—then all agreed as to their long detestation of the writings and those were handled accordingly, and then Mr Hay said, "It is all very well to agree about the writings—but what do you intend to do with the *man*— surely when women are banished from society for their faults, you will never admit such a villain as that", and then Sir Charles and all said that *they* should never receive him, and Mr L growled out his indignation at his having dared to write to Sir Charles at all, which I do think the greatest assurance.'†

Lady Eastlake's report that Ruskin had intended to make a statement probably came from Dr Acland who had now heard from Ruskin as we learn from Millais's next letter to Mrs Gray from Glenfinlas:

Friday June 23rd
I have delayed writing until I could tell you that at last my work is over. Tomorrow I expect will be my last day on the

---

* The Rev. Charles Hugh Terrot (1790–1872), Bishop of Edinburgh, 1841–62.

† Lockhart, on account of ill health, had retired from the editorship of the *Quarterly Review* the year before and had spent the winter in Rome with Robert Hay, an old friend, and one of the oldest contributors to the *Quarterly*. Ruskin, in 1847, had proposed to Lockhart's daughter, Charlotte, although he seems to have cared almost as little for her as she did for him. All the same, Lockhart must have felt a special interest in the matter.

rocks, and on Tuesday or Wednesday Collins and I are going
to see Loch Lomond* . . . I have had another letter from Dr
Acland saying that he had heard from Ruskin, I suppose giving
his explanation of his conduct, for the Dr begs of me not to
speak against him as "*I may pledge myself to more moral blame of
him than I should*". Furnivall also has written to me, and he had
also received a letter from Ruskin, who professed the greatest
enjoyment of the scenery about him, drawing the greater part
of his time, adding that he hopes to astonish his friends with the
result.† Sir Walter and Lady Trevelyan were staying with Dr
Acland.

Although it would not be the most pleasant subject to look
on, I should like you to see this portrait, as you all know him so
well. Every man, woman, and child here recognise it at once.
One very common looking fellow who removes the fallen timber
in the woods, made some strange remarks about him. He said
that he was the queerest looking man he ever saw, *and not like
other people*. Directly he saw the likeness he asked after the original, saying that he was a poor sickly looking gentleman, and
had *very dull eyes*. He seems to have left an odd impression in
everybody's mind . . .

I am very sorry that the decision is likely to remain until
November but it scarcely matters now that the result is certain.
I expect when he meets her again he will be as tender in
enquiries after her health, and evince as much interest in her
welfare as though nothing had happened. I will write again
as soon as I have reached a resting place.

Millais and Collins left Glenfinlas on June 28 for a walking tour
but were back at the New Trossachs Hotel by July 3. Soon afterwards Collins returned to London but Millais stayed on with Luard
because he was expecting his friend John Leech to come and stay for

---

* While Luard remained at Glenfinlas to finish a picture he had started.
Millais became more and more attached to Luard during their stay at
Glenfinlas. Luard would cheerfully clean Millais's palette and brushes for
him, and read aloud to him Ruskin's Edinburgh Lectures! (Letter of
June, 1854, from Millais to John Leech: Sir Ralph Millais's Collection.)

† This is Ruskin's letter to Furnivall of June 9, p. 213.

a few days. On the 9th he was writing to Mrs Gray: 'For the last three days I have been painting a little girl and as I desire to give her a present for sitting I appeal to you to get enough *Rob Roy* tartan to make the young lady a dress.* The better way will be to buy as much stuff as would do for an ordinary-sized woman and then she can patch up the dress when it gets old, put new sleeves to it and that kind of thing . . . Tomorrow I expect Leech—he has been delayed by the illness of his wife. I will take him to the most interesting scenes about here and then we shall away.† I am sure the decision will not be until November as it is always the case that they are deferred to the extreme limit of the time announced. Let me know if

---

* A picture entitled *A Highland Lassie* or *Head of a Scotch Girl*, dated 1854, is reproduced in A. L. Baldry's book (*Sir J. E. Millias, His Art and Influence*; Bell, 1899), and is stated there to be painted from Miss Euphemia Chalmers Gray; and in M. H. Spielmann's *Millais and His Works* (Blackwood, 1898) the same picture is said to be painted from Lady Millais. In Millais's *Life* it is listed among his works for 1854 but the name of the sitter is not given. When it turned up at a sale in 1911 it was in a frame bearing inscriptions to the effect that it represented Mrs Ruskin. It is now in the Delaware Art Center, Wilmington, U.S.A., and still said to be a portrait of Effie. In fact it bears no resemblance to Effie, nor did Effie and Millais meet during the whole of 1854. It is almost certainly the portrait of the little girl described in this letter.

Mrs Gray sent the tartan which arrived after Millais had left but it was presented to the girl by Luard who had stayed on to finish his picture.

† Millais had written several times to Leech about this coming visit to Glenfinlas, but had asked Leech not to come until he had finished his picture as he wanted to be free to go fishing with him. Leech had never fished for salmon, which were plentiful that year, unlike the year before (simply, Millais complained, because he had not brought his own fishing tackle with him this time in order not to be distracted from his work). On June 13 he had written to Leech that his painting had been held up because he had fallen down and hurt his thumb—his right one this time—which was bandaged 'as though it was up the bore of a flute', but on the 18th he wrote that the background was almost completely finished: 'I have only a few more bubbles to paint in the smooth of the waterfall, and I will delay them until I can paint them from the permanent saliva globes proceeding from the wee partie's [Leech's baby daughter] little mug when it has got *breezes* or Zephyrs.' (Sir Ralph Millais's Collection.) Ruskin's disgust if he had heard this joke can be imagined, for he hated babies and when staying with Effie with the Henry Aclands at Oxford in July, 1848, had been made sick every morning by their insistence on having their baby at the breakfast table. (Letter from Effie to her mother, July 20, 1848; Morgan.)

John James Ruskin, *c.* 1860 (he died in 1864), the only known photograph
of him apart from two of head and shoulders taken at the same sitting.

The Gray family photographed at St Andrews in August, 1855. Back row, left to right: George, Jeanie (the old family nurse), Mr Gray, Sophie, Millais. Second row: John, Albert, Mrs Gray, Alice, Melville, Effie.
(*See p. 264.*)

it is settled now. I have just written to Ruskin at the desire of the
Deverell family (of whom the Countess will tell you) to try and obtain
for one of the younger sons a clerkship in Mr Ruskin's House. They
have already applied to him on the subject and asked my interest in
the matter which I could not refuse. I have written simply stating
the poverty of the family and how much they would be benefitted by
his getting some employment. There is only one boy who has a
situation of 70 or 80 pounds a year on which all the family have to
live . . . Before Collins left we went to the old room and took tea with
the Minister, and since then, I have made a sketch of him to hang up
in his new house.'

Effie had by this time gone to St Andrews with the rest of the
Gray family where she was eating and sleeping well, walking long
distances, bathing and teaching the children on the beach because
the weather was so glorious. She had had no recurrence of her '*Tic*'
and any friend who met her was astonished to see how well she
looked. All this she told Rawdon Brown in a letter of July 15, adding
that as they had heard nothing from the lawyers there was no doubt
her case would not come up until November; she then repeated to
him every word Lady Eastlake had told her about her dinner for the
Bishop of Edinburgh and Lockhart.

Millais meanwhile was at Glenfinlas, still waiting for John Leech
who had been further delayed. At last, bored and impatient, he
decided to wait no longer, and on July 13 set off to join his friend at
the Peacock Inn, Baslow, near Chatsworth. Leech was there with his
wife, Ann, and baby daughter, Ada. Millais wrote to Mrs Gray from
Baslow the day after he arrived there to say that he had received yet
another letter from Dr Acland, the third, which he enclosed because
it could not but give the Countess pleasure. 'The few words he says
upon Ruskin are of quite a different nature to what he first thought,'
Millais went on. 'He is a truly good man, and too gentle to be hasty
in his judgement; I should not like him to hear that I made use of his
letter in any way so burn it after you read it . . . I hope the poor
martyr of Perth is getting daily happier. I hope that one day soon
she will not forget to let her drawing master know this from her own
hand . . . Now that Mr Gray has authority over his daughter again,
he can command her to improve. her writing by setting large
copperplate style of copies for the small people. I remember that she

told me that he [Ruskin] was dissatisfied with that part of her education.'

Millais would not have to wait long now for a letter from Effie herself. On the very day he was writing this she was unexpectedly granted her decree of nullity.

# THE MARRIAGE ANNULLED

❃

The reason for the speeding up of the case is given in a letter from
Effie's proctor, Mr Glennie, to Mr Gray. Effie, who was still at St
Andrews, copied it and sent it off to Rawdon Brown the day it was
received, July 20:

15th July 1854

You are aware that on the 4th Inst the cause was concluded
and set down for hearing and that nothing more could be done
until the meeting of the Courts in November—I put myself in
communication with Mr Ruskin's Solicitor, whom I found to
be a gentlemanly right-thinking man. He saw at once the
Cruelty of your daughter being kept in suspense for some
months for a sentence she must ultimately have obtained. He
accordingly sent a Document for Mr Ruskin's signature author-
izing a Proctor to appear and consent to a day being appointed
for the Hearing of the Cause and I have now the great pleasure
to inform you that this morning the Case was heard and the
Judge has signed a sentence declaring the pretended marriage
a nullity and that Miss Gray is free from all bonds of matri-
mony. On Monday an Official Copy of the Sentence will be
sent.

Mr Rutter had informed Mr Ruskin on July 1 that, as in November 'the Woman' would be able to obtain Nullity of the Marriage
without a proctor appearing for his son, he considered that the
sooner the Sentence was pronounced the better, *not*, as Mr Glennie
said, because he saw the cruelty of keeping Effie in suspense, but
because if it were delayed she might run Ruskin into debt![1] He had
therefore instructed Mr Pott* to prepare 'a proxy' to be sent to

---

* Frederick William Pott of 13 Godliman Street, Doctors' Commons,
whom Mr Ruskin had been to see the day after Effie's flight.

Lausanne (where the Ruskins were then staying) for John's signature.

This proxy, which Ruskin signed at Lausanne on July 5, is the second document that was bought by Sir Albert Gray in 1924 and relinquished to Alexander Wedderburn. It is endorsed 'Mr Pott's Questions and Mr J. Ruskin's Answers'.[2]

The five questions put to Ruskin suggested possible defences on his behalf, all of which Ruskin dismissed. He confirmed that, as far as he knew, the marriage was valid when solemnized and that it had not been consummated. Asked whether 'the Lady's conduct' might have induced a supposition that she was not 'at this moment a pure virgin', he replied, 'The Lady's conduct has been without reproach' and 'I have no doubt her case will stand any examination'. It was then put to him that 'The Lady's conduct having given rise to so much disagreement and her habits being of so extravagant a nature, to consider the expedience of allowing the case to proceed without hindrance, merely giving a sufficient opposition to allow the Lady to obtain her decree without the appearance of collusion'. To this Ruskin replied, 'I certainly wish the case to proceed with as little hindrance as possible.'

The Decree of Nullity granted to Effie in the Commissary Court of Surrey on July 15 is very long and written in the usual unpunctuated style of all such legal documents. The damaging part to Ruskin came towards the end: '. . . the said marriage . . . between the said John Ruskin and the said Euphemia Chalmers Gray falsely called Ruskin was had and celebrated whilst the said John Ruskin was incapable of consummating the same by reason of incurable impotency.'[3]

Although the case was conducted with all possible privacy,* the verdict of the Court must soon have leaked out and one can imagine with what glee Lady Eastlake passed it on to her friends. Ruskin himself must have been as pleased to be done with it as Millais or the Grays, and on August 13 he was writing in his diary at Sallanches, near Chamonix, 'How little I thought God would bring me here again just now—and I am here, stronger in health, higher in hope,

---

* 'Nothing could have been more privately done,' Mr Rutter wrote to Mr Ruskin when sending him a copy of the sentence. No reporters were present and it was not even noticed in *The Times*. (Letter of July 19. R–CT.)

deeper in peace, than I have been for years.' He was not aware as yet of the number of enemies that had been made for him. Mr Rutter, when sending Mr Ruskin a copy of the Sentence and of the Grays' Depositions, suggested that they should not be shown to his son as they might 'distress his mind and interrupt his pursuits', and Ruskin later confirmed that he did not look at them.[4] It was only gradually that he came to realise how damaging had been this charge of impotence which, by not refuting, he appeared to have admitted.

Sixteen years later he was to write, 'The Decree of Divorce was passed against me because I had never fulfilled a husband's duty to his wife, and it was assumed necessarily in my declining to give any answer that I was impotent . . . I only was able to retain my own life and power by . . . coming from it as I would from any pestiferous room—and as far as I could, forgetting it in intense work. My father and his lawyer managed the suit, and only asked me a few necessary questions. I am in Law unmarried and in my conduct to my wife—I boldly say and believe—guiltless though foolish.'[*][5]

Away in Switzerland he was trying to be aloofly philosophical about what had happened to him. To Dr Acland he complained of too much sermonising in his letters. 'The more I see of the human race,' he wrote to Acland from Chamonix on July 18, 'the more I think they are divided into classes—intensely fixed in their natures— Creatures made to honour and to dishonour, as the Potter willed.[†] At least I find it a marvellous hard thing to Unbake myself—which I have been trying to do more than usual lately, in consequence of the self-examination I have been led into by this matter.

'As for the extent of the misfortune itself, I believe I know it to the utmost of its possibilities—and did so at the first hour of its happening, as far as it regards myself only. But I am full of fear for another person, and can only keep myself steady by occupation in other matters, knowing myself perfectly powerless in this.'[6]

There is little doubt that the person he was full of fear for was Millais.

Furnivall was all this time pressing him to make some kind of

---

* The idea that throughout his marriage his conduct had been foolish rather than culpable was later stressed in a letter to Joan Severn: 'I was wilful—foolish—boundlessly idiotic in marrying Effie.' (May 15, 1875. *Illustrious Friends*, by Sheila Birkenhead, p. 247. Hamish Hamilton, 1965.)

† Romans ix. 21.

statement in his own defence and at last he wrote openly to Furnivall about his marriage:

19th
Chamouni, 18th August

My dear Furnivall,

I have just received your kind letter—I have a good many others to answer; I hasten only to reply to the most important part of it.

I hardly know how much I owe to myself in this matter—and whether—even supposing I owe *everything* to myself, I am likely to gain much by a defence which could be founded only on statements of my own—As to the accusation of having thrown my late wife in Mr Millais' way—with the view supposed by Lady Eastlake, I should as soon think of simply *denying* an accusation of murder. Let those who say I have committed murder—prove it—let those who believe I have committed it without proof, continue to believe it.

The entire history of my married life is due to you—for you are one of *the three* people who have been perfectly staunch to me.* But I cannot give it you on paper in a days hard work of writing—an hours talk will set your mind at rest as soon as I return—I do not know at present what steps to take with reference to the public—on this I shall slowly consult with my friends—One great difficulty is that no one will ever believe that Effie's general character in her domestic life was what it was—what it *must* have been in order to render my conduct explicable—For instance—would the kind of temper indicated in the following dialogue—which I happened to put down one day as an example of our usual intercourse—be believed in a woman who to all strangers behaved with grace and pleasantness.

Effie is looking abstractedly out of the window.

John. "What are you looking at, Effie."

E.    "Nothing."

* The other two were Lady Trevelyan and Mary Russell Mitford (see p. 245). The fact that Dr Acland could have written a letter to Millais which would give Effie pleasure shows that he could not have been perfectly staunch to Ruskin.

J.      "What are you thinking of then?"
E.      "A great many things."
J.      "Tell me some of them."
E.      "I was thinking of operas—and excitement—and—
        (angrily) a great many things."
J.      "And what conclusions did you come to."
E.      "None—because *you* interrupted me."
Dialogue closed.

This appears little—but imagine every question asked in a kind tone—every answer given with a snap—and that continuing the whole day—Imagine this behaviour in daily intercourse attended by the most obstinate opposition in serious things—and by an *utter* ingratitude for *all* that was done for her by myself—my father—and my mother—not merely ingratitude—but ingratitude coarsely and vulgarly manifested—imagine her for instance speaking of her husband—his father—and his mother—as the "Batch of Ruskins" and you may understand—though I do not see how at present I could make the public understand—why I used no persuasion to induce my late wife to change the position which we held towards each other—no persuasion of late times would have availed—for she hated me as only those hate who have injured. I have not time for more to-day.

Ever yours
J Ruskin[7]

It was not only Lady Eastlake who believed that Ruskin had taken Millais to the Highlands with an ulterior motive. Jane Boswell was to write to Mrs Gray on September 15, 'I never doubted the taking John Millais to the Highlands was a regular deep laid scheme, which doubtless J.R. imagined could not fail, judging the world by his own wicked self.' And George Gray believed it for the rest of his life.

Millais himself, however, did not believe it at this time as is shown in his letter to Mrs Gray of July 27; but before that he had written to Effie direct. Mrs Gray had immediately communicated to him the good news of her release, and at last, after all these months, he felt free to write to her:

Friday night. [July 21–22]
The Peacock Inn
Baslow Chatsworth
Derbyshire

My dear Countess

I cannot see that there is anything to prevent my writing to you now, so I will wait no longer. I consider that I have a special right to be amongst the first of your congratulating friends, for no one has been so keenly interested in the trials you have gone through, or is so happy at this blessed termination—I had so thoroughly convinced myself of the improbability of ever speaking to you again that I find my brains unable to keep pace with the sudden alteration of affairs, and that I am writing this in a state of incredulity. I did not hope to hear of the decision until Nov$^r$ and when I came down this morning I was surprised to find your Mother's letter upon the breakfast table, for I knew at once the news it contained. The best news I have ever received in my life. May God give you health and peace of mind to enjoy the new life you have entered upon, and I think from your late pedestrian performances at St Andrews you are not wanting in the former—I will say nothing of the past. Recalling bygone events can only be distressing to you. You may always feel happy in having done your duty, for you have done John Ruskin even a greater service than yourself. You were nothing to him but an awful encumbrance, and I believe secretly the source of all his sullen irritability. Love was out of the question in such a nature so that by the separation you have caused him no more pain than a temporary exhibition of grief such as would naturally follow after your living so many years with him. Now dear Countess do not be distressed with any more backward thoughts but pray to God that the future may be as happy as the past has been otherwise, and that you may not grow less earnest in your appeals to Him than you were in adversity. This time last year there seemed no more chance of what has happened than that the moon should fall, and now you are Miss Gray again. If you could see me I am sure you would pity me for I am scarcely able to write commonsense I am so bewildered. I cannot separate you in my mind from what appeared to be your inevitable doom and when I see you I shall not be able to believe but what J.R. has got a duplicate Countess. By the bye what am I to do with the little portrait I did of you with the foxgloves? I have never sent it him, and now I suppose it is impossible and yet I do not like to keep it after giving it him—This will appear to you an absurd thing to talk about, but I am so crazed with trying to realize your freedom that I am simply unequal to express myself—It is past twelve o'clock—for I could not attempt to write to you till they had all gone to bed—and I have not said one thing I would wish. I have been painting out of doors all day, or rather pretending to paint—so that I might be away from my friends and have some quiet to think upon this wonderful change.

I feel half frightened at the thought of meeting you again, like the time when you returned to the cottage after visiting Bowerswell.

I must see you before returning to London, *if you will invite me.* Oh Countess how glad I shall be to see you again, this is all I can say now, and you must imagine the rest. I can never be sufficiently thankful for God's goodness to me—I really believe that I should have grown a selfish callous fellow if this alteration had not come about. Take all care of yourself *and write me a letter to assure me that you are the same Countess I knew at Glenfinlas.* Since the time of my first hearing of your intention to separate from J Ruskin I have been in a constant state of anxiety, so much so that I am now quite dull in my head. I have been striving nightly to think upon what I must soon be about, but the subject flies from me immediately—however I think I can show poor Ruskin that he cannot write me down in a week. Here I am going off into a wretched bit of bombast; that is not the spirit I hope to work in—When I come to my senses I will tell you about what I am going to set about and every other subject you care to hear. Although it is but a short time since I saw you last at Edinburgh it seems years,* and I am possessed of a strange feeling of witholding myself. Many a day I have cursed the exhibition of my liking for you before Ruskin and this has brought on a caution I never had before. I tell you

* This shows definitely that Effie and Millais had not met since November 10, 1853, the evening Millais left Edinburgh.

everything as I know you will not misunderstand my meaning. I assure you Countess I have had a share of bitterness after I left you that night reading Tom Taylor's life of Haydon,* and when your sister Sophie came to me to Gower St, which I don't wish [to] recall. If I remain up much longer the girl will be coming in to lay the cloth for breakfast so I must finish this— I have lost no rest, for I could not sleep tonight. *Write me [a] line by return of Post*—If I have done wrong in writing to you take no notice of my letter beyond asking your Mother to write a word in answer.

Ever yours<br>
John Everett Millais

I should think you find it rather difficult to return to your old signature—Effie Gray. You must now grow so fat that cab-men will refuse to take you as a single fare. Remember me to your family and thank your Mama for the good news.[8]

He did not have to wait long for Effie's reply for on the 26th he was writing again most revealingly:

My dear Countess

I have done nothing but read your letter all day long. What a blessing it was to see your writing again. You are doubtless quite right in not wishing that I should visit Bowerswell just yet. It never struck me that there was any reason why I should not, but I understand what you mean perfectly. I will wait patiently until you say I may come. I hope I will not tumble into a fit when I see you, the changes that have taken place have been an awful trial to my wretchedly nervous disposition. I suppose that I am desperately happy (at least I ought and wish to be) but I cannot yet believe this, and have all day long been endeavouring to persuade myself of the truth by reading your welcome letter. Yes Countess I am *very happy indeed* and

---

* Ruskin had written to his father from Edinburgh on November 10, 1853, 'I am immensely interested in Haydon's life . . . It is a precious book.' Benjamin Haydon, the artist, had committed suicide in 1846, aged sixty. Tom Taylor (1817–80), dramatist, art critic and later editor of *Punch*, was a great friend of Millais's. His biography of Haydon had been published in 1853.

will show you that I am not shut up at 25. The thought of being near you again numbs my senses in an odd way, so that I almost fear what I look forward to with such ["desire" crossed out] pleasure, meeting you again. I am so glad to hear that you are happy now, may God always keep you so. I scarcely know what to write about first, it seems as though I must send you a hundred letters before talking about what I am now doing—First I must make a confession to you and that is, I did not destroy all your old letters, but kept one until I heard that you were going to get free again, and then I burnt it like the others. It was the last but one. Now I am clear of concealing disobedience to your commands, I will go on with answering your questions—The people I am with are perfectly kind and agreeable. Leech you know something about from some letters I received from him at Glenfinlas. I was more indebted to him, during the miserable London period last year, than to any other of my friends: I went out hunting with him, sometimes twice a week. It was about the only thing that gave me some amusement—if risking one's neck can be called such. Through disregard of casualties, I became, in hunting twice, a very good rider, and derived a good deal of advantage from the excitement which is too great for the time to permit of other thoughts —Good little Halliday was the only person I could get a word from about you, and I used to bore him to death after he had seen you—such awful nights I used to have setting [*sic*] with him in his gloomy chambers hearing everything about you and the people dining at Herne Hill. Once when he dined with you* I returned from poor Deverell's who died whilst I was in the house. A short time before his death I used to sit up by his bed and read to him, and walk home in the snow 12 or 1 in the morning. About that time also Hunt left England and I think I was the most miserable creature in London—but what matters now?

What a good brave girl you have been to get your freedom. I used to be terribly distressed in thinking on the advice I had given you, for there was such frightful responsibility attached to your position. When you tell me to write more clearly, I don't quite understand whether you mean that it is difficult to

* This was the dinner-party of February 2, described on p. 133.

read or not. I am sure it must be unless I am careful, for I have
great difficulty myself sometimes in making it out. To day I
have been painting upon the lawn in front of the house which
is a beautiful place overlooking Chatsworth and its grounds.
Leech is here with his wife, sister, and baby, nurse, and maid.
The child takes up the attention of the 5 nearly all day. They
lost their first and are dreadfully anxious about this second and
only one, a pretty little girl with blue eyes, 5 months old.* I
have only been about three small sketches since the finish at
Glenfinlas. This year I have no out door painting to speak of,
but I have two glorious subjects† which I commence immediately I get back, and you shall see what the results will be.
If it does not equal your wishes, have nothing more to do with
me. I will tell you the subject in my next, for I cannot speak
of that now. I have numbers of things I should be doing for
publishers and people but I am quite put out for the present.
Tennyson has chosen me to illustrate his poems for Moxon the
publisher,‡ and I ought to be about them. If you were with me
I could do them all in a week. Yesterday I received a long letter
from Hunt at Jerusalem, the first words are expressing his delight at hearing of your coming deliverance, for I wrote to him
about that directly I knew it myself, as he was so interested
about you and me, having guessed how matters stood long
before he started for the East. I would send you the letter as it
is interesting, but there are orders in it which obliges me to
send it to London.

*What has become of the tooth?*§ I shall look forward to trotting

* This child survived and in September, 1855, they also had a son.
Leech died of angina in 1864, aged forty-six. His widow died soon afterwards. A water-colour drawing Millais made of Leech while they were at
Baslow is now in the National Portrait Gallery, one of the best portrait
heads he ever did.

† *The Blind Girl* and *L'Enfant du Regiment,* afterwards called *The Random
Shot.*

‡ Millais contributed eighteen of the fifty-four illustrations for Edward
Moxon's special edition of Tennyson's *Poems* published in 1857.

§ Effie still had one of her baby teeth which had remained in because
there was no second one to push it out. Millais, in his letter to Mrs Gray
of April 27, described how he had helped to extract the tooth of Halliday's
charwoman, adding, 'It was a little shaky child's tooth like the one the
Countess has.'

up the hill of Kinnoull with you. *Tell me if I can amuse you in any way* by drawing for you? Whenever anything occurs which I may sketch I will, but just now all fun is swallowed up in wonder at the fluctuation of my life. This writing I am afraid is awfully unintelligible but it is of course the fault of the pen. What a comfort it is now to know that I may write to you without the fearful hesitation, and dread of the old correspondence. Although I tell you to refrain from speaking of the past I keep on myself returning to it; for the contrast is so great it thrusts itself upon me. When do you think it likely I may come and see you? Do not hurry ["against your" crossed out] so as to give people the chance of blaming you in any shape although beyond a few close friends it scarcely matters what the World says, the public will always be unkind if they can. I am quite of opinion that it would be far from good taste my seeing you now. I saw Lady Eastlake just before I came North, and she particularly told me that I was not to go near Perth. She appeared to me to know all about what had taken place last year very soon afterwards, for I noticed the first time I met her, unlike most people she never mentioned my stay with you in the Highlands, or your name. The day of the opening of the R A. [April 28] she came to me and for the first time spoke about you. That day the news was circulated of your *aweyegoo.* In future I must always call it this as I am sometimes puzzled to give it a name. The better way perhaps will be not to say a word about your little portrait to J R.* I am sorry to have to mention his name to you. Poor little Countess what suffering you have gone through. I wish I could see you for one moment to tell you more than I can write in a week. Write to me as often as you can without injuring the education of the small Grays, or wearying yourself. You know how a letter from you is received by

Your loving master

Always understand that I am to be remembered to your family. Sophie was *so good when she sat* to me at Gower St.

---

* Millais kept this little foxglove portrait which had delighted Ruskin so much at Glenfinlas that he had mentioned it three times in his letters to his father.

Give Alice a kiss for me if she does not consider it a liberty.*
I have forgotten the day it is, so cannot date this. I received
your letter this morning, I could not send this by the afternoon's
Post.†

The next day, July 27, Millais was writing to Mrs Gray about
Ruskin:

In regard to my feeling towards J R I cannot but think he is
more to be pitied than any other man I know, and I confess
now, that like Mr Gray I could pass him without experiencing
much feeling beyond pity. He has behaved *most badly*, but he is
half mad, and possibly embittered by discovering—when too
late—that he ought never to have married—in that case according to his strange education and bringing up he is not to
be judged so severely. You know what I thought of him at the
time of his wretched treatment of the Countess, but now I hope
to grow every day less intolerant towards him. I am quite
hurt to hear that he appears to be so ill‡—this may seem strange
to you but I cannot wish him but to be peaceful, and in health to go
on writing as he likes. Now *she* is out of his possession I can forgive him, and I know she will also. If I recall his behaviour the
old antipathy comes on, which is so painful to me that I can
only trust for my own sake to forget it. I *will* not believe that he
desired her to fall, for in the beginning I cannot imagine a man
of education to be such a devil, neither do I think there was any
evil intention in his asking me to accompany him to the Highlands, but *I do not doubt* but what he was more than indifferent
afterwards. There was an amount of cool impudence about his
visiting Bowerswell in spite of his insane conduct to Effie,
which at once declares him to be inhuman. *No man* could have
face enough to confront the family of a girl he had so awfully

* Alice had a much happier life than Sophie. She married in 1874
George Davey Stibbard who was very much beloved by all the Gray family.
He was a partner in the legal firm of Hillier, Fenwick and Stibbard which
subsequently became Stibbard, Gibson & Co. They had no children. Alice
survived him for thirty years and died at Bowerswell in 1929, aged eighty-
four.

† This letter is postmarked 27th so presumably it was written on the 26th.

‡ There is no confirmation that Ruskin was ill at this time.

ruined. If I was to ponder much upon the subject the thing which would make me most savage would be his brutal want of generosity to her. After his mistake he should have put up with everything. I believe that no living woman ever behaved as she did. If there had been the slightest warmth in his blood he would have loved her for her endurance. At the time I assure you it drove me almost mad to think how they lived together. The very writing of this reminds me of agony I went through— As you say let us only remember now to thank God for her restoration. I don't know how to thank you enough for all your kindness to me during this trial.[9]

Millais went with Mike Halliday to Winchelsea in August to start painting the backgrounds for his two pictures, *The Blind Girl* and *The Random Shot*. To Furnivall he was still being very wary, writing to him from Winchelsea, 'In answer to your questions about Ruskin's late-wife I believe she is at Perth or in Scotland, and I imagine he is in Switzerland, all I know for certain is that I am here,'[10] but to Hunt he wrote on August 25: 'Mrs Ruskin that was is entirely free and is now Miss Effie Gray again. Ruskin is in Switzerland, dancing probably over cascades. All London has of course been in arms over the affair, and my name is mixed up with the reports—so much for that.' He went on to say that he was much stronger, stouter and happier and was growing whiskers which Halliday considered a great improvement.

His trials were not over, though. Having waited for so long and been so patient, Effie kept him waiting another six months for a glimpse of her. Perhaps she was emotionally exhausted; perhaps the opinion of the world counted too much with her; perhaps she was too sure of him; or maybe she waited for his sake so that no breath of scandal should touch his career. To Rawdon Brown she wrote on October 9: 'I am not fit to marry anybody, believe me, and after what I have suffered could not do so without very much time for thought and deliberation—and you know it would never do to be wretched twice.' But before this both Effie's former schoolteachers, the Misses Ainsworth, who still had a great influence over her, had written voicing the opinion of half the world—Miss Harriet to Mrs Gray on July 31: 'One opinion only obtains, that *he* [Ruskin] is a great scoundrel, and it is thought he will not show his face again in

London for some time, if ever. Those to whom the real reason cannot be told, are speculating on Effie's motive for obtaining a divorce instead of a separation, and wonder who is to succeed Mr Ruskin. Millais is much spoken of, but I always contradict the report and declare it has arisen from *his* determination to throw them together in order to injure *her*. And however estimable he may be, I should be very sorry for Effie to think of him, as a marriage with him would in some measure strengthen Mr R's hints, that Effie was actuated by other than the real reasons for seeking a divorce.' And a month later Miss Mary was writing to Effie herself in exactly the same strain: 'Millais . . . is the person to whom you are generally given. I deny it positively and I do not scruple to say I hope and trust no such thing will *ever* take place.'

A letter from Lady Eastlake, however, of August 10 seems to show that Effie really was in love: 'But all that is *over*, and another life lies before you, my dearest child—and one that cannot but sparkle brightly to your view—for your heart, however mistrustful it may have become, is now really engaged. I knew it was so, and can only honour you for having held it in tight subjection at a time and during trials when a little sophistry might have argued you into believing that you were not bound to do so. All I hope and believe is that out of your past sufferings that good may have sprung, that all *delusions* may be powerless upon you, and that you may view your future with *safer* eyes. But don't think more of it than you can help; be sure that you do more than enough for him in letting him look forward to the privilege of making you really happy—and let neither his happiness nor misery disturb that rest of body and peace of thought which you so much need. Think only of *yourself*—it won't be *selfishness*. I should better liked to have shipwrecked him—with canvas, colours and brushes—on a desert island for two years—and then rescued him. I like him very much—but I do not *want* him yet awhile. I wanted my Effie to be *untroubled* till she was fit for this life's work again, knowing all the time that the two dear people were safe enough to come together at last. But all is overruled—and now my only refuge is in hoping that you will disturb yourself about his waving locks as little as you can, and give him just the scantiest *parish* allowance to keep him from starving.'[11]

This is just what Effie appears to have done, though there are no more letters from him to tell us how near he was to starving. He certainly wrote to Effie* but the letters have not survived. How importunate were they, one wonders, how intimate? Did Effie realise what this waiting meant for him? He had ended his letter to Hunt from Winchelsea, 'Now I am going with H [Halliday] to smoke a sigaret upon a stile—What a difficult thing it is to behave properly. At this place there are lots of pretty girls who insist upon coming out bonnetless in the moonlight and invitingly passing and repassing us, and I have an almost insurmountable desire to stop them and speak, as most youths would, and when I get back to my bedroom I think what a fool I have been, and make up my mind to begin again.' Perhaps Lady Eastlake had chosen her words carefully when she wished him shipwrecked upon a *desert* island.

* 'I have been such a correspondent with *Miss Gray* that I have in part been kept by her from writing to you.' (Millais to Holman Hunt, May 22, 1855.)

# THE PORTRAIT FINISHED

❋

The Ruskins did not return to England until October 2. Cholera had been raging in London which was probably the reason why they delayed their homecoming. Ruskin noted in his diary at Dover: 'Drove to Canterbury—under very different circumstances from those of six years ago, and very happy.' Six years ago he had arrived back in England with Effie after a tour of Normandy.

On his way home he had written to Lady Trevelyan from Paris owning that although he had had times of 'painful feeling' when he first went abroad, he had now got over his distress and darkness and was feeling very full of plans and promises and hopes.[1]

Yet it must have been a difficult homecoming for him in many ways, and a letter to his old friend, Miss Mitford, written on the 3rd, four hours after he set foot in Denmark Hill, reveals his loneliness and doubt:

Two letters were put into my hands when I arrived, and the first I opened was yours* and the first words my eye fell upon: "The only fear is, lest I should do too much."!

Could any happier—kinder—sweeter welcome have been given me ... God willing I will come to see you about the middle of next week ... I cannot come sooner, because it is necessary that I should now show myself for a few days in London in order to convince my friends—and some—who are otherwise than friendly—that I am the same person I used to be. You will perhaps not easily believe that of all my friends,

* This letter from Miss Mitford was written on October 2 and is given in full in *Mary Russell Mitford, Correspondence with Charles Boner and John Ruskin*, ed. Elizabeth Lee (Fisher Unwin, 1914). It is very long and is mostly to do with the writer's own health. In December, 1852, she had been involved in a carriage accident and had never since been out of pain. Much to Ruskin's grief she died on January 10 of the following year, aged sixty-six.

*you* are the only one whose tact—whose sympathy and feeling—
I ought rather to say—have been unerring, during the trial I
have had lately to go through. Some wrote to me asking
questions, which very little common sense might have told them
*never* could be answered; others wrote in useless and inappro-
priate condolence—some in the style of Eliphaz and Zophar*—
and the rest kept a terrified silence—depriving me of the pleasure
I might have had in hearing from them about their own affairs.
*You only* knew what to do.[2]

Some time during the next two months Millais at last finished the
Glenfinlas portrait which had caused him so much misery, but
unfortunately there is no record of it. There were only the hands left
to be painted which might have been done in two sittings,† though
knowing how slow and meticulous Millais was they probably took
more. As the Gower Street house had been given up and as Millais
had not yet moved into Langham Chambers, it is probable that the
sittings took place at 17 Hanover Terrace, Regent's Park, the house
of Charles Collins's mother.‡ Anyway the finished picture was on
show at Hanover Terrace before it went to Denmark Hill. Lady
Eastlake saw it there and reported her impressions of it to Effie:

Well darling, and now last but not least, for a few words on
that other *E* who interests me more and more. He has been in
several times and has now quite worn off his shyness with me,

* Two of Job's three comforters.
† After the last sitting in April, Millais had written, 'I have very little
more to do from him; two days more will suffice.' See p. 178.
‡ We know that Gower Street had been given up because Millais, while
he was still at Winchelsea and before Ruskin returned to England, had
told Hunt that another artist was in possession of the house and using his old
studio; and we know that the sittings did not take place at Langham
Chambers because Ruskin asks for Millais's address there *after* receiving
the finished picture (see letters, pp. 247–8); moreover Ruskin not only
addressed these letters to Millais care of Charles Collins at Hanover Terrace, but asked whether he (Millais) was still staying there. Although this
is not proof that the picture was finished there it seems highly probable
that Millais temporarily made use of Collins's studio. Millais did, however,
have what he called 'a painting room' above the stables of his parents'
cottage at Kingston so it is just possible that Ruskin drove over there from
Denmark Hill for the final sittings.

and does himself *justice* for I see into his refined intelligent nature, and into the sound religious principles which animate him. On the last 2 occasions Mamma and Jane [her sister] have been in the room so he has not been able to talk on the one dear subject, and this has perhaps given me the opportunity of judging of him with more impartiality. Immediately after my last hurried note to you I drove to Hanover Terrace and saw that picture which he has finished. I thought I could not have borne to look at it, and yet felt that I should be wrong to let the sight of it escape me. It was a very foggy day, and I could only see that it was a *marvel* of art and beg to bring Sir Chas the next day—So we both went, and a better light showed us beauties which I had not discovered before and enabled Sir Chas to pronounce it "a first rate work of art". He was *enchanted* with it, and enthusiastic like myself—and both of us forgot and *could* forget the *subject*, while we hung spell-bound over the art. I could not have believed that any portrait of him could have given me any pleasure, but in truth the personality of the portrait utterly vanished before the skill of the painter. Sir Chas said over and over again that it was "one of the remarkable pictures of the world"—and we could liken it to nothing but Van Eyck, for with all minutia of finish, a greater breadth and grander feeling pervades the whole. As we came away Sir Chas remarked to me that Millais stood in a most beautiful and interesting position—whether to the eye of painter or moralist— fairly started in a career of great distinction—his toil over—his pleasure to come—with unsullied reputation—finely constituted mind, and splendid person—And darling I listened and *assisted* with a *glowing* heart, taking a tenfold pleasure in the praise unknown to Sir Chas—or not quite unknown for I am sure he understands in a quiet way why I take such interest in the fine young painter. I share the *parental* feeling for you so strongly, that all this from a man so well able to judge, and never profuse in expression, was balm to me as I know it will be to your dear mother.*

* This letter causes some confusion because it is dated January 2, 1855. Lady Eastlake starts her letter, however, by saying that it is an immense time since she has written. She then describes many events of the past few weeks and it becomes apparent that her visit to Hanover Terrace must have

This was the picture about which Lady Eastlake had written eight months before, 'Truly I think it useless his finishing a picture which *nobody* will ever *look* at.'

The next we hear of it is from Ruskin himself:

Denmark Hill
Monday 11th [December 1854]

Dear Millais

We have just got the picture placed—in I think the very light it wants—or rather—for it cannot be said to *want* any light—in that which suits it best. I am far more delighted with it now than I was when I saw it in your rooms. As for the wonderment of the painting there can of course be no question—but I am also gradually getting reconciled to the figure's standing in the way. On the whole the thing is right and what can one say more —always excepting the yellow flower and the over large spark in the right eye, which I continue to reprobate—as having the effect of making me slightly squint—which whatever the other faults of my face may be—I believe I don't. My Father and mother say the likeness is perfect—but that I look bored—pale —and a little too yellow. Certainly after standing looking at that row of chimnies in Gower Street* for three hours—on one leg—it was no wonder I looked rather uninterested in the world in general. But the more they look at it the more they come into it. Please send me your proper address, as I may often want to write to you, now. I need not, I hope tell you how grateful I am to you for finishing this picture as you have.

Have you given up all thought of *architectural* design? I am just getting the workmen to be able to do something—and if you would sometimes do a design for them to carve in wood or stone it would be such a priceless help.†

Faithfully and gratefully yours
J. Ruskin

---

taken place *before* December 11 when the picture was hanging at Denmark Hill.

\* In Millais's studio on the ground floor at the back of what is now No. 7 Gower Street (partitioned into three offices) chimneys can be seen across Gower Mews.

† This refers to Ruskin's Thursday evening drawing classes at the Working

Best regards to Collins if you are still staying in Regent's Park.[3]

Millais took six days to reply. Perhaps he sent Ruskin's letter to Perth and waited for Effie's opinion before answering it. It is just possible, though, that he did not intend to answer it at all until Ruskin wrote again impatiently on the 16th, 'Why don't you answer my letter—it is tiresome of you—and makes me uneasy.'[4]

Two days later Millais replied:

18 December

My dear Ruskin,

My address is Langham Chambers, Langham Place, but I can scarcely see how you conceive it possible that I can desire to continue on terms of intimacy with you. Indeed I concluded that after finishing your portrait, you yourself would have seen the necessity of abstaining from further intercourse.

Yours truly
John Everett Millais

The barrier which cannot but be between us *personally*, does not prevent me from sympathising with all your efforts to the advancement of good taste in Art, and heartily wishing them success.[5]

It does seem incredible that Ruskin, knowing as he must have done that Millais was probably going to marry Effie,* should have imagined that he and Millais could remain friends, yet the bitterness of his reply to Millais's letter shows that he had not expected even this eventuality to interfere with their relationship:

Denmark Hill, Camberwell
20th December 1854

Sir

From the tenour of your letter, received yesterday, I can only

---

Men's College, 31 Red Lion Square, founded on October 31 of this year. As far as is known, Millais never again attempted architectural design.

* Mr Ruskin had written to William Alexander on December 14 this year: 'The reports are that she [Effie] will marry Millais whom you saw her with at Edinburgh. She left home in April to get the marriage dissolved no doubt for that purpose.' (R–CT.)

conclude that you either believe I had, as has been alleged by various base or ignorant persons, some unfriendly purpose when I invited you to journey with me to the Highlands, or that you have been concerned in machinations which have for a long time been entered into against my character and fortune. In either case, I have to thank you for a last lesson, though I have had to learn many and bitter ones, of the possible extent of human folly and ingratitude. I trust that you may be spared the natural consequences of the one, or the dire punishment of the other.

I remain,
Your obedient servant
John Ruskin[6]

It was left to Mr Ruskin to fire the last salvo. This he did with his usual clumsiness, whereas Ruskin's shot may perhaps have reached Millais's heart:

Denmark Hill 20 Decr 1854

Sir,

Something passed between us when I called to see my Son's portrait about its being exhibited and I said I had no objection.

I have now the greatest objection and it cannot for *any* purpose leave my House—I may also add that although it is my practice to pay an artist and a friend always a sum beyond the price demanded for his pictures, I must beg you will allow me to consider all accounts between you and me settled by my late payment.*

The only service I believe my Son has rendered you is in having directed public attention sooner to the presence of a Genius that ultimately would have filled its space without any aid of his and the only return he sought was your friendship— By your last letter I see, even this is denied him, not to my regret on *his* account but on yours for I had not imagined that so strong a Capacity could so easily have been imposed upon, deluded, misguided and duped even by the most artful, and I

---

* A note in Mr Ruskin's account book reads: 'Dec 4 John's portrait Millais £350 Insurance 8/9.' (Bembridge.)

am grieved to think that so much strength in the artist can be
accompanied by such utter weakness and blindness in the Man.

I am Sir

Yrs obediently

John James Ruskin

From the following letter from Mr Ruskin to Millais's friend,
Charles Collins, it is learnt that not only did Millais deign to reply to
this but that Collins, whom Ruskin must have met at Hanover
Terrace, had tried, and perhaps was still trying, to prevent a final
break between Ruskin and his friend:

28 December 1854

Sir,

As the confident [*sic*] between Mr Millais and my Son I
trouble you with this—you have seen my letter to Millais and
his reply in which he says that in imputing weakness to him—I
may be mistaken. God Grant I may—He certainly has a retort
ready that I have one nearer to me who has been weak before
him—My Son caught by a pretty face married contrary to his
parents *judgement* but not to their *commands*—Miss G concealed
the embarrassed circumstances of her Father—courted my Son
and was united in her Father's House at Perth, none of his own
Friends attending the Ceremony*—He found at once that the
Woman had no Love for him and he lived with her accordingly
—She soon filled his House with men of her own finding till he
could not get a single hour for study without stealing away to
his Father's House—In that house she professed the greatest
pleasure in being with her Mother in Law up to the marriage
day, but no sooner she secured my Son than she used her
utmost efforts to take him entirely from his parents and to make
him a mere man of the Town. She wasted my property in the
most reckless manner making away with £15000 in six years,†

* This is not true. John's friend, William Macdonald, was best man at
his wedding. Mrs Ruskin did not go because she had a superstitious dread
of Bowerswell; Mr Ruskin because it was thirty years since he had slept in
a friend's house. (*Effie in Venice*, p. 19.)

† This charge of wanton extravagance was Mr Ruskin's most reiterated,
and most unjust, accusation against Effie—as unjust as Ruskin's enemies
saying that he had 'fled the country' when he went abroad on May 9.

but she would have been pardoned had she proved a Helpmate
to my Son or a Daughter to Mrs R but she was neither—every
kindness was lost upon her—she returned for care and fondness
only neglect and even contumely, altho' herself both lowly born
and lowly bred. Foiled in her attempt to make my Son break
with his parents she turned round and left him, telling him she
had laid her plans and was too clever to be defeated by him—
With the artfulness and falsehood inherent in her Character she
told the World that those men whom she had forced on my
Son destroying his domestic Quiet, were brought by him and
left with her for improper ends, the latest and most preposterous
falsehood ever invented by the most abandoned woman, and
Millais whom my Son with the purest motive and single eye
to his Improvement in art, asked to join his Circle, among
rocks and Waters which he wished him to study, was one of
those whom she proclaimed to be among the persons brought
improperly about her—In Scotland Mr Millais' Conduct was
most improper when he left his work to follow my Son and Wife
to Edinburgh—My Tone to Mr Millais may have seemed harsh
for I did feel that he of all men should not have so readily
ranked himself on the side of my Sons enemies and slanderers.
I however speak for myself not for my Son. He has taken his
part rightly or wrongly and scorns to propitiate those who give
credit to any reports against him. He will neither say nor write
a word in his own defence. I like the position matters are now in,
my Son's admiration of the Talents—his praise of the artistic
Labours of the preRaphaelites will bate no jot of their fervour
or Intensity but it is clear to me that Mr Millais is not the man
to understand or appreciate the Graduate and all personal
Intercourse should at once terminate now and forever.[7]

Hall Caine had a story, which he claimed to have got from
Rossetti, that Ruskin's father, in his rage against Millais, threatened
to put a penknife through the Glenfinlas portrait and that Ruskin
smuggled it out of the house and took it to Rossetti's studio for safe-
keeping.[8] This dramatic story has often been repeated but never
corroborated. Hall Caine was born in the year the picture was
finished and did not meet Rossetti until 1880. Mr Ruskin was
certainly not the man to destroy his own property, especially a

picture which had cost him £350 and which he believed to be painted by a genius.

Moreover there are two other stories which contradict Hall Caine's—the first that on the day Millais married Effie (July 3, 1855) the portrait was seen by a visitor to Denmark Hill hanging over the dining-room fireplace,[9] and the second that in 1857 it was hanging in Ruskin's bedroom at Denmark Hill.[10]

After Mrs Ruskin's death in 1871, when Denmark Hill was sold and Ruskin moved to Brantwood, he gave the picture to Dr (afterwards Sir Henry) Acland, who must have had a special interest in it seeing that he was present when it was begun. It remained a treasured heirloom in the Acland family until 1965 when it was sold at Christie's by Sir Henry's grandson on July 16. It was bought by Mrs Patrick Gibson for 24,000 guineas, the under-bidder being the Tate Gallery.

# REUNION AT BOWERSWELL

❊

The time was drawing near when Effie and Millais were to meet again. Lady Eastlake had been to Venice in the autumn of 1854 and had brought back for Effie a present of a seal from Rawdon Brown and was waiting for someone to take it to Perth. Effie wrote to Brown on January 5, 1855: 'Your seal has not yet arrived! Your hint about the initials was not lost on me. *Really* I see you *will not* be pleased till you get me married, as you told me—but why all this hurry? . . . why grudge me my happy security and quiet Life now?'

Brown's *Giustinian* had at last been published in December, and in this same letter Effie wished him 'everything good and happy and much success and comfort in the introduction into public life of my "God Child" as you graciously term the pretty Book which I have now examined with care'. She went on to tell him that she was riding, taking cold dips, teaching the children and decorating and furnishing the large drawing-room at Bowerswell which had been left empty since the completion of the new house in 1847.

But soon the happy family at Bowerswell were stricken with influenza. They all went down with it except Effie herself who nursed the entire household for a month. Mrs Gray also had erysipelas all over her face and head, and her condition caused grave anxiety, especially as she was soon to have what Effie called 'an addition to her flock'.

At last, however, on February 12, Effie was writing to Rawdon Brown, 'I am expecting your long unacknowledged seal this week by the hand of Millais. Lady E said she would keep it until someone would bring it and as she *alone* knew that I had permitted him to come here for two days this week, she said she would give it to him. I have not seen Mr Millais for more than a year, and I shall tell you in my next letter about his visit, in the meantime you will say nothing about it.'

This long awaited meeting was a dreadful anti-climax, as perhaps it was bound to be. It was not until March 21 that Effie wrote to Brown about it and even then, before mentioning Millais, she informed him that her mother had had 'a little Boy the night before last and by means of that wonderful agent Chloroform she was spared all sense of suffering for two hours'.* She then went on about other matters and it was not until nearly the end of her long letter that she told him the only thing he must have wanted to know: 'Well, Millais came in the middle of the snow, bringing in his hand your seal *which is lovely* . . . This visit was only two days long, very anxious and distressing in many ways. The cold was intense—Mr Millais was very ill—so did I become, and I have coughed ever since and the Doctor will not let me out until the fine weather comes. This must not alarm you for I am very happy and well indoors, but we thought better to tell Millais to come back in May when his Picture which he is doing for this Year is gone in—and he might come and stay with us, when we could settle things for the future, as really with the cold hand of past sufferings opened by remembrance and Mama's illness not over it was better just to let the visit go by unnoticed. He could not stay longer and now he is better. Sir Charles and Lady Eastlake pet him next to me I think.'

This, of course, was Millais's very first visit to Bowerswell. How different their meeting might have been if Effie had allowed him to go the previous July, directly after the annulment as he had wanted to do.

He had postponed finishing his other pictures, and it was *The Rescue* which he exhibited at the 1855 Academy— a fireman rescuing two children from a burning house at night and delivering them into the arms of their distraught mother—a subject inspired by an actual fire he had seen when returning from a dance with his brother William. It was not finished until nearly midnight on the last day for sending in, and Charles Collins sat up with him painting the firehose. On varnishing day he had a terrible row with three members

---

* This child, called Everett after Millais, was Mrs Gray's fifteenth and her last, born two days after her forty-seventh birthday. (Seven of her children had died young.) He was christened in the drawing-room at Bowerswell on the same day that Effie and Millais were married. He became a partner in the stockbroking firm of Vivian, Gray & Co., and died in 1891.

of the hanging committee who had skied it. He threatened to resign until it was lowered three inches and tilted forward.[1]

The Private View was on Monday, May 1, and Millais may well have been apprehensive lest Ruskin, because of the breach between them, should condemn or ignore this picture which he himself believed to be his best work to date—painted in a heat of enthusiasm almost as great as the fire itself. But no personal considerations affected Ruskin's artistic judgement. In his *Academy Notes* (a kind of printed circular letter begun for the first time that year) he wrote of *The Rescue*, 'It is the only *great* picture exhibited this year; but this is *very* great.'*

A little sidelight on the Ruskins' attitude to Millais at this time is given in a letter from Mrs Ruskin to her husband written after reading an account of the pictures in that year's Academy, including Millais's *Rescue*: 'The papers very interesting today. Millais deserves punishment but I shall be glad if John thinks so far well of it as to be able to say something in its favour if asked his opinion about it.'[2]

(The next year Millais exhibited six pictures at the Academy, including *The Blind Girl* and *The Random Shot*. Ruskin did not mention these in his *Notes*, but two of the others—*Peace Concluded* and *Autumn Leaves*—he praised extravagantly, saying, 'they will rank in future among the world's best master-pieces; and I see no limit to what the painter may in future achieve', and, 'Titian himself could hardly head him now'. When, therefore, in his *Notes* the following year he condemned with almost equal vigour one of Millais's three exhibits of 1857— *Sir Isumbras at the Ford* (called by Ruskin *A Dream of the Past*)—Millais knew there could be nothing personal in the criticism and he took it very much to heart.)

Millais wanted to return to Bowerswell before May, but Mrs Gray, a week after her confinement, had the worst illness of her life, 'a kind of cholera', and the household was in great distress. Effie wrote to Rawdon Brown on April 16 that she would not like Millais to come until she could attend to him.

* In the same *Notes* he was fairly rude about Sir Charles Eastlake's *Beatrice*, an insult which Lady Eastlake sought to avenge in an unsigned review (for the *Quarterly* of March, 1856) of the first three volumes of *Modern Painters* and the first number of *Academy Notes*. The review, which is forty-eight pages long, begins by abusing his writing and ends with an attack on his moral character. Lady Eastlake died in 1893, aged almost eighty-five, having been a widow for twenty-eight years.

In another month's time, all was settled between them, and on May 22 Effie was again writing to Brown (now in London on account of his mother's death) to thank him for sending her a present of money. 'I shall buy my *marriage dress* with this and as it was to be covered with Venetian Lace at any rate, you can think how pleased I shall be to wear it as from you . . . I hope I shall be happy. I have the greatest reason to be thankful about everything connected with the future as far as I can see. Only think how pleased my parents are that the very next place to this, belonging to our oldest friends, being let most unexpectedly as they have to go abroad with, I fear, a dying Daughter, last week Millais immediately wrote to me to take it for a year as he also wishes to live in the Country for his health and quietness* . . . I regret much you have not seen Millais again. I should like you to know him better but it takes long to know anybody well. I suppose we shall be married about the first week in July. He comes down here after next week. The marriage will be very quiet. I do not wish anybody but my immediate relations and his if they like to come. Neither of us are the strong of the earth. Sometimes I am dreadfully nervous. He is worse, but I think this is temporary with us both.'[3]

On this same day, May 22, Millais was writing to Hunt with even greater apprehension: 'Next month please God I shall be a *married man* . . . I am going to be married so quietly that none of my family come to the wedding—Good gracious, fancy me married my old boy, I feel *desperately melancholy* about it which is rather different to most bridegrooms, but callous to all results as it is quite impossible to foresee the end of anything we undertake . . . I take this fearful risk in desperation, I hate wasting my life, and fretting away in *Bachelorism*, and cannot myself change for worse (I may it is true make this girl wretched and so increase my state) but it is worth the risk and you must pray for me my dear old friend . . . She dislikes naturally coming to London after her life in it, and I much fear it will never cease to live in her memory, and will always affect her spirits, but time will show. I have so little faith in my own ability to blot out this ruin in her life that I am often very desponding in the

* This house was Annat Lodge. The owner was George Payne Rainsford James (1799–1860), a writer of historical romances. In 1858 he became Consul-General in Venice where he died. The Millais's took the house and lived there for the first two years of their married life.

matter, but I cannot see how this marriage could have been otherwise, everything seems to have happened to work out this end.'[4]

Was the marriage a little too inevitable? Many people must have felt, as did Ruskin himself, that Millais was merely doing the chivalrous thing. Ruskin had been ill and had gone to Tunbridge Wells to recuperate. From there he wrote to Furnivall on June 3 a letter which shows that his bitterness against Effie was every bit as great as hers against him:

It is a week since I received your interesting letter—in a dull place like this the time slips by like oil—and I find myself as much in arrear as in busy London—I had not much however to say in reply. I could do nothing—you could do no more, now—although it may perhaps be well that I should mention to you my surprise throughout this matter, at your treating it with Millais as a jest—or at least—a thing to be jested upon. Ordinary love—if true, admits not such treatment—Love which has passed the limits of conscience and ['reas' crossed out] prudence —still less—and even if any conceivable good could have been effected by light language—I cannot understand how you could bring yourself to use it, of an act which involved so solemn a sealing of fate—for good or evil—of such a mind as his; (wholly irrespective of any results to others). I am not able to calculate the probabilities on either side. I do not say that Millais does wrong *now*—whatever wrong he may *have* done. I am not sure but that this may indeed have been the only course open to him; that, feeling he had been the Temptation to the woman, and the cause of her giving up all her worldly prospects,* he may from the moment of our separation—have felt like something of a principle of honour enforcing his inclination to become her protector. What the result may be, to him I cannot

---

* Effie's worldly prospects did indeed look bleak at this time. The capital settled on her by Ruskin had been returned to him at the annulment; she had not a penny of her own and her father was not in a position to give her an allowance. They would be entirely dependent on Millais's earnings which at this time were very variable and uncertain. In the past few years he had helped to defray some of the expenses at Gower Street, so when his parents decided to give up the house and move to Kingston, they probably knew already of his plans to marry Effie, and that he would need all he could earn for his own household.

conjecture;—I only know that if there is anything like visible retribution in the affairs of this life there are assuredly, dark hours in the distance, for her to whom he has chosen to bind his life.[5]

# EFFIE MILLAIS AT LAST

❊

Millais arrived at Bowerswell on June 9, more than three weeks before the wedding. His brother William came on the 25th, the only one of his family or friends to be with him on the occasion.* Two short letters from Millais to Charles Collins take us up to the wedding day itself:

Tuesday forenoon [June 19, 1855]

We are going out for a ride. There is a visitor here and Mrs Gray and the Countess are in Conversation, and I betake myself for employment to writing to you. Yesterday was the Parents' anniversary marriage day, and people were dining here, and playing bowls in the evening.† This morning we went to see the house we have taken—such a *sweet place*, truly comfortable, and pretty, as you will see. It was very strange and delightful going over the house and the servants peering at us to see their future master, and mistress. This day fortnight is *thee* day . . . I long to get back and settled in this nice place . . . We have *often* beau ideal rides such as P.R. James [the owner of Annat Lodge] would delight in, as it would satisfy his mind that his stories are not altogether exaggerated. The Countess

---

* William Millais himself married twice—in 1860 Judith Boothby by whom he had a daughter, and, after her death in childbirth two years later, Adelaide Fraser by whom he had a son and two daughters, one of whom, Mrs Mary Earle, is still alive.

† The Grays had been married on June 18, 1827. The bowling green at Bowerswell can still be identified. The house is now a home for old people. Until the end of the last war it was still owned by the Grays. Effie's brother, Melville, lived there until his death in 1946 at the age of ninety-eight. Mr Gray died in 1877, aged seventy-nine, and Mrs Gray in 1894, aged eighty-six.

looks so beautiful in her riding habit, and the horse she rides is so *perfect* that it is quite wonderful to see her. I wish you were here, old fellow, as it is really nice and I am not so greedy but what I would willingly give you a share of the pleasure—I think I am pretty friendly with them all. Last night I won *seventeen* shillings at whist, with Mr Gray, who in consequence is very happy. This is the kind of thing and *very like her* although a few

lines. She is without the least exaggeration *5ft—6 inch. I have measured.* Write to me again *soon. I am getting resigned to my fate,* but have lost my voice with a bad cold.* My love.

*Tuesday morning* [July 3]
Here is *the* day at last. I find myself positively *not* in the least nervous, and very happy. I don't see the Countess until 2 when we are to be married . . . Well, last night I slept well and awoke

* Ruskin too caught a bad cold when he went to Bowerswell to stay before his marriage in April, 1848.

refreshed this morning, not so with the Countess who had no sleep, and I believe [is] rather headachy this morning. Everything is prepared, and there is no mistake about it. The room we are to be married in is full of beautiful flowers, and it does not want *four hours* to put me into another state of life—God knows but I trust a better one. There must be I suppose a great deal of vagueness in taking this step. I am completely in the dark, and uncertain about the probable close of the matter but all seem very happy.

A brougham is to be here at 3 and away we go by train to Glasgow, and down the Clyde. Fancy I have just been writing Mrs Millais on some directions. I confess I wish all this part was over. I am throwing myself blindly to the waves, without being able to realize *in the least*. It happens to be a most lovely day which is a *great* blessing, but I feel feverish, and slightly out of sorts, an exaggerated sensation of going to an Evening party at fifteen years of age. How strange it is. I am only hopeful it may be the right course I have taken which can only be known from experience. I cannot promise to write again for some little time. I know I have all your prayers which is not a little comfort to me. This is a trial without doubt as it either proves a blessing or a curse to two poor bodies only anxious to do their best . . . There are some startling accompaniments, my boy, like the glimpse of the dentists instruments—My poor brain and soul is fatigued with dwelling on unpleasant probabilities so I am aroused for the fight.[1]

Effie spent the morning quietly in her room. 'I saw from my window the young men playing at Bowls,' she wrote afterwards in her diary, 'whilst I sat reading and thinking of my past Life and my Life with Everett that was to come. Jeanie [the old nurse] came in and told me that the Bridegroom looked so merry and pleasant it put one in good spirits to see him. I felt the same. Indeed I said to myself this is no time for anything but happiness and comfort while I look back and see what wonderful things have happened to myself, my family and Everett, how much cause I have to bless God for this day . . . Mr Anderson [the Minister of Kinnoull] having arrived . . . Papa came to take me down and said, "Come away, my dear Lassie, this time I feel happy in putting you into good hands." My bridesmaids, very youthful ones dressed in white, were standing at my door waiting to follow us downstairs, Eliza Jameson and my two little sisters.* In the Dining room was William Millais, Mr Anderson, Everett and myself with Papa to sign the Contract. I did so at several places. I felt very happy. The last time I had signed any paper or Document was a little more than a year before when in Doctors Common I was sitting in a Lawyer's room and signed my signature Euphemia Chalmers Gray . . . to get free of a hateful and loathesome Contract . . . I now bound myself by the same signature for Life to another with every feeling of confidence and happiness. Everett was more agitated. He said afterwards he felt very much inclined to throw down the pen and ask what play he was performing in and refuse to sign. I have no doubt to us both it seemed very like this, but so much to me has gone before like a play that I looked on this as the 3rd Act happily concluding and leaving the spectators and the Actors equally pleased by a conclusion which finished off in the most approved style of the Romance or Drama. Neither Everett nor myself having the formal manners of the Grandisonian period made any public demonstration on the occasion of meeting for the first time that day. On the contrary I think a looker on might have fancied we were very indifferent to each other . . . The Drawing-room† was beautifully arranged with natural flowers on stands . . . I had some exquisite roses in my hair . . . We particularly wished the marriage to be a quiet one . . . but when my cousins, all the Servants and the children were assembled the party looked quite a large one. Mr Anderson gave us a short but suitable address. When he told us to join hands I pressed Everett's very tightly and felt very happy. I wished to assure myself that I really was being married and being bound for Life to a man in whom I was to place the Love of all my future Life. I did so most unreservedly as my conscience and heart both told me undeniably. When we went away I did not feel any sorrow . . . We got through the town.‡ The Curtains [of the brougham] were down. Everett said it was like a dream. He got very agitated and when the Railway had started the excitement had been so much for him that instead of the usual comfort I suppose that the

* These three had also been her bridesmaids when she married Ruskin.
† The large drawing-room which Effie had recently furnished. She had been married to Ruskin in the small drawing-room.
‡ They had to cross the River Tay before they reached the town.

Brides require on those occasions of leaving, I had to give him all my sympathy. He cried dreadfully, said he did not know how he had got through it, felt wretched; it had added ten years to his Life, and instead of being happy and cheerful, he seemed in despair. I bathed his face with Eau de Cologne, held his head and opened one of the windows and he soon began to get better. We were approaching Glasgow ... We were very anxious not to be thought like new married people. I put off my white shawl, put on dark gloves, my grey plaid and black veil, and so habited we reached the Queen's Hotel.'²

That evening they went down the Clyde to Rothesay where they spent the night in a very uncomfortable hotel but the next day they crossed over to Brodick on the Isle of Arran.

Millais's dread of the honeymoon was very understandable, for he, like Ruskin, was almost certainly a virgin, and the thought of Ruskin's failure must have increased his own nervousness a thousand-fold. All seems to have gone well, however, as soon as they got to Brodick where they remained for fifteen happy days in glorious weather. Afterwards they went up to Inverness, and from Inveraray on the way there, Effie wrote home with greater warmth than she had ever shown: 'Everett is so happy and well .... I am so happy with him. You can imagine how much I appreciate his natural character. I really think if it was not rather wicked to say so that I would almost go through much misery—I was going to say all I had suffered—rather than miss being with him a day.'

Millais sounded no less happy. On July 29 he told Mrs Collins that they were both different creatures already and that he was so proud of such a wife—everybody looked at her and paid her such attention; and to Mr Gray he wrote on August 2, 'My dear Father, I look forward with some pride, I can tell you, to the day that I bring back to Perth your altered girl. She has such rosy cheeks and has become so jolly you will find her a different looking woman.'

Only once was Ruskin mentioned in their letters—by Effie, writing on August 4 on their way home: 'Drove on to the Tummel Bridge, the very road I went with "The Party" as Everett calls him—the day after the 10th of April 1848. You may imagine I remember it very distinctly. Such an extraordinary change did not produce great grief either in Everett's mind or my own. We were both particularly happy and were both as gay as could be.'

At the end of their honeymoon they went for two days to St Andrews where the Grays were enjoying their usual annual holiday and where they were all photographed in the family group reproduced on p. 227. Effie afterwards wrote in her diary: 'We did not get very settled for some time. First we went to St Andrews to see the family who were all strengthening themselves with golf, sea bathing and fresh fish.'

Effie and Millais returned to Perth to take up residence at Annat Lodge and there on May 30 of the following year the first of their eight children (four girls and four boys) was born. Millais dashed off a note to Hunt: 'Just a line to say that another PRB has just come into the world. My wife was taken ill last night and is now the mother of a fine little boy.* She got through it better than anyone could have expected.'

One wishes one could ring down the curtain on them at this point 'in the most approved style of the Romance or Drama' with the assurance that they lived happily ever after. Alas, it was not so.

Millais's fears that he would not be able to 'blot out the ruin' in Effie's life were to some extent justified. She imposed on her family an absolute ban of silence with regard to her first marriage,[3] yet the wound underneath would not heal. Perhaps the chief cause of this was that she never fully recovered her health. Nine years after her second marriage she was complaining to her father that she was worn out and could not sleep at all without chloroform pills provided by Dr Simpson; and in October, 1870, she wrote to Mrs La Touche that she 'had nearly died of all those years of distress and suffering' with Ruskin which 'still hurt' her 'dreadfully' and that her 'nervous system was so shaken' that she would 'never recover again'.[4] Acute insomnia was to plague her for the rest of her life. Eight confinements and one really bad miscarriage in the course of thirteen years did not help her to regain her strength. As she lay awake in 'the dark hours' she no doubt brooded over the past. Hatred as much as love can bind one to another.

---

* Called Everett (known as Evie in the family). He married in 1886 Mary Hope-Vere and died in 1897, leaving one son who died unmarried. He was an authority on scientific dog-breeding and introduced the Basset hound into England.

Unfortunately Millais's own forgiving attitude towards Ruskin, as evinced in his letter to Mrs Gray of July 27, 1854, changed after his marriage to an antagonism as great as Effie's own. 'I can scarcely trust myself to speak of Ruskin,' he wrote to Hunt in the first year of his marriage, 'who certainly appears to me (now that I know *all* about his treatment of my wife) to be the most wicked man I have known in my life. This I say *without hesitation* and methodically.'

Effie suffered also a certain amount of social ostracism as the result of the scandal over the annulment. It is true that all her old friends, with the exception of Lady Trevelyan, remained staunch to her, and that she made many new ones, even among royalty—the Tecks, for instance, and the Lornes—and later on the Prince and Princess of Wales came regularly every year to Millais's studio to see his pictures;* nevertheless, the fact that Queen Victoria would not receive her meant that the more conventional among the aristocracy followed the Queen's example, and when the time came for Effie's four pretty daughters to come out, it was very often their father who had to take them to parties because their mother had not been invited.† This would have hurt Effie deeply and perhaps partly accounted for the fact that her relationship with her daughters was not a very happy nor a very close one. She idolised her eldest son‡ who did not turn out very well; her second son died at the age of

* In 1871, the first time that the Prince and Princess of Wales visited the studio, Millais, probably out of shyness, told Effie to keep out of the way. She went out and afterwards he was furious with her for doing so as the Princess had asked to meet her. The two eldest girls were presented instead. (Letter from Effie to her mother. Morgan.)

† It seems it was not only Effie whom the Queen blamed. In spite of the fact that she sent Princess Louise to ask Millais on his death-bed whether there was anything she could do for him, she refused to have her portrait painted by him because she understood that 'he had seduced his future wife while painting her'. (*Victoria, R.I.* by Elizabeth Longford, p. 419. Weidenfeld and Nicolson, 1964.)

‡ In 1871, when 'Evie' was sixteen, Effie took him alone with her on a sight-seeing jaunt to Germany and Paris. In Paris, staying at the Grand Hotel, he caught smallpox very badly and nearly died. The manager wanted to turn them out; no one would come near them; their food was left outside the door. Effie nursed him entirely herself as she could not get a nurse. Effie's letters to Millais during this harassing time have been preserved in the Bowerswell Papers and show her at her very best—courageous, resourceful, devoted, and most unselfish, urging him not to come as he could do no good and would only run into the danger of infection himself.

nineteen (a terrible grief for her and for Millais) and, feeling that she had over-indulged the eldest boy, she became over-strict with the two youngest. Her daughters, who all adored their father, as did the boys also, found her something of a martinet. Although a woman of great feeling and with a great power of endearing herself when she wished to, she was undemonstrative by nature and had a cold manner. As she grew older she became, outwardly at least, sterner, and her reserve was taken for lack of feeling. The comparatively few letters of hers to Millais to have survived in the Bowerswell Papers, written over the course of many years, might easily have been written to her father or her brother, and the handful of Millais's to her are no warmer. This does not, of course, prove any lack of devotion on either side. Effusiveness in letters, as in personal contact, is a very individual thing. Restraint in letter-writing, though, was certainly not a characteristic of the Victorian age.

In the first few years of their married life they were continually worried about money. Millais, with a rapidly increasing family to support, was obliged to work too hard and too quickly, and although his work was selling, prices were influenced by the critics who continued to tear him to pieces. At this time he did many book and magazine illustrations to help augment his income. Effie helped him in every way in her power when she was not feeling too ill— taking over all his correspondence, keeping strangers away from him, finding models for him,* sitting to him herself for hours in uncomfortable poses,† making the costumes for his historical pictures and playing the piano to him in the evenings to soothe him after a hard day's work. She was a very accomplished pianist and he had always loved music.

* Millais wrote to Hunt in the first year of his marriage: 'Effie . . . is the best Jackall for her Lion husband (I hope this doesn't appear conceited) in the procuring of models you can conceive, going into strange habitations and seizing adults and children without explanation and dragging them here, and sending them back to their homes with a *sixpence* when I should have been doubtful between a sovereign and thirty shillings.'

† Effie herself had first sat as the model for the blind girl in Millais's picture of that name exhibited at the Academy in 1856. 'It was dreadful suffering,' she wrote. 'The sun poured in through the window of the study. I had a cloth over my forehead and this was a little relief but several times I was as sick as possible, and nearly agued in [the] other two days I sat in the open air, and when the face was done Everett was not pleased with it and later in the year scratched it out entirely.' (Effie's diary, 1856.)

By 1863, when he became a Royal Academician, the tide had turned, and his success, financial as well as artistic, was assured. The year before he had taken a house in London, 7 Cromwell Place, after several furnished lodgings, and there he and his family lived for the next sixteen years. Effie, not unnaturally, wanted security for him rather than fame, and when Sir Charles Eastlake died in 1865 she pressed Millais to put himself forward as a candidate for the Directorship of the National Gallery.* Fortunately for his career as a painter he would not even consider doing this, much to Effie's annoyance.

There were temperamental differences between them too which most clearly showed themselves when, in the autumn of 1865, they travelled abroad together for the first time to Paris, Venice and Florence.† Effie's delight at being in Italy again was intense and she wrote to her sister Sophie on October 24 from the Europa Hotel, Venice, where they had arrived the evening before: 'If George is able to bring you abroad, or if you and Alice ever marry people who will bring you, I do hope you may enjoy all these wonderful places as they deserve. If with Everett it would be impossible for you to do so or not to be immensely influenced by his perpetual fault finding at everything and his petted temper. He is so bad a sight seer at home that you may perhaps a little imagine what he is here. I am extremely thankful that neither you nor Alice are with us for you would not be allowed to admire anything in a natural way.'‡

What a contrast in behaviour between Ruskin and Millais in Venice, yet one cannot help sympathising with Millais when he wrote to Mrs Gray in the train on the way to Florence that he had been badly bitten by mosquitoes in Venice whatever Effie said to the contrary, that it wasn't enough for him to praise anything *once*, and that there had been 'too much Mr Brown'.

If he was bored by Effie's sight-seeing, Effie might very well have been bored by his obsession with sport, for if originally he took up

* Eastlake had become Director of the National Gallery in 1855. He was succeeded by William Boxall.

† Millais had not been abroad since the age of eight when his family had returned to Jersey after living for two years at Dinan.

‡ Sophie (now twenty-one and soon to suffer her breakdown) may be forgiven for thinking when she read this that Effie's heart would not be broken if Millais became too fond of his sister-in-law or of anyone else.

salmon fishing, stalking and grouse shooting as some compensation for having to spend so much time in Effie's beloved Scotland, they rapidly became an addiction, and as soon as he could afford to do so he hurried through his work in order to spend two solid months in some hired shooting-lodge with a few sporting cronies while Effie for most of that time was at Bowerswell or St Andrews with the children.

Did his work suffer from these long holidays or was he, in the course of indulging in his passion, able to further his career as a portrait painter by making contacts with influential people? He has been accused of debasing his later work to suit the requirements of public taste and Effie has often been blamed for this.* According to Holman Hunt, however, it was Millais's own contention at the height of his success that a painter 'should hold up the mirror to his own times' and that the only way to be sure of doing so was to find 'people willing to give him money for his productions' and 'win honours from contemporaries'. 'What good would my labours hundreds of years hence do to me?' Millais is reported to have said to Hunt. 'I should be dead, buried, crumbled to dust. Don't let us bother ourselves about the destinies of our work in the world, but as it may bring us fortune and recognition.'⁵

Fortune and recognition certainly came to him. (He was earning more than £25,000 a year at the end.) In 1879 he moved from Cromwell Place to 2 Palace Gate, opposite Kensington Gardens, a neo-renaissance mansion designed by Philip Hardwick† to his specifications, with marble hall and marble staircase and forty-foot studio on the first floor. (How Ruskin would have hated it.) In 1885 he was created a baronet, and a month after Lord Leighton's death in January, 1896, he was elected President of the Royal Academy. But already he was a dying man and he knew it. In the autumn of 1892 he had noticed a swelling in his throat and a huskiness which

* It has been cynically said that if Ruskin had remained married to Effie he would have ended up by writing *Bubbles*. Incidentally, the idea that Millais painted *Bubbles* for commercial purposes is a most unjust one. It was sold with its copyright to the *Illustrated London News* whose proprietors then sold it to the producers of Pears Soap. No one was more furious than Millais when he discovered the use that was to be made of it, but having parted with the copyright, he was unable to prevent it. (Millais, Vol. II, p. 189.)

† Philip Charles Hardwick (1822–92), son of the better known architect who designed Euston Station.

steadily increased. It was cancer of the throat. He showed great courage throughout his long illness and died peacefully, with Effie beside him, on August 13, 1896, aged sixty-seven, and was buried in the crypt of St Paul's Cathedral next to Turner. On the day of his death Beatrix Potter, who was then thirty, wrote of him in her secret journal: 'I saw him last in November, walking in Knightsbridge, "how is my little friend? can't speak, can't speak!" He looked as handsome and well as ever, he was one of the handsomest men I ever saw ... He gave me the kindest encouragement with my drawings (to be sure he did to everybody!) . . . He was an honest fine man.'[6]

There is some slight evidence that at the end Millais forgave Ruskin,* but they never met again after that final sitting for the Glenfinlas portrait. Ruskin never lost interest in Millais or concern for him, and continued publicly to praise his work whenever he considered praise was justified.

Effie survived her husband by only sixteen months. Her eyesight was very bad for the last few years of her life and she could not see to read. In 1893 she had undergone an operation on her eyes which did no good, but a passage in Beatrix Potter's journal, written on the day Millais was elected President of the Royal Academy, February 25, 1896, shows her with unimpaired vitality: 'Met Lady Millais in Gloucester Road. She was being bullied by a lady in a velvet mantle, so I merely insinuated the remark that she must be receiving more congratulations than she could attend to, whereupon she seized my arm to cross the street, expressing a wish to die together, there being a procession of female bicycles. I thought it a characteristic mixture of graciousness and astute utility, she walking with a black crutch-stick, but most amusingly elated.'[7]

She still had much to go through—Millais's tragic death, and then, a little more than a year later, the sudden death of her favourite eldest son from pneumonia. She herself died at Bowerswell on December 23, 1897, in her seventieth year, and is buried in the old graveyard of Kinnoull on the banks of the Tay, as peaceful and lovely a spot as where Ruskin lies in the churchyard at Coniston.

* Valentine Prinsep, R.A., wrote in his reminiscences of Millais that Millais had once told him during his last illness, 'I have no enemies, there's no man with whom I will not shake hands—except one, and, by Jove, I should like to shake him by the hand now.' (Millais, Vol. II, p. 393.)

# APPENDIX

❀

## Letters from Mr and Mrs Ruskin to Effie during her Engagement

London 21 Nov<sup>r</sup> 1847

My dear Effie

I do not write letters generally on a Sunday but I think I cannot do better than perform an omitted duty in writing a few lines to you on such a day. I have not had the pleasure of addressing you since my son has obtained your consent to a Union, on which I feel very sincerely convinced (take place when it may) I shall have good reason to congratulate both myself and him—I have never yet seen the young Lady nor should I know where to go in search of one more likely in my mind to make my Son entirely happy or as reasonably so, as a Wise man ought in this world to expect—I only trust he may prove as well adapted for you as you seem to be for him—you have both fine qualities and good talents and your tastes and dispositions are sufficiently alike, differing only enough to make an agreeable variety, to prevent the monotony perhaps Insipidity of entire agreement.

Mrs Ruskin had various opportunities of sending pretty messages—by your late intimation, I have been somewhat remiss—but you have been no less in my thoughts—and my Son and his Mother both knew that my silence might be taken as entire acquiescence in plans so promising of happiness to my Son.

From all you saw, or might guess at here, you may fancy that my opinions have not been always what I now express and that my approval comes late—but dearest Effie—my objections were never to *one* but to *two*—I cannot perhaps correctly say two—my son never had two Loves but he certainly during your visit to London had fully one and a half and I was kept extremely uncomfortable with a double source of anxiety—my son's happiness and Honour—*

The young Lady that caused my uneasiness had, happily penetration enough to see that my Son only offered her half a heart and another Swain having fortunately brought her an entire one, the affair terminated *en regle* and agreeable to all parties—Whatever encouragement Circumstances led me to give my Son in his other pursuit, I can truly say that I am much more satisfied now that his success has been at Perth—I never saw the young Lady in question, I cannot therefore say I admired her—now I am only restrained from declaring myself your most devoted admirer by knowing that you have much more of this stile [*sic*] of Phraseology than you care for and that my son's letters may at present be suspected to run a good deal in the same strain—

It is very pleasant for all parties that there are as far as yet discovered, no dissentions to this union, a point of some importance to the chief actors for it is lamentable to witness how often the happiness of the young is interrupted or marred by the contentions among their elders, always ready on occasions matrimonial, to come forth with bundles of objections, misunderstandings, whims and eccentricities, so that in a party of perhaps forty the only contents are the two carried off in the post Chaise—I earnestly hope that you will neither be visited by trouble nor by regret after the Ceremony, I cannot express a higher opinion of your merits and Character than by at once most readily entrusting my Son's future happiness in your Keeping—I humbly trust that the union will have not only the approval of friends on Earth but of Heaven and that under the happiest and holiest Influences you will both long live to enjoy each other's Society so living as to lay the foundation of a happiness that may be eternal.

Give my kindest regards to your Mama and Papa George

* At the time Effie was staying at Denmark Hill in the spring of 1847, John had proposed to Charlotte Lockhart and had not, as far as Mr Ruskin knew, been refused by her. Charlotte married James Hope in August, 1847. Lady Eastlake wrote to Effie about this passage in Mr Ruskin's letter, 'the "loves of my son" are horrid and monstrous now to think of'. (Letter of May 9, 1854.)

&c. Accept of the same yourself—in all which Mrs Ruskin joins me.

I am My dear Effie Yours very affectionately
John James Ruskin

4 Denmark Hill Dec$^r$ 11th
1847

My dear Effie

You have so much to write and read that I shall make this as short as I can which will serve the double purpose of saving your eyes and mine promising that you must not infer from it any shortcoming in all a true mother's feelings towards you— Many thanks my love for your letters—The note John spoke of sending to Mrs Gray was one intended to be written by me regarding your going abroad with us before your marriage and to thank her for her very kind and considerate letter while John was with you. I desired John to do the latter stating how much I was obliged and felt the kindness, and as former was set at rest by your papa's decision I thought it unnecessary to enter into the subject farther—indeed my Love I should have been truly glad had John brought you his Wife home with him—but for some reason which I do not write about, but your Mama will understand—these same reasons operate against your marrying till you are upon the point of setting off on your travels—were it not so I should not have waited till April before having you with us—if John could have by any persuasions have prevailed on your parents to have parted with you sooner. I should be sorry indeed if you could leave your home and so many dear and near relations without some grief, but it is not like going to India, you can so frequently see them and then you will be very differently situated from most who marry—John being our only son you will be to his parents as his wife a treasure invaluable and I feel certain it will be the strongest desire and delight of both Mr Ruskin and myself to promote your happiness and guard you from all that might injure or annoy you—We have so few relations to love or care for that you will come in for a tenfold share of both—all day long in whatever I have to do about the house I do nothing without some thought and reference to you—you know my love all we have will be yours and John's and I am continually thinking of what may most insure your pleasure and comfort. You know we intend you shall have your own special apartments here—that you may come to when you choose and remain as long as you like—but I do not mean to make any alteration till we can plan things together. I wish we were nearer love, you know not how I long to see and hear you again—It gave me much comfort to know your Mama was better. I trust nothing will retard her recovery.* My best regards to her and most earnest wishes that she may long enjoy health and see her children's children promising and happy as her own—a better name than Melville cannot be, both for sounds and profit, from all acounts from all parties of Uncle Melville if as it is said children take after their name-fathers. My kind regards to your papa, George and the little ones—I hope you keep well and all your charges better or well, you must be very happy just now being so employed in making others so—your letter which came today was sent to Folkestone—I hope John may be home in a day or two—but his father and I have rather denied ourselves the pleasure of having him at home the Influenza being so prevelant and in many cases so fatal here—but you will know of all his movements. Mr Ruskin has sent in three very nice Annuals which I shall put by carefully for your Drawing Room Table. Can I do anything for you in London—I have desired John several times to ask if your papa paid for trifles sent by Steamer—I much fear I shall not get flowers as I used from poor Keel, but I shall try if you let me know at any time that you wish for some—God bless you My Dear child

> Prays always
> Yours most sincerely
> Margaret Ruskin

* On November 30 Mrs Gray had given birth to a son, Melville, who lived to be ninety-eight, and married for the first time when he was ninety-one. He died at Bowerswell and is well remembered there today.

# SOURCE NOTES

❀

Unless otherwise stated, all the letters which are quoted in the text are now in the Bowerswell Papers, Pierpont Morgan Library, New York. Exceptions are John Ruskin's letters to his father which are in Yale University Library and those from Millais to Holman Hunt which are in the collection of Mrs Elizabeth Burt. All are hitherto unpublished, except where so indicated in the following notes.

The following abbreviations are used:

*Bembridge*: Educational Trust Ltd, Ruskin Galleries, Bembridge School, Isle of Wight.

*Hunt*: *Pre-Raphaelitism and the Pre-Raphaelite Brotherhood*, by W. H. Hunt (Macmillan, 1905).

*Huntington*: Huntington Library, San Martino, California. (The passages quoted appeared in the *Huntington Library Quarterly*, November 1956, in an article by Frank Fogle on Ruskin and Millais.)

*James*: *The Order of Release* by Admiral Sir William James, G.C.B. (John Murray, 1947).

*Leon*: *Ruskin the Great Victorian* by Derrick Leon (Routledge & Kegan Paul, 1949).

*Millais*: *The Life and Letters of Sir John Millais* by J. G. Millais (Methuen, 1899).

*Morgan*: Bowerswell Papers, Pierpont Morgan Library, New York.

*R–CT*: Ruskin–Cowper Temple Correspondence, Pierpont Morgan Library, New York.

*Stuart Wortley*: a typescript by the Hon. Clare Stuart Wortley now owned by Sir Ralph Millais, Bt. She was Effie's grand-daughter and spent ten years before her early death in 1945 annotating Effie's letters and transcribing about half of them into five volumes of typescript.

*Whitehouse*: *Vindication of Ruskin* by J. H. Whitehouse (Allen and Unwin, 1950).

*Works*: *The Works of John Ruskin*, Library Edition, edited by E. T. Cook and Alexander Wedderburn (George Allen, 1903–12).

## RETURN FROM VENICE

Note 1. Quoted in James, p. 90.

2 & 3. Partly quoted in James, pp. 190–1.

4. Effie's letters to Rawdon Brown are included among the Bowerswell Papers. Brown died in 1883 and in July, 1896, during Millais's last illness, Effie asked George Cavendish-Bentinck, the son of Brown's executor, to send her back her letters. They had been mixed up with the family papers and could not be found, and it was not until after Effie's death that they were returned in 1900 to Effie's daughter, Mrs Stuart Wortley, afterwards Lady Stuart of Wortley.

## TROUBLES AT HERNE HILL

Note 1. *Effie in Venice*, ed. by Mary Lutyens, p. 340 (Murray, 1965).

2. Ibid., p. 175.

3. Quoted from a copy of Ruskin's letter in a MS written by Effie's brother, Sir Albert Gray. Sir Albert left out Ford's name and even the word 'Foreign' from Foreign Office, doubtless because Clare Ford, an old family friend, was still alive when it was written (he died in 1899). The MS, now owned by Sir Ralph Millais, Bt, was undated but evidently written some time during the 1890's. It gives particulars of the Ruskin marriage and annulment and of Ruskin's parentage with some hearsay reports but no new facts.

4. *At John Murray's*, by George Paston (Murray, 1932).

5. Morgan.

## EFFIE'S DISCONTENT

Note 1. Morgan.

2. The letter (which was undated) is quoted in James, pp. 194–195, but is misdated July 22, 1852, and the meeting ascribed therefore to the first Duke of Wellington.

3. Mostly quoted in James, pp. 196–7.

4. Stuart Wortley.

### ENTER MILLAIS

Note 1. Stuart Wortley.

2. Millais, Vol. I, p. 91.

3. Hunt, Vol. I, p. 57.

4. *Some Reminiscences* by W. M. Rossetti, Vol. I, p. 70 (Sands, 1903).

5. Millais, Vol. I, p. 12.

6. James, p. 171.

7. Hunt, Vol. I, p. 257.

8. Letter to Mrs Thomas Combe quoted in Millais, Vol. I, p. 116

9. Stuart Wortley.

10. Partly quoted in James, p. 199, but misdated April 10.


### A LONDON SEASON

Note 1. Partly quoted in James, p. 201, where a passage from another letter of June 20 to Rawdon Brown has been inadvertently added to it.


### TO THE HIGHLANDS

Note 1. William Bell Scott's autobiographical notes are in the collection of Mrs Janet Camp Troxell of Connecticut, U.S.A., and contain the following passage:

> The only one of the P.R. Brotherhood that he [Ruskin] was personally acquainted with was the favourite of the Academy, Millais, whom he had thus carried off to Scotland to initiate him into the only class of painting he, Ruskin, knew anything about or cared for, landscape. But although the critic was interested only in landscape, the born painter was a man as well as an artist, and more catholic and universal in his loves. Already apparently before they reached Northumberland, the handsome hero had won the heart of the unhappy Mrs Ruskin, whose attentions from her husband had it seems consisted in his keeping a notebook of the defects in her carriage or speech. More than that the lovers had evidently come to an understanding with each other, founded apparently

on loathing of the owner of the notebook. Mrs Ruskin used to escape after breakfast, and joined by Millais was not heard of until the late hour of dinner. Lady Trevelyan hinted remonstrance, took alarm in fact, but not caring to speak confidentially to the lady who acted so strangely in her house, got Sir Walter to rouse the apparently oblivious husband. Her quick eye had of course discerned something of a telegraphic nature between the lovers, and she was mystified by Ruskin's inexplicable sillyness as she inadvertently called it to me. Sir Walter was also mystified, having pretty good eyes of his own, but was less given to forming conclusions or speaking of what was passing, he agreed however to take Ruskin into his confidence. But that innocent creature poo-poohed him. Really he didn't *believe* there was any harm in their *pleasing* themselves. He did not see what harm they could do: they were only children! He had often *tried* to keep her in order. Years after when I could venture to talk over the affair with Sir Walter, I asked him how he explained this mode of taking the warning. He confessed to having thought over the matter, and was inclined to conclude that John Ruskin wanted to get rid of his wife; had it been any other man he would have so concluded, but then the individual in question did not know much about love-making.

2. A small part quoted in Leon, p. 181.
3. Quoted in *Works*, Vol. 12, p. xx.
4 & 5. Passages quoted in Leon, p. 182.
6. Quoted in *Works*, Vol. 12, p. xxiv, but with slightly different punctuation from the original.
7. Morgan. After Charles Collins's death in 1873, his widow Kate, second daughter of Charles Dickens, married Carlo Perugini, the artist. As Mrs Perugini she became a great friend of Effie's daughter, Mrs Stuart Wortley, and after Millais's death gave her Millais's letters to Collins and to Collins's mother, Mrs William Collins; hence their inclusion in the Bowerswell Papers.

### GLENFINLAS

Note 1. To his father of September 30, 1853, at Yale, and to F. J.
Furnivall of October 16, 1853, reproduced in *Works*, Vol.
12, p. xxiv.

2. Pen and lamp-black study, given by Ruskin to his Drawing
School at Oxford and now at the Ashmolean Museum.
Reproduced in *Works*, Vol. 12, Plate 1.

3. Millais's letter to Collins of July 3.

4. From Effie's diary of April, 1856. See Note 2, pp. 284-5.

5. Millais, Vol. II, p. 390.

6. Quoted in *Works*, Vol. 12, p. xxiii.

### RUSKIN'S PORTRAIT BEGUN

Note 1. Quoted from Millais, Vol. I, p. 201.

2. Ruskin's published Diaries (Joan Evans and J. H. Whitehouse, Oxford, 1956-9) follow the *Works*, Vol. 12, p. xxiv,
in dating the following passage July 20, thus adding to the
confusion: 'Millais's picture of Glenfinlas was begun on
Wednesday; outlined at once, Henry Acland holding the
canvas, and a piece laid in that afternoon. None done on
Thursday—about an hour's work on Friday.' Examination
of the original diaries, which are in the Ruskin Galleries,
Bembridge School, Isle of Wight, enable one to construct a
calendar which indicates that, according to Ruskin's diary
recollection, the picture was begun on Wednesday, July 27,
and that the passage quoted is not part of a dated diary
entry at all. Nevertheless, Thursday, July 28, is the date to
be preferred, since although Ruskin had headed his letter
merely Thursday his father had added July 28th. Moreover,
he was writing to his father every day, whereas the passage
in the diary was written later from memory.

3. Letter of December 12, 1853, Bembridge.

### MILLAIS IN LOVE

Note 1. This letter, among five others from Mrs Ruskin to John, was
bought by F. J. Sharp at the Ruskin sale at Brantwood in

1931 and lent by him to Effie's daughter, Mary Millais. The text quoted is from Clare Stuart Wortley's copy and was partly quoted in James, p. 211.

2 & 3. Mostly quoted in Leon, pp. 184–5.

4. Yale. Clearly dated by Ruskin Thursday 17 August although the 17th was a Wednesday. Another part of the letter is quoted in *Works*, Vol 12, p. xxiv.

### Slow Progress

Note 1. Quoted but undated in Leon, p. 185.

### The Party Breaks Up

Note 1. Bembridge. Quoted in Whitehouse.

2. Author's collection.

3. Quoted in Leon, p. 187, but joined to a later letter giving the impression that Millais left immediately for London. He did not leave until November 10.

4. Millais, Vol. I, p. 216.

### Edinburgh

Note 1. Quoted in Leon, p. 190.

2. Letter of November 6, partly quoted in Leon, p. 190.

3. Partly quoted in Leon, p. 191.

4. Quoted in *Works*, Vol. 12, p. xxxiv.

### Return to London

Note 1. Yale. Quoted in Leon, p. 192. Ruskin's handwriting when writing to his mother was larger and more legible than usual.

2. Letter of December 14, 1853; Bembridge.

3. Quoted in Leon, pp. 192–3.

4. Bembridge.

5. Quoted in Leon, p. 192.

6. Letter from Naples of December 12, 1853; Morgan.

7. Quoted in *Works*, Vol. 12, p. 192.

### MILLAIS AND MRS GRAY

Note 1. Quoted in James, pp. 207–8.
  2. Quoted in James, pp. 208–11 with omission of postscript.
  3. Millais, Vol. I, p. 221.
  4. Partly quoted in James, p. 213.

### UNHAPPY NEW YEAR

Note 1. Mr Ruskin wrote to his old friend William Alexander of Leith, Edinburgh, on December 14, 1854, 'My Son had in 1840 nearly died of a Broken Heart from attachment to a French young Lady [Adèle Domecq] whom he resigned in obedience to his Mother who objected to the R. Catholic faith. In 1846 Miss Gray was rather forced upon us and my Son wanted a Young Companion he asked Mr Gray to let his daughter travel with his family which was declined; my son proposed marriage to which, fearful of another blow to his Constitution, we consented, though disliking the restless undomestic character of the girl.' Copy of a letter in Mr Ruskin's handwriting sent by Ruskin to William Cowper Temple in June, 1871; R–CT.
  2. Hunt, Vol. I, p. 365.
  3. Sir William Rothenstein (*Men and Memories*, Faber, 1931, Vol. I, p. 367) reported that F. J. Furnivall 'was staying with Ruskin when Millais came to paint Ruskin's portrait'. This appears to be the origin of the subsequently much repeated error that the sittings took place at Denmark Hill. Furnivall was 75 when Rothenstein first met him and his memory must have been faulty.
  4. Sir Albert Gray's MS.
  5. Not Dr John Brown as suggested by the editors of the published edition of Ruskin's diary.

### SOPHIE AS GO-BETWEEN

Note 1. Passages towards the end quoted in James, p. 214.
  2. Partly quoted in James, p. 214.
  3. Partly quoted in James, pp. 216–17, but misdated March 5.
  4. Mostly quoted in James, pp. 217–18.

## The Truth at Last

Notes 1–3. Mostly quoted in James, pp. 219–22, but the important second sentence of Millais's letter of March 15 beginning 'You will better understand . . .' omitted.

## Plans for Escape

Note 1. Passage quoted in James, p. 222, misdated April 7.

## Effie's Flight

Note 1. Quoted in James, p. 223.
2. Quoted in *Works*, Vol. 36, p. 163, but misdated April 2. Rawdon Brown did not arrive in England until the 4th.
3. Quoted in James, p. 224.

## Ruskin's Defence

Note 1. Letter of April 25, 1853, from Mr Gadesden of Ewell Castle, Surrey, to Mr Gray; Morgan.
2. Ruskin to F. J. Furnivall, April 21, 1853, quoted in *Works*, Vol. 36, p. 164.

It has been said that Rossetti was also at Denmark Hill on April 25 but this can be disproved by reference to Rossetti's letters to Ford Madox Brown of April 19 and May 23, 1854, and to William Allingham headed 'Monday, ½ 6 o'clock, (April 1854)', which show that it was on the 24th that he was lunching there, the day before Effie's departure. *Letters of Dante Gabriel Rossetti*, ed. Doughty and Wahl, Vol. I, pp. 186–7 and 200 (Oxford, 1965).
3. Morgan. Copy in Mrs Gray's handwriting. Quoted in James, pp. 225–7, with omission of last sentence.
4. R–CT. Ruskin sent these letters to William Cowper Temple on June 18, 1871, in a last effort to clear himself in order to marry Rose La Touche. He underlined several passages in them for Cowper Temple's special attention.
5. Stuart Wortley.
6. Bembridge. The document is given in facsimile in White-house.
7. R–CT. Letter of June 2, 1868, quoted in Leon, p. 410.

### LADY EASTLAKE RAMPANT

Note 1. Quoted, with passage omitted, in James, p. 229.

2 & 3. Quoted in James, pp. 231 and 234.

4. Morgan. From a parcel of eighty letters from Mr Ruskin to W. H. Harrison bought by Clare Stuart Wortley at Christie's in December, 1937.

5. Bembridge. Quoted in *Works*, Vol. 36, p. 165, but misdated April 24 (which was before Effie left).

6. Hunt, Vol. I, pp. 415–18. Also in *Works*, Vol. 12.

7 & 8. R–CT. Quoted in *Letters of John Ruskin to Lord and Lady Mount-Temple*, edited by J. L. Bradley (Ohio State University Press, 1964); letters of March and June, 1868.

### RUSKIN GOES ABROAD

Note 1. Huntington.

2. Partly quoted in James, p. 239, with paragraph from letter of May 3 added.

3. Mrs Camp Troxell's collection, Connecticut, U.S.A.

4. Bembridge. Quoted in *Works*, Vol. 36, p. 169, and in *Letters from John Ruskin to F. J. Furnivall*, edited by Thomas J. Wise, 1897, but in both places Millais's name has been replaced by dots or stars.

### EFFIE'S ORDEAL

Note 1. Huntington. This letter is undated but as Millais ends it by saying that he has a great deal to do 'before starting to-morrow evening' it may be ascribed to May 22.

2. Letter of May 25, partly quoted in James, p. 240.

3 & 4. Stuart Wortley. All the official records of the Ruskin annulment case have unaccountably disappeared. Sir Albert Gray copied them some time in the 1890's from the Registry of the Commissary Court of Surrey and these copies were in turn copied by Clare Stuart Wortley.

5. Hunt, Vol. I, p. 419.

## The Marriage Annulled

Note 1. R–CT.

2. Bembridge. Quoted in Whitehouse, p. 13.

3. Stuart Wortley.

4. R–CT. Letter headed Waterloo Day (i.e. June 18) 1871 to William Cowper Temple enclosing Mr Rutter's five letters: 'You will see that the lawyers advised me not to look at depositions, nor did I.'

5. R–CT. Letter of September 20, 1870, in an unidentified handwriting but evidently dictated by Ruskin. Quoted in *Illustrious Friends* by Sheila Birkenhead (Hamish Hamilton, 1965).

6. Bembridge. Additional Letters 1827–69 set up but crowded out of Vol. 36 of *Works*.

7. Ashley MS 3922, British Museum. Quoted in *An Ill-Assorted Marriage. An Unpublished Letter by John Ruskin* (25 copies Privately Printed by Clement Shorter, 1915).

8. Quoted in James, pp. 241–3, with omission of some relevant passages.

9. Mostly quoted in James, pp. 240–1.

10. Huntington.

11. Quoted in James, pp. 243–4.

## The Portrait Finished

Note 1. Letter of September 24, *Works*, Vol. 36, p. 175.

2. Quoted in *Works*, Vol. 12, p. xxxvii.

3. Morgan. Addressed to Millais c/o Charles Collins at 17 Hanover Terrace. Quoted in James, p. 245, omitting postscript.

4. Morgan.

5. Morgan. A retained copy in Millais's handwriting. Quoted in James, p. 245.

6. Quoted in James, p. 246.

7. R–CT. Copy of a letter in Mr Ruskin's handwriting sent by Ruskin on June 18, 1871, to William Cowper Temple together with another letter from Mr Ruskin to William Alexander (see Note 1, p. 280, *Unhappy New Year*). Ruskin

wrote a note on these letters: 'Two important letters of my Father's to Alexander and Collins.'

8. *Recollections of Rossetti* by Hall Caine (Cassell, 1928), p.173.

9. *Ruskin and his Circle* by Ada Earland (Hutchinson,1910),p.70.

10. G. P. Boyce's Diary for November 19, 1857, reads: 'Adjourned to Millais house, just taken, No 16 York Terrace, at about 4, and not finding him in waited and had a long and very pleasant chat with his wife, who has a lovely and passionate face, and whose manner is particularly engaging and ladylike withal. At her request, and afterwards backed by Millais, stayed to dinner, after which she left and I had a long chat on divers subjects with him. He spoke about Ruskin, whom he thinks desperately ill off [of] and of the portrait he painted of him in Scotland, which he thought the finest thing in the way of portraiture he had yet done, and said he wanted it for the exhibition (R.A.). He seemed astonished when I told him I had seen it in Ruskin's bedroom.' Quoted from *The Old Water-Colour Society's Club*, 1941 (19th Annual Volume), p. 26.

## REUNION AT BOWERSWELL

Note 1. Letter of May 22 to Holman Hunt; see Note 4.

2. Letter of May 7; Bembridge.

3. Partly quoted in James, p. 249.

4. The only letter from Millais to Holman Hunt which is in the Bowerswell Papers. It was sent to Millais's daughter Mary by Hunt's widow in August, 1923. Hunt had marked it 'Private' and erased many passages. Parts of this very long letter are quoted in James, pp. 246–8.

5. Huntington.

## EFFIE MILLAIS AT LAST

Note 1. Partly quoted in James, p. 249.

2. Effie's diary, now owned by her grand-daughter, Mrs Esmé Prowse. This vellum-covered notebook contains only one long entry of twenty-four pages dated April 5, 1856. It records the wedding, honeymoon, and the painting of

Millais's two pictures, *Autumn Leaves* and *The Blind Girl*, in the winter of 1855–6.

3. Stuart Wortley.

4. From the copy of Effie's letter to Mrs La Touche in the Bowerswell Papers written on October 10, 1870, and quoted in James, pp. 254–6, with the omission of these particular passages. Effie has been much criticised for this letter but correspondence in the Bowerswell Papers shows that she wrote it only after great provocation.

5. Hunt, Vol. II, pp. 372–3.

6. *The Journal of Beatrix Potter from 1881 to 1897* transcribed from her code writings by Leslie Linder (Frederick Warne, 1966), pp. 418–19. Beatrix's father, Rupert Potter, was an excellent amateur photographer and took many photographs for Millais to help him with his painting. See Beatrix Potter's journal, pp. 63, 71, 96, 100, 119, 154, 283.

7. Ibid., p. 408.

# INDEX

✳

Academy, see Royal Academy
*Academy Notes*, 255
Achray, Loch (the Trossachs), 60, 63
Acland, Dr (Sir Henry); at Glenfinlas, 72–6; hears from Ruskin, 224–5; on R. and Effie, 206, 208–9, 227; letter to R., 231; given R.'s portrait, 252; letters to Millais, 205, 211, 215, 225, 227, 232*n*; Trevelyans stay with, 225; mentioned, 150*n*, 224, 226*n*
Ainsworth, the Misses, 129, 241–2
Alexander, William, 218*n*
Anderson, Rev. John, 261–2
Annat Lodge (Perth), 256*n*, 259, 264
Anne (Strachan), Ruskin's nurse, 142–3
Annulment Case: first mooted, 151; possibilities of, 155, 157, 168, 177, 180–1; Ruskins unsuspicious, 169, 177, 179; medical opinion, 180; citation served on Ruskin, 182, 184; R. remains passive, 187, 214*n*, 217, 231; R.'s defence, 187, 188–93, 230; R. suffers from, 204, 231, 244; Mr R.'s handling of, 187, 218*n*, 231; lawyers' letters about, 187, 192*n*, 214*n*, 218*n*, 229, 230*n*, 231; Effie's letter to Mrs R., 184; E. fears retaliation, 207; E. comes to London for examination, 214, 216; visit secret, 219; depositions, 218–19, 231; doctors' report, 218; damages, 186*n*, 199, 218, 218*n*; expected date of hearing, 217, 225–7, 234; final hearing, 229; privacy of, 187, 230; expenses, 218*n*; marriage settlement, 189*n*, 218*n*, 257*n*
Avonbank School, 129*n*, 135*n*

Baslow, Peacock Inn (Derbyshire), 227, 234, 238*n*
Battledore and Shuttlecock, 65, 72–3, 75, 123*n*
Bell Scott, William, 54, 87, 120*n*, 212
Bellini, 108
Ben Ledi (the Trossachs), 65, 67*n*
Beveridge, John, 106, 109, 111
Bishop, Mrs Thomas (*née* Cecilia Northcote), 116–17, 128, 145, 164

Blackburn, Mrs Hugh (*née* Jemima Wedderburn), 113, 115
*Blackwood's Magazine*, 45–6
Boswell, Jane, 144, 160–3, 167, 171, 175; on Ruskin, 159–60, 165, 168, 233; on Mrs R., 159, 168; letter to Mrs Gray, 233
Bowerswell (Perth), 22 *et passim*; Effie at, 25, 111–12, 194, 235, 268–9; E.'s diaries at, 206*n*; Millais at, 254, 259–62; M.'s sketch of party at, 86, 115; William Millais at, 84, 259; Ruskin at, 27, 42*n*, 115, 117, 125, 240; Mr R.'s dislike of, 115, 117; Mrs R.'s dread of, 171*n*, 250*n*; drawing-room at, 42*n*, 253, 254*n*, 261–2; suicide at, 171*n*
Bowerswell Papers (Pierpont Morgan Library, New York), 184, 220*n*, 226*n*, 265*n*, 266
Boxall, Sir William, R.A., 197
Boyle, Hon. Mrs R. (E. V. B.), 133
Brantwood, 3*n*, 208*n*, 252
Brig o' Turk (Perthshire), 58, 102–3, 220; Ruskins at, 62–5; Millais returns to in 1854, 211, 214, and in 1856, 220*n*; hotel at, 62–5, 88; Millais at hotel, 62–5, 76, 219, 225
British Museum, 34, 133
Brodick (Isle of Arran), 263
Brown, Rawdon, 8, 28–9, 31, 42*n*, 50, 56, 73, 95, 112, 118, 132, 229; appearance, 205; in London, 168–70, 173, 177, 194, 256; consulted by Effie, 168–9; calls at Denmark Hill, 170; plays doubtful part, 169, 176, 207; passes on gossip, 205; on Ruskin, 169, 171; invited by R. to stay, 174–5; calls on Grays, 177*n*,; meets Millais, 205; Millais finds a bore, 267; back in Venice, 223; gives Effie seal, 253; and wedding present, 256; letters to E., 199, 200, 207; death, 205*n*; and Venetian State Papers, 176; *Giustinian at the Court of Henry VIII*, 29, 56, 73, 95*n*, 132, 170, 173, 205–6; read aloud by Effie, 96, 205*n*; Ruskin helps with,